T0330001

THE POLITICAL ECONOMY OF DIGITAL MONOPOLIES

Contradictions and Alternatives to Data Commodification

Paško Bilić, Toni Prug, and Mislav Žitko

BRISTOL
UNIVERSITY
PRESS

First published in Great Britain in 2021 by

Bristol University Press
University of Bristol
1–9 Old Park Hill
Bristol
BS2 8BB
UK
t: +44 (0)117 954 5940
e: bup-info@bristol.ac.uk

Details of international sales and distribution partners are available at bristoluniversitypress.co.uk

British Library Cataloguing in Publication Data
A catalogue record for this book is available from the British Library

ISBN 978-1-5292-1237-2 hardcover
ISBN 978-1-5292-1239-6 ePub
ISBN 978-1-5292-1238-9 ePdf

Cover design by Liam Roberts
Front cover image: iStock/Vasif Bagirov

Bristol University Press uses environmentally responsible print partners
Printed in and bound in Great Britain by CPI Group (UK) Ltd,
Croydon, CR0 4YY

FSC
www.fsc.org
MIX
Paper from
responsible sources
FSC® C013604

Contents

List of Figures and Tables

Figures

Tables

Preface

Marxian political economists do not necessarily focus on media, communication, and data as they usually consider it a peripheral phenomenon to the reproduction of capital. This is becoming an increasingly weak position given the dominance of big tech and its insertion into some of the core mechanisms of contemporary capitalism. On the other hand, Marxian political economists of communication focus on the material conditions and power relations within media and communication, accepting that their analysis deals with phenomena within the capitalist mode of production but rarely including the mode of production as their immediate object of study. Such division of labour usually results in misunderstandings and entrenched positions that do not move our understanding of corporate tech giants forward. Debates between these sub-fields are rare. When they do occur, they usually take the form of reverse mirrors in which one theoretical concept raises different concerns in the context of the other subfield. At the same time, these subfields are filled with internal struggles. To forge this collaboration, we had to allow our pre-existing knowledge and assumptions to be tested by the empirical and theoretical material brought to the table during the writing process.

This book is the result of many discussions, debates, arguments, and meetings that took place over a span of three years. During that time, all three of us adjusted, stretched, and changed some of our starting positions while trying to maintain an understanding of the inherent unity of capitalist production and circulation as well as an understanding of the central concepts of surplus value and value form. We do not argue that we have solved all problems posed by our object of study in this process. But we have tried to bring diverse perspectives to improve our understanding of the common problem: the enormous economic, political, and social power of a handful of tech companies fuelled by hunger for data commodification. To do so we also went against the grain of some of the usual Marxian starting points such as cognitive capitalism and the audience commodity debates. Whether we were successful in our interpretations, interventions, and extensions of the existing Marxian conceptual apparatus remains for the readers to decide. In any case, we hope that this truly collaborative effort will help push some of the debates within Marxian critiques of political economy and critical political economy of communication forward, and that our work on social forms and their social and economic determination will provide inspiration for future studies and publications.

Parts of the book were presented at the following events: European Sociological Association's mid-term conference in Zagreb (2018) and congress in Manchester (2019), International Labour Process Conference in Vienna (2019), Algorithmic Spaces workshop at the University of Copenhagen (2019), Women's Studies School in Zagreb (Centre for Women's Studies, 2020), School of Socialism in Belgrade (CPE, 2020), Association for Heterodox Economics (online, 2020), and other events and seminars. We would like to thank many people who have provided their thoughts, suggestions, and critiques to different aspects of the book: from the initial stages in which the full scope of the project was not fully clear, to the final stages in which specific issues and details of the project emerged. Special thanks goes to Peter Golding, Tomislav Medak, Brian Beaton, Bjarki Valtysson, Eran Fisher, Jernej Amon Prodnik, Stipe Ćurković, Hajrudin Hromadžić, members of the Centre for the Politics of Emancipation (CPE) in Belgrade, and many others with whom we discussed the ideas from the book. We would also like to thank Paul Stevens from Bristol University Press for commissioning the book as well as for his cordial communication and advice during the entire book-writing process. Our gratitude goes to anonymous reviewers for their valuable insights and comments on the book proposal and the final manuscript.

Introduction: The Context of Digital Monopolies

Reports, debates, and calls for challenging the power of tech giants are common in business and daily press. Outrage over socially damaging practices is found across the public sphere with issues ranging from tax avoidance and anti-competitive behaviour to disinformation and hate speech distribution, privacy abuse, surveillance, and labour disputes. These regular signs of dissatisfaction put the political system on notice and create a sense of urgency for political action in the form of regulatory and policy responses.[1] Despite widespread debates and clear indicators of their excessive power, very rarely do we encounter discussions as to what does it actually mean to hold a monopoly and what are the specific features of digital monopolies in the capitalist mode of production. Digital platforms as monopolies lead to a peculiar set of economic, political, and social configurations and consequences, whose negative tendencies remain to be adequately understood. In this book, we provide theoretical and empirical arguments for a better understanding of the character and consequences of digital monopoly platforms in contemporary capitalism.

Much of the existing research on digital platforms tries to follow the latest technological developments by providing entirely new theoretical concepts. It is, however, common that new concepts suffer a double fate. First, they become outdated when new products and services appear in radically new forms, when they take the shape of new technological forms and social forms of wealth. Techno-optimism surrounding so-called user-generated content on social media and its alleged democratization potential in the public sphere is one case in point. Second, over time they are often exposed for reducing the explanatory power of the conceptual apparatus they build on. Over time, it became clear that user-generated content is a way for social media companies to gather and process data, and ultimately to profit from platform usage and accumulate capital and wealth. We try to avoid both problems by sticking with the classical Marxian theoretical frameworks while preserving the methodological space for new concepts and theoretical insights. Focusing on profit making as the driving force of capitalist firms, we alter the existing concepts and theoretical insights only when we come across empirically observed entities that play a functionally important role in profit making, yet whose role is not understood clearly enough with existing concepts and theories. Our approach is historical in that it tries to understand the genesis of current developments in order to relativize technological novelty and demonstrate its continuity whenever there is a case to do so. It is also empirical in that it tries to understand the relevance of contemporary technological developments by studying traceable socio-economic relations, legal and regulatory interventions through document analysis, market reports, industry reports, official statistics, and publicly available data. Empirical research helps us locate areas where extensions of chosen theoretical frameworks are necessary, in the process uncovering problems with new categories introduced in recent decades. It also helps us to determine the scope and character of our own categorical and theoretical innovations.

We start from a seemingly obvious set of research questions: given the nominally competitive character of developed economies, why is there a single company for socially and economically important functions such as web searching, social networking, and online retailing? This is especially intriguing in the context of a seeming paradox that some of those new services are offered to end-users free of monetary charge. Answers to these questions cannot be given by looking at our present situation alone, nor can they be brushed aside with techno-determinist notions of network effects and the supposed autonomous logic of networked technologies. We have to observe these processes from a historical and political economy perspective. A historical approach allows us to trace how dominant digital platforms are established, what social and economic forms do they and their constitutive socio-economic elements take, providing us with a set of theoretical insights for grasping their monopolistic positions and plausible alternatives. Specifically, what kind of policy and regulation driven initiatives have the potential to reduce the current dominance of capitalist monopoly platforms? Can regulation provide us with long-term solutions that may alleviate the negative effects of the capitalist driven development? What social forms of production coexist with the dominant capitalist one? Do they constitute elements for building long-term plausible alternatives to the dominant capitalist mode of production in some sectors and types of products? How exactly are they functionally integrated into the logic of capital and to what extent?

In the process, our approach enhances the visibility of inherent contradictions of contemporary capitalism, especially between the public and the private, obfuscated by analytical frameworks that normalize and naturalize capitalism's presence as the best and only desirable form of production. We will argue that the control over markets by GAFAM (Google, Apple, Facebook, Amazon, and Microsoft), as they are sometimes labelled collectively in capital markets, is enabled by a set of beliefs that emphasize the self-regulating, inherently progressive, and wealth-enhancing character of capitalist production and markets, whose functioning has to be enabled and supported by liberal political institutions. Our contribution challenges such idealizing of commodities and markets by pointing out that understanding production, allocation, and consumption as social, historically specific, and transitory reveals the co-existence of various social forms of production, to different degrees utilized by and functionally integrated into the dominant capitalist mode of production driven by the central goal to extract surplus value.

Tech industry is among the most concentrated in the US economy (L. Davis & Orhangazi, 2019), while tech companies are among the most profitable ones (Orhangazi, 2018). In February 2020, Google held a more than 90 per cent market share on web search across all platforms globally (StatCounter, 2020b). Facebook is the most used social medium internationally with a more than 60 per cent market share in February 2020 (StatCounter, 2020c). Amazon held 49 per cent of the US e-commerce market in 2018 (Lunden, 2018). Amazon is also leading the global, cloud infrastructure market with 33 per cent, followed by Microsoft with 18 per cent, and Google with 8 per cent (Richter, 2020). Google dominates smartphone operating systems with more than 70 per cent market share for Android OS in February 2020. Apple's iOS is second with 28 per cent (Net Market Share, 2020). The leading mobile phone manufacturer worldwide is Samsung with more than 30 per cent market share, followed by Apple with more than 25 per cent (StatCounter, 2020a).

GAFAM's collective annual revenue in 2019 was $899 billion (Table 1.1). If they were a national economy they would be ranked on the 18th spot among countries ordered by GDP in 2019 (World Bank, 2019), just behind the Netherlands ($909 billion) and above Saudi Arabia ($793 billion). Nonetheless, it is still rather common for some

Table 1.1: Selected financial data for GAFAM

Company	Market cap (6/3/2020) $ billion	Revenue (2019) $ billion	Net income (2019) $ billion	Fortune 500 rank
Alphabet Inc.	903.61	161.9	34.34–21.2%	15th
Apple Inc.	1281.66	260.17	55.25–21.2%	3rd
Facebook Inc.	527.81	70.69	18.48–26.1%	57th
Amazon Inc.	957.80	280.52	11.58–4.1%	5th
Microsoft Corporation	1264.65	125.8	39.2–31.2%	26th

Sources: NASDAQ, Company Form 10-Ks, Forbes Fortune 500

tech companies to operate with low profitability, or even with losses, in favour of growth, global market expansion, and future profits. For example, Amazon recorded only 4.3 per cent net income of their total revenue in 2018, which was still a record for the company. It operated with losses for years. Uber recorded a net loss of $1.8 billion in 2018. Regardless of their performance, investors reward such business models and support their continued global growth. GAFAM are the world's most valued companies holding a $4.9 trillion market capitalization in March 2020 and occupying top spots of all publicly traded companies, positions previously reserved for banks and oil companies. Together with Netflix, they were responsible for 24 per cent of the S&P 500 market capitalization on NASDAQ in June 2020 (Borodovsky, 2020).

Much of the technologies upon which they built their commercial success rely on early and risky public research and innovation. The initial 'angel investor' and one of the main reasons for the Silicon Valley success is the US Department of Defense, which provided a multitude of contracts even before World War I (Leslie, 2000). Packet-switching, TCP/IP and email were developed under the funding of ARPANET in the 1960s and 1970s (Abbate, 1999). Early principles of cloud computing were discussed in the 1960s in the debates on time-sharing and the delivery of computing along the principles of public utilities (Mosco, 2014). Microsoft built its Windows OS on the foundation of the major research on human–computer interaction at the Stanford Research Laboratory and MIT in the late 1960s (Myers, 1998). Google's Page Rank algorithm grew out of the National Science Foundation (NSF) grant awarded to Stanford University in the early 1990s. Facebook's servers are running on Linux and other types of open source software (Zeichick, 2008). Apple's iPhone technologies were developed through multiple government research programmes, military initiatives, public procurement contracts, and tax policies. This made Apple the champion in recognizing technologies with commercial potential and applying engineering skills to integrate them into complex products by prioritizing design and user satisfaction (Mazzucato, 2013). In addition to public investments, independent engineering communities played an important role in developing some of the key components for many technologies and their applications in commercial systems. In particular, Free Software and Open Source (FLOSS) production played a role for Google and Apple whose core technologies are difficult to imagine without FLOSS (Hubbard, 2004; Burnette, 2008; Al-Rayes, 2012; Papadimitriou & Moussiades, 2018). The robustness of publicly funded technologies and FLOSS enabled layering of software applications and smooth running of commercial services once the internet was privatized and commercialized in the 1990s (Abbate, 1999; Greenstein, 2015). Privatization opened the door for the ideological combination of neoliberalism and technological determinism that gave birth to the rise of GAFAM's oligopoly (Smyrnaios, 2018). Financialization and venture capital were the main drivers. Once tech companies enter financial markets, new competitive pressures play a role in how companies are managed, how capital is accumulated and reproduced, and how labour is controlled and remunerated. Financialization creates enormous wealth disparities between institutional equity holders, corporate owners and top management, small contingents of full-time employees, and a long tail of service workers, gig-workers, assembly workers, warehouse workers, and other part-time and outsourced workers (Prado, 2018; Wright, 2018).

Despite the influx of venture and financial capital, the majority of tech companies were unable to establish profitable businesses and the dot-com crash of the early 2000s resulted in enormous financial losses that ultimately brought the digital economy back to the drawing board. Stock market wealth fell $8.3 trillion between its peak in the first quarter of 2000 and the third quarter of 2002 (Greenstein, 2015). Companies that survived, or were established after the crash, such as Google (incorporated in 1998), Facebook (founded in 2004), and Amazon (founded in 1994)[2] approached the emerging digital economy with a different mind-set. The primary goal was to grow the international user base, provide most services free or at competitively low prices, and attract revenue from advertising and other industries interested in reaching global consumers. Through widespread usage platforms collect and analyse more and more data, the scale and scope of which is difficult to overstate. Currently, more than 90 terabytes of data is generated every second online. More than 83 thousand Google searches are performed every second. More than 82 thousand YouTube videos are viewed every second (Internet Live Stats, 2020).

Platforms frame users' engagement by pulling together access to a wide range of digital datasets (for example, news, advertising, music, videos, textual documents, personal contacts, and so on). At the same time user engagement with those datasets leaves traces on a multitude of behavioural aspects exploited by platform owners (for example, age, geolocation, language, time spent online, search history, consumption habits, likes, political preferences, purchasing power, and so on). Software and algorithms allow these engagements to occur almost seamlessly. Yet, gathering data is not enough to establish a monopoly. In order to shape the data in the social form of commodity, making it economically valuable and profitable, a number of conditions have to be met. First, there needs to exist a large number of users, which makes data analyses unique and useful in terms of scope and scale.

Second, patented software and algorithms have to be constructed and deployed as means of production to produce and continuously update and interpret data, providing standardized data output required in order to monetize the platform, either by selling access, or by making the platform attractive to advertisers. The construction of a digital platform requires highly skilled labour and substantial research and development investments. When these productive activities leading to commodification affect private activities of citizens as political subjects – influencing, for example, how citizens find, contextualize, and discuss news material – the social form of economic activities affects political processes in ways hidden inside algorithms and data processing. These filtering, aggregating, and, in general, data-processing procedures – known only to the producers and concentrated within GAFAM companies – currently lie beyond comprehensive policy regulation, presenting a threat to democratic processes and governance in general.

Third, the market regulatory framework, in particular antitrust regulation, favours the growth of large companies instead of competition between producers that is a nominal modus operandi of the capitalist economies. In our approach, we see regulation as a concrete configuration of institutional settings, actors, and legal codes within a struggle to protect and/or promote specific interests. Within the capitalist mode of production, regulation often serves the purpose of promoting a specific regime of accumulation aiding capital to reproduce itself. There are significant political and social costs to imposing, implementing, and changing regulatory frameworks, which makes it a field of long-term struggles over a variety of outcomes.

The challenge of studying digital monopoly platforms has created a sense of urgency in reshuffling existing theoretical and methodological concepts in fields ranging from science and technology studies, media studies, data science, labour process theory, and gender studies, to more traditional fields such as economics, sociology, political science, and information science. Mainstream economics placed the development of platforms in a lineage of perfect competition within the so-called two-sided or multi-sided markets (Rochet & Tirole, 2003). The increasing power of tech giants gave rise to terms such as the platform society (van Dijck et al, 2018) and platform capitalism (Srnicek, 2017, 2018). Studying algorithms received even more attention in recent years (see F. Lee & Björklund Larsen, 2019). There is a widespread understanding of the connection between data and algorithms (Dourish, 2016) with some authors celebrating datafication as a science changing process (Kitchin, 2014) bringing in a new economy (Mayer-Schönberger & Cukier, 2014).

With increasing corporate power, there is also widespread understanding of the inherent politics of algorithms (Introna & Nissenbaum, 2000; Gillespie, 2014) and the need to unpack the black box of technology (Pasquale, 2015) in order to understand the mechanisms of data collection and processing. Bringing more transparency to otherwise opaque algorithms (Burrell, 2016) would make algorithms more accountable (Diakopoulos, 2015; Ananny & Crawford, 2018) and ethical (Ananny, 2016; Mittelstadt et al, 2016). There are also calls for relativizing infatuation with big data analytics, which undoubtedly brings a host of biases and misunderstandings (boyd & Crawford, 2012). Some argue for a critical assessment of techno-euphoric innovation and privatization within an algorithmic ideology (Mager, 2012), while others demand a critique of datafication on corporate platforms (van Dijck, 2014). At the same time, there is a need to separate what is novel about current developments and what is a repetition of familiar trends in the development of capitalism, already described by Marx and various strands of Marxist theory.

On related Marxian approaches

We contextualize the impact of corporate entities collecting and analysing data by putting the economic actors' central goals, profitability, and accumulation of capital, at the forefront of the entire analytical approach. Our aim is to provide theoretical and empirical insights into producing, circulating, and regulating commodities in the context of monopolistic digital platforms relying on algorithms and data to accumulate capital and generate wealth. To study digital monopolies from such a vantage point, it is necessary to reflect on related Marxian approaches. In particular, the predominant starting points for grasping the intense use of information and knowledge in contemporary capitalism is the cognitive capitalism perspective (for example, Hardt & Negri, 2000, 2004; Vercellone, 2007; Moulier-Boutang, 2011). Inspired by Marx's fragment on machines and the general intellect thesis, it provided concepts such as immaterial labour (Lazzarato, 1996), free labour (Terranova, 2000), knowledge commodity (Vercellone, 2007) and the closely related analysis of social media within the so-called social factory (Scholz, 2013), or the digital labour and the audience commodity debate (for example, Fisher, 2012; Fuchs, 2010, 2014b).

The crux of the argument is that even though social media users engage with platforms without a monetary exchange and perform their activities during leisure time, we can still regard them as being exploited while engaged in such activities. User activities were theorized as a form of unproductive labour that nonetheless contributes to capital accumulation and social reproduction of inequality, a theoretical approach closely resembling some Marxian feminist perspectives. Put differently, these authors viewed social media activities as a form of unpaid labour that creates value for platform owners (for example, Fuchs & Fisher, 2015).

This theoretical reach moved the attention of scholars, and ultimately even some policy makers, towards understanding how free-of-charge services allow companies to accumulate capital. It was essential in moving the terms of debate within media studies away from participatory and celebratory accounts of the internet and user-generated content towards critical analyses of how participation aids profit-seeking mechanisms. Theorists from a contending Marxian approach argued that value is generated in circulation where it is extracted by renting digital spaces to advertisers. For this approach, the cost of reproduction of knowledge commodities is close to zero since consumption does not deplete them. This makes it necessary to impose intellectual property rights to secure profitability from otherwise valueless knowledge commodities (for example, Teixeira & Rotta, 2012; Rigi & Prey, 2015; Rotta & Teixeira, 2019).

The theoretical argument of our book is that neither of these perspectives paint a complete picture of the role of platforms in contemporary capitalist society, nor do they shed full light on the unity of production and circulation within the capitalist mode of production. In fact, while attempting to prove a point that user activity contributes to the accumulation of capital, digital labour approaches remained trapped in the social factory metaphor. On the one hand, by capturing the mainstream logic of 'prosumers' in which internet users are viewed as users of technology and producers of their own content, the distinction between production and circulation became blurred and irrelevant. On the other hand, the authors closer to the circulation perspective often omit the fact that digital spaces and data from which the platforms are profiting from also need to be produced and constantly updated. Moreover, they miss the point that profitability largely depends on the number of users a platform is able to attract and on the non-monetary exchange occurring between users, who give up data on their on-line behaviour in return for free of monetary charge services provided by platforms. Taking either the productivist or the circulationist perspective makes it difficult to theorize production, consumption, labour, and commodities within a capitalist mode of production as a whole, unless a thesis about a completely novel form of capitalism is accepted, such as theories that postulate a shift from Fordism to post-Fordism. Authors within this line of argumentation often emphasize exploitation of unpaid internet user activity, or the unique ontological characteristics of knowledge commodities, which become benchmarks for the latest transformations of capitalism.

We argue that there is much to be gained by understanding how production and circulation operate in unity, instead of conflating the two or giving advantage to either one of them. From our perspective, there is an overarching logic of surplus value extraction, which determines the social and economic forms of all inputs (elements and actors) within the capitalist mode of production and shapes the immediate technological form (whether in the form of software or not) within the capitalist mode of production. This umbrella logic, expressed by the category value-form, determines the social and economic forms that it encompasses. Platforms and their free-of-charge services are used without monetary exchange on most services, Google and Facebook being the most prominent examples. Yet these 'pre-commodities' are the output of capital and wage-labour inputs within the broader system of surplus value extraction. User activity, at the same time, results in the exchange between platform users, who grant (knowingly or not) access to data on their on-line behaviour, and platform owners who provide free-of-charge services in return.

As platforms attract users, data accumulates and allows platform owners to engage in a monetary exchange in which user data acts as raw material input into production of adverts (which we theorize as 'intermediate commodities'). These peculiar commodities are exchanged for money to interested advertisers producing commodities in a traditional sense (which we theorize as 'final commodities'). 'Pre-commodities' (free services provided by platforms), 'intermediate commodities' (targeted advertisements), and final commodities (products purchased for consumption) are tied in a dynamic balance. 'Intermediate commodities' would not be appealing to advertisers if 'pre-commodities' and technological forms were not widely used by a diverse range of internet users on a scale large enough to enable aggregation of user preferences that enables a more fine-grained matching of users and advertised final commodities. Furthermore, 'pre-commodities' could not be offered free-of-charge to internet users if there was no profit from selling 'intermediate commodities', whose sole purpose is to ensure quicker and more voluminous sale of 'final commodities'. All producers of final commodities are under pressure to sell their products as quickly as possible, both in order to realize the value of their products and extract surplus, and to shorten the time capital spends in circulation in the form of final commodities offered for sale and various related expenditures such as marketing, distribution, and storage. Capturing this full chain of capitalist production allows us to remain within the unity of production and circulation of surplus value. Grasping a peculiar character of these objects as three types of commodities allows us to see their role in this productive chain, avoiding speculating on the ontological significance of labour and commodities for the transformation of capitalism.

Which capitalism?

Capitalism, in our understanding, remains the same mode of production based on surplus value extraction regardless of the fact that contemporary technological forms of data and knowledge have peculiar features, both as useful objects and when they become commodities, and that new types of labour involve cognitive skills, management, communication, and even unpaid social media activities. Granted, contemporary character of digital knowledge, communication, and data, especially their quantity and inter-connectivity, are indeed new types of inputs and outputs of the capitalist mode of production, which makes capitalism's determinate form on digital platforms (or simply its business model in a more conventional jargon) specific and unique to our historical period. However, the traditional determinate abstractions of the capitalist mode of production such as capital, wage labour, surplus value, and commodities, along with central causal relationships such as exploitation remain unchanged even if the full process of capital accumulation becomes increasingly complex and reliant on technology, data, and legal forms. The key point is that many Marxian approaches studying digital media sometimes conflate general and determinate abstractions as evident in granting the specificities of digital production and circulation both systemic and trans-historic qualities. Despite the fact that contemporary technological forms play a novel role within the capitalist mode of production, sometimes exhibiting seemingly non-capitalist attributes by offering products free of charge, there is nothing systemic in this novelty. The logic of profit-driven production keeps finding ways to include and commodify new inputs and outputs. To explain our theoretical position further, we combine Marxian perspectives that are rarely put into a fruitful theoretical dialogue: New Readings of Marx and more broadly value-form approaches, some aspects of the Monthly Review School of monopoly capitalism, critical legal theory, and the Frankfurt School theory.

Before we proceed by outlining the key theoretical elements of these schools of thought useful for our analysis, a methodological note on using and extending Marx's work is required. For many readings of Marx, one of the goals was to find the true kernel of Marx's work (Heinrich, 2009, pp 89–90). In our view, and in the light of how Marx's work was published, translated, and made available,[3] it is more scientifically defendable to take Marx's work as not finished, as argued, for example, by Michael Heinrich.[4] A key element that enables us to have a far more accurate impression of Marx's work is the publication of all the known economic writings of both Marx and Engels through the *Marx-Engels Gesamtausgabe* (MEGA[2]) project. Introducing the recently published collection of articles by the authors involved in or related to the project, the editors passed their judgement in a fashion similar to Heinrich.[5] Hence, rather than treating it as a body of work from which we have to reconstruct a final version of the theory that would be most faithful to the original texts, our approach is to improve Marx's work in ways conductive to theoretically and empirically grounded investigations of contemporary phenomena. This, however, stands in agreement with Heinrich that openness of Marx's work 'is not to be confounded with arbitrariness' and with the notion that Marx's project 'is committed to a certain aim: to overcome capitalism' (Heinrich, 2009, p 96). Refining our understanding of Marx's methodological approach is an important step in respecting those points. Whether our work can be classified as interpretation, or reconstruction and extension of Marx's work, a question that occasionally becomes an important topic of debate among Marxists (Reuten, 2000), is less of our concern.

From our perspective, scientific work ought to be able to hold its ground in relation to both its empirical object of study and its community of researchers, regardless of how we classify its relationship with the work it builds on. A faultless interpretation of Marx's work may not be able to pass either of those two tests. Marx's central object of study, the capitalist mode of production, along with the conditions and potentials for overcoming capitalism, may differ to such an extent in contemporary times that several features of Marx's work that require altering, or even uprooting in order to reflect those changes, may disqualify such work from being classified as an interpretation of Marx. Grasping as accurately as possible the contemporary social and economic determination of forms and their causal relationships within production and circulation as a single whole, along with conditions for social change, is the criterion that matters for us, rather than faithfully interpreting any work. Having said that, Marx's work and Marxism, especially those works we find among value-form literature, remain for us the best available approach for understanding both the contemporary forms of production and circulation as well as conditions for emancipatory and lasting social change beyond the domination of the capitalist mode of production.

Reading Marx's work by focusing on social and economic determination of forms was first proposed by Rubin (1928/1973), whose work was re-discovered in the 1970s. Related approaches developed into a variety of value-form theories that emerged from New Readings of Marx in the 1960s and 1970s in several countries as a way to challenge the traditional Marxist political economy (Backhaus, 1980; Heinrich, 2009; Elbe, 2018). These readings included Marx's preparatory manuscripts, focusing not only on the resulting theory but also on the methods, often interpreting the work of Marx through the lens of the Frankfurt School and their focus on the commodity form and the irrational social consequences it carries. However, instead of focusing on ideology critique and culture industry, the NRM approach focused on the critique of political economy as a whole as well as on its constitutive elements. Marx's critique of the Trinity Formula and its three sources of revenue (capital, land, and labour) as described by political economists of his time serves as an insight into the methodology of social forms. He argued that political economists mix a category belonging to a specific social organization of production (capital), with general categories such as land and labour found in all forms of production. This creates 'the illusion of the economic', the impression that there is only one, general, and the most natural, way of producing (Murray, 2002a).

Marx argues that there is nothing natural about the capitalist mode of production since 'the capitalist process of production is a specific social form of the production process in general' (1864/2015, p 884). In our book, we take the social form approach and consider Marx's critique of political economy as the science of social forms (Elbe, 2013), which helps us construct the range of general and determinate abstractions (Murray, 1988, 2016) that the capitalist mode of production acquires on digital platforms. We consider general abstractions such as production and labour as the highest levels of abstraction, useless from the perspective of social sciences as they say nothing on the social character of the object of study. They are followed by simple abstractions such as commodity and wage labour, and finally by determinate or concrete abstractions, such as wage labour, commodity, and surplus value in the capitalist mode of production. Determinate abstraction are the most important ones. Grasping their differences from single and general abstractions is essential in order to understand the character of the mode of production, its specific nuances, tendencies and real mechanisms at work (Smith, 1997, p 190).

The Frankfurt School theory, especially in the works of Adorno, Horkheimer, and Marcuse, is closely tied to the concept of commodity fetishism. Marx famously described commodity fetishism as a mystification detaching commodities from their social and material conditions. Marcuse (1998, 2007) extended this approach to criticize technology as a mode of organizing and perpetuating social relations for the purpose of control and dominance. He argued that a true transformation of capitalism must also take into account the transformation of dominating technological forms (Marcuse, 1971), technical solutions that solve problems and meet needs, but in a peculiar setting of the capitalist mode of production, are shaped by its social and economic forms. Marcuse's broad approach allows us to discuss the contingency of technical designs (Feenberg, 1996) that, once produced, simply become normalized in society. Their capitalist becoming and character tends to disappear out of sight once they are in common use. The technological form of capitalist digital platforms is what is visible in the experiential realm of everyday users through engagements with algorithms, recommendation systems and databases.

Marcuse's broad approach helps us understand that platform users enter unequal social relations as they are embedded in the capitalist mode of production and a chain of commodities (pre-, inter-, and final commodities) contributing to profits of the owners of technical objects. It is quite ironic that in the time of digital media, once celebrated as democratic, open, and inclusive we see a return to the classical Frankfurt School argument of passive consumers through the experience of technological form. The passive consumers of today are not cultural dupes and manipulated consumers of ideologically charged mass media content produced by platforms. Internet users engage with most algorithmic systems free of charge in exchange for their personal data. However, they have no power to change or re-programme structural settings of their search algorithms, Facebook news feeds, Android OS, or Amazon Web Services. They are sucked into platform usage and exposed to content they are engaging with and mostly producing and sharing themselves. This creates a strong technological fetish, which blurs the economic processes unfolding in the background. In oligopolistic conditions, there are limited or no alternative services at all to choose.

Value-form and related approaches, including our own development of theory of social and economic determination of form, critical legal studies, and historical studies of the role of legal forms help us challenge one of the main benchmarks of neoclassical economics, the notion of perfect competition. If the neoclassical understanding of competition turns into an analytical anchor, monopoly and other forms of the so-called imperfect competition can appear only as forms of deviations from the norm. Perfect competition and monopoly emerge as polar opposites with perfect competition leading the way as a regulatory ideal, while monopoly is positioned at the other end of the spectrum, as the most extreme form of a defective market. However, just as competition should be thought of as an intricate process rather than a state, monopoly entails more than a simple definition of a product market with a single seller. Monopolies are recurring conditions of the drive for capital accumulation, and their historical co-existence with competition (Christophers, 2016), differing on various levels of the organization of production and valorization across sectors.

Consider advertising-funded digital platforms: platform providers face little competition, while content and app producers compete fiercely for our attention, hoping to valorize their labour through advertising or additional sales. It therefore becomes essential to understand conditions that lead up to concentration and centralization of capital, along the way unpacking processes such as the creation of large corporations, sales efforts, mergers and acquisitions, financialization of capital, social inequality of economic distribution, and dominance of transnational corporations. Crucial for the discussion of digital platforms is the mediation of capital through legal code, either in the form of antitrust regulation or intellectual property rights (IPR). The present IPR regime is not a foreign element to capital accumulation, but an additional set of rules imposed upon the familiar logic of capitalist development in order to enable its functioning in new conditions. The regime contributes to inequalities in international relations and results in extraction of surplus value from peripheral countries.

Chapter structure

In Chapter 2, titled Production, Circulation, and the Science of Social Forms: Theoretical Foundations, we outline the core of our analytical approach. We explain the pivotal role of value-form analysis, discuss the internal association of value and money and present various approaches to Marxian understanding of the unity of production and circulation. We argue that in the capitalist mode of production the production process is not a domain where value simply lingers. Instead, the exchange relation comes as the final moment of the production of value since it validates and socializes the production process. To understand the full complexity of this process we move on to outline different levels of abstractions and social forms within the capitalist mode of production, moving beyond neoclassical and mainstream analyses that naturalize capitalist production and exchange, and ignore its transitory, historical existence. We utilize three different types of abstractions, general, simple, and determinate, to capture how we understand production in general (general abstractions), shared features of various social forms of production (simple abstractions), and production within a specific mode or social form of production. A specific mode of production occurs when the social and economic determination of form is most complete (determinate abstractions), and when operating mechanisms and interactions that develop within the given form of production result in causal relationship, such as that of exploitation or extraction of surplus value in the capitalist mode of production. To close out the analytical framework for analysing digital platforms, we use the concept of technological form to underline how different modes of production result in different types of configurations of technologies. The concept serves as the link between experiential dimensions of technology usage and the underlying production process that frames technology in a certain way. Finally, we present production on digital platforms. Self-organized engineering communities and public investments played an important role by producing public wealth through non-capitalist social forms of production utilized by capitalist digital platforms. We conclude by outlining the business model on advertising-funded digital platforms offering their key products free of monetary charge, yet being embedded in a broader chain of commodification and surplus value extraction.

In Chapter 3, titled Marxian Perspectives on Monopolies, we critically discuss how monopoly is conceptualized as aberration from perfect competition in mainstream economics or as a stage in the development of capitalism that leads to the dominance of the giant trans-national corporation from a Marxian perspective. Competition is an important aspect of linking production and circulation. Once labour is expended and an output produced competition comes into play, giving rise to extra surplus value because of conditions such as the adoption of a new production method. At the same time, monopoly is already present at the start of the capitalist process as a monopoly over the means of production. Therefore, competition and monopoly do not serve as exclusive points or stages, but as processes within a continuum of accumulation and expansion of capital. The limits and boundaries that shape competition, monopoly, and accumulation are framed by technological, institutional, and political factors. The law has the capacity to constitute abstract objects as commodities, which in specific conditions enter the circuit of capital and augment capital accumulation. This is particularly the case with any digital content where the direct association of capital form and legal form is necessary for the inclusion of such content in the capitalist mode of production. Legal form, we will argue, is constitutive for the movement, operations, and exchange of commodities, as well as for formatting of capital itself, enabling the construction and production of wealth under specific conditions suitable for the capitalist mode of production. Moreover, IPRs result in intellectual monopolies, which enhance commodification, sharpen income, and wealth inequality.

Chapter 4, titled Platforms, Advertising, and Users, evaluates commonly used theories of platform economy and platform capitalism, looking at different ways in which advertising was conceptualized from a Marxian standpoint, critically engaging with theories of user activity, particularly with those that conceptualize it as forms of digital labour. Mainstream approaches provided some of the earliest examples of the platform economy under concepts such as multi-sided markets and zero-price markets in cases where platform services are offered free of charge. However, these theories regularly neglect the fact that multi-sided markets are not balanced and that they do not benefit all actors and all sides of the market equally, nor do they render the social and economic operations of digital monopolies visible. Theories of platform capitalism and platform imperialism provided Marxian interpretations of platforms. However, they come with a set of theoretical deficiencies. Zero-price theories contribute by pointing out that there are non-monetary exchanges occurring through the usage of platforms (that is, data and users) and that producers' profit motivation and costs of production have to be included in the analysis instead of the mainstream marginalist approaches. Advertising is conceptualized as a sales effort from a monopoly capitalism perspective, consumption of advertising as commodity production from an audience labour perspective, and as circulation from close readings of *Capital*, Volume 2. In our understanding, the latter helps situate advertising within a broader perspective of the unity of production and circulation. Finally, we argue how digital labour perspectives, while focusing on user activity as labouring and by conflating production and consumption, lose sight of some of the broader processes of capital reproduction.

In Chapter 5, titled Financialization and Regulation, we look at research and development, labour management, and financial profits within GAFAM. Concentrated and centralized capital allows these companies to impose high entry barriers to competitors who struggle to gather capital and are unable to develop new outputs without comparable access to user data as a key raw material resource. GAFAM uses accumulated capital to reproduce and invest in the development of new outputs and commodities through the production process that depends on flexible but overworked, exploited labour, as well as on inputs from globally dispersed gig workers performing various low-paid tasks. At the same time, financial profits are unevenly distributed to corporate owners and top managers creating enormous income disparities within the tech workforce in general. We then focus on the history of Google's corporate development by looking at how corporate risks changed between 2005 and 2019 in annual market reports, particularly with regard to the technical infrastructure, organizational changes, competitive pressures, advertising risks, and stock performance, legal and regulatory risks. Finally, we analyse the role of state(s) and regulation in the expansion of data-driven business models, focusing especially on how antitrust regulation is unable to transcend the liberal order of the capitalist mode of production, how unchallenged mergers and acquisitions perpetuate GAFAM's oligopoly, and how capital accumulation on a world scale leads to global inequalities.

Chapter 6 is titled Controlling, Processing, and Commercializing Data. It starts by discussing privatization and commercialization of knowledge from Free Software inputs and publicly funded science and research. Free Software advocates were producing software under a set of various legal forms attempting to bypass privatization and commodification. Yet, business-oriented engineering communities slowly introduced and promoted a variety of more permissive licences under the brand Open Source, thus enabling quicker and broader software commercialization. This is not a new development in the history of capitalism since the capitalist mode of production always displayed a tendency to absorb and exploit various 'gifts of nature', cultural achievements, unpaid labour, scientific discoveries, and so on. Even though Google and Facebook provide their key outputs free of charge, their technological form sits on top of public wealth produced by FLOSS and public research that gets deeply embedded in and subordinated to the capitalist mode of production, all with the goal to extract surplus value, enabled by patents and the international intellectual property regime. These technological forms set the rules of data engagement for all actors worldwide including internet users, advertisers, search engine optimizers, website owners, news industries, and others. Tech giants continuously observe, process, and resell background usage data to create technological and economic enclosures that the existing legal forms, algorithmic operations, and regulatory instruments make difficult to penetrate, unpack and grasp by outside actors such as civic organization or democratic institutions.[6] Disinformation and surveillance are only partially the result of weakening liberal democracies. More importantly, these societal outcomes are determined by the extraction of surplus value operating in the background of widely used technological forms.

In Chapter 7, titled Conclusion: Contradictions and Alternatives to Data Commodification, we discuss alternatives for controlling monopolies, imagining alternative technological forms, recognizing public wealth and value and the role of data for democratic development. While acknowledging current initiatives for curbing corporate power through digital taxation policies, we also outline the long-term limits of such thinking, because it does not challenge the surplus value extraction model held together by the capture of public wealth and legal forms aiding commodification and capital reproduction. Instead, we argue that what is needed is a broader notion of surplus, stretching beyond surplus value, covering other social forms of production, along with redistribution of outputs for various democratic purposes, as well as public attentiveness to technological forms conducive to democratic aims and outcomes. Currently, data on a variety of human activities is firmly enclosed within the circuit of capital, both as a technological form, whose technical characteristics we are unable to alter, and as a commodity and private property resulting in economic inequality and all kinds of negative externalities. Through democratic takeover and control of data, human development would stop being a side effect of the drive towards capital accumulation and would move towards post-capitalist sustainable development based on forms of public wealth.

Production, Circulation, and the Science of Forms: Theoretical Foundations

The starting point of the research presented in this book is defined by the simple fact that the platform economy, however one conceptualizes it, has been a part of the capitalist landscape for more than two decades. This empirical reality can be approached from different theoretical traditions and levels of inquiry. Our principal goal is to show that this relatively new reality of contemporary capitalism can become intelligible within the Marxian theoretical framework, and that, in turn, the Marxian approach is responsive enough to include insights from other theoretical traditions and schools of thought. We start from a rather abstract level of Marxian theory of value and social forms in order to proceed to the more concrete features of actually existing platform capitalism. Starting from the presentation of the inner workings of the Marxian research programme is important for several reasons. Most importantly, delineating key assumptions brings more epistemic clarity. Furthermore, certain strands of post-Marxism, most notably *Postoperaismo* and proponents of the cognitive capitalism hypothesis, have formulated their understanding of the so-called knowledge economy on the assumption that Marxian value theory, in its most prominent aspects, is obsolete.

We will have more to say about the issues raised by *Postoperaismo* and related approaches in Chapter 4, but for now it will suffice to show that the key notions and concepts of the Marxian theory can be used to explain the rise and functioning of platform capitalism. This epistemic claim can be expressed in more historical terms: it implies that the rise of platform capitalism does not represent a radical break with the logic of capital accumulation that drove the capitalist development in the 19th and 20th century, notwithstanding all the disruption and breakdowns, real or imaginary. Thus, the novelty of digital platforms must be found on the more concrete level of inquiry, which overlaps and corresponds with the analysis of financialization, another phenomenon that marked the end of the post-Fordist regime of accumulation. From a Marxian perspective, the theory of money is the key for understanding the operations of financialized capitalism, for without settling the issue of the roles and functions of money in a capitalist economy financialization remains a set of loosely connected events and processes that usually appear as a parasitic burden on the back of the 'real economy'. We will deal with some aspects of financialized platforms in Chapter 5. Likewise, platform capitalism and in particular digital monopolies that have occupied its commanding heights must be accounted for with a theory of value in order to make sense of them and all of the surrounding buzzwords.

The value-form and the Marxian research programme

Following Tony Smith's suggestion, the central categories of Marxian value theory can be elaborated using Lakatos' notion of scientific research programme. Lakatos developed the notion of scientific research programme as a way to replace Kuhn's paradigms and avoid the pitfalls of Popper's falsificationism. Without going into details and particularities of the debates in the philosophy of science, the key feature around which a research programme is structured consists in the distinction between a theoretical hard core and a protective belt. In the first step Smith repeats Lakatos' definitions. Hard core consists of basic assumptions and postulates that participants of a research programme take as inviolable and which make theoretical or empirical investigation possible in the first place, while evolving theories, auxiliary hypothesis, and empirical conventions can be found in the protective belt of a research programme (Smith, 1997, p 177). Participants in a research programme will strive to make suitable changes in the protective belt in order to improve its explanatory scope and predictive power. In the second step Smith introduces ordering of basic social forms as 'the hard core of the Marxian research programme devoted to the study of capitalism' (Smith, 1997, p 178). From our perspective, basic propositions and methodological principles of *value-form theory* comprise the hard core of the Marxian research programme.

The position that we are aiming for is somewhat similar to Smith's formulation to which we will return shortly. However, a couple of additional points are required for the sake of clarity and proper scope. Value-form theory at its base seeks to explain the functioning and the development of the capitalist economy in the light of its fundamental contradiction, namely that the production of useful objects undertaken by independent private units must, at a certain point, enter the relations of exchange. Put differently, 'the products of labour necessarily have to take on a social-universal form which is the value-form' (Reuten, 1988, p 51). In other words, privately organized production – privately bought and organized labour power and other inputs – must be socially validated through relations of exchange, otherwise it will remain socially non-existent (Reuten, 1988).

One should thus note two things concerning value-form theory. First, in contrast to other conceptualizations grounded in the reading of Marx that places extensive attention on and give primacy to the sphere of production, value-form theory puts more emphasis on the combined effects of production, circulation and realization. On the most general level, what becomes essential is 'the whole process of reproduction of capitalist social relationships, and of realisation of value and surplus value' including 'forms of money which develop in a capitalist system and the roles which money plays in and around the circuit of capitalist reproduction' (Kincaid, 2007, p 140). Unlike traditional Marxism, where 'the difference between Marx's critique of political economy and classical political economy is widely reduced to surplus value, exploitation and crisis theory', value-form readings emphasize the analysis of forms, the role of money and fetishism, with the critique of Trinitarian formula from the classical political economy and social forms playing a far more prominent role (Heinrich, 2009, p 89).

Common to all varieties of value-form theories is the notion of the unity of production and circulation, that is, the production process is not a domain where produced value somehow lingers, separated and autonomous from the relations of exchange. On the contrary, the exchange relation comes as the final moment of the production of value inasmuch as it validates the privately taken decisions and choices about what, how and for whom to produce. Therefore, on the one hand, 'the exchange relation establishes that the dissociated activity of particular labour – producing particular useful objects – becomes associated', while, on the other, this social validation enables capitalist enterprises to remain private and dissociated for the following sequence of the production process (Reuten, 1988, p 50). Furthermore, as Heinrich argues, coming to terms with the unity of production and circulation is of some methodological import because 'only after capital is depicted as the unity of production and circulation are we at the point where we can deal with the fundamental properties of empirically existing individual capitals' (Heinrich, 2012, p 149). Heinrich's comment here is simply a restatement of the point we made earlier, namely that to situate platform economy in the contemporary capitalist landscape one first must have a general account of capital, how it gets formed and how it moves through different stages of production and circulation.

Internal association of value and money

The unity of production and circulation brings us to the second point related to the internal association of value and money. Considering that value is first and foremost a social relation, and taking on board the insight that this social relation appears 'as a tangible characteristic of a thing' (Heinrich, 2012, p 59), the question that remains is how should the link between these two spheres be conceptualized. It is precisely here that money as a form of value enters the stage. The discussion within the varieties of value-form theories, starting from the *Neue Marx Lektüre* group and continuing within the extended New Reading of Marx (NRM) literature,[1] has brought about the consensus that Marx's theory of capitalism developed in the *Grundrisse* and the first volume *Capital* crucially differs from pre-monetary theories, both classical and neoclassical. Classical political economy, steered by the works of Ricardo, moved toward a double system of measurement of value, built around two separate axes – one articulated in terms of embedded labour, the other given in monetary terms. The consequence of the double measurement has been the partition of, as Bellofiore and Riva put it, objective and external phenomena of monetary exchange from the 'independent' value dimension (Ricardo Bellofiore & Riva, 2015, p 29). The same is true for the neoclassical economics in which money is even less significant, reduced to the function of the medium of exchange with zero importance for the determination of 'real variables' such as economic growth, employment, and so on.

   Value-form analysis purports to represent Marx's value theory as 'monetary theory of value' (Heinrich, 2012), or more specifically, to disclose and explain the 'distinctive, monetary, nature of the capitalist mode of production' (Murray, 2016, p 280). Unlike pre-monetary theories, including quite a few Marxian attempts to determine value of a commodity strictly on the grounds of socially necessary labour time, in the value-form analysis value and money are closely tied together. This means, 'Money is the necessarily displaced social form of wealth and labour in those societies where the capitalist mode of production dominates' (Murray, 2016, p 278). It is a displaced social form because the value of commodity cannot be measured directly, that is, the output of value-producing labour can be grasped in quantitative terms only in the form of money. Two consequences of the proposition that value cannot appear without mediation of money form, repeatedly emphasized by Murray, are the following. First, the relation between commodity form and money form, where they presuppose each other conceptually, yet exclude each other in the actual process of exchange (Murray, 2016, p 283). Second, the inadequacy of Marxian schemes that posit value and money form (price) as independent and dependent variables, respectively.

If the value of a commodity could be straightforwardly equated with the socially necessary labour time required to produce it, then Marxian value theory could be rightly seen as an attempt to show how labour values determine relative prices. In that case, instead of the unity of production and circulation, the analysis of value would begin and end with the analysis of commodity production. In an effort to reassemble the Marxian research programme, value-form theory decisively preserves the notion of labour, that is, of value-producing labour, but the unilateral causal relationship between labour embedded in commodities and market prices is abandoned. Labour, to be sure, still produces value. However, abstract labour has to be validated and rendered socially necessary to produce value. Murray sums up this point in the following manner: 'We learn that such validation occurs only in commodity circulation and that there is no way to tell whether labour is "socially necessary" apart from the circulation of commodities' (2016, p 228). The controversy facing the value-form approach starts with the question about value measurement in the sphere of production and continues with the need to elaborate upon the new status of market forces that the unity of production and circulation apparently entails. Value-form approach is particularly useful for understanding platform capitalism as the direct association between labour and value is severed for products such as Google's web search and Facebook's social networking service. As these products are offered at zero prices, their social validation occurs indirectly through the circulation of final commodities produced in other sectors of the economy. For Google and Facebook, while main outputs are offered free of charge and take the form of pre-commodities, the exchange that validates them is achieved via advertising in the form of intermediate commodities. We explain this further at the end of this chapter.

Various approaches to the unity of production and circulation

One way to resolve the first question concerning measurement is to follow Heinrich's footsteps. Since he takes value – a social relationship, not a thing – and magnitude of value to be simultaneously determined in production and circulation, his 'solution' is to accept that, in order to be socially validated, value must somehow be present in the course of production, but deny any possibility of measurement of value before exchange takes place. For Heinrich, the only thing that can be measured in production is concrete private labour time expended before exchange, but value-constituting labour time (the magnitude of abstract labour) can be expressed only through money. It is therefore specified only when exchange occurs. Heinrich's outline in which the sphere of production comes out as a kind of black box, opens the door to criticism that the roundabout way of specifying the magnitude of value carries the danger of turning value theory into perhaps coherent, but essentially untestable set of assumptions, jeopardizing in turn its scientific credentials (Cockshott, 2013). More generally, value-form approach is charged with the lack of analytical depth arising out of conflation of money with the substance of value and neglect of antagonistic relation between capital and labour in the sphere of production (Saad-Filho, 2002).

As value-form theory moves away from traditional Marxism that gives full analytical primacy to the site of production, uneasiness emerges because bringing circulation into the picture might imply a withdrawal from the Marxian research programme all together. The solution for some proponents of value-form theory has been found in pre-commensuration, which indicates, '[c]ommodities produced do ideally represent an amount of value, ideal money. In this sense, the actual abstraction in the market is anticipated by an ideal abstraction and the actual commensuration in the market is anticipated by the ideal pre-commensuration' (Reuten, 1988, p 54). We can find the same line of reasoning in Bellofiore and Riva. They write,

> The unity of between production and circulation is established on the market, but that unity actualizes a movement from the inner (production) to the outer (exchange). In our view, Marx's argument is that values, as congealed human living labour in the abstract – after production and before exchange – count as 'ideal' money magnitudes anticipated by agents. (Ricardo Bellofiore & Riva, 2015, p 33)

Notwithstanding the undeniable importance of measurement of value (that is, the magnitude of value) in production, certain key insights that have been forming and ripening over time within value-form theory can be upheld even without the comprehensive resolution of the measurement issue. Carchedi's defence of abstract labour as material substance of value is a case in point. Whereas any run of the mill value-form theorist would endorse the view of abstract labour as social relation constituted in exchange, Carchedi affirms the materiality of abstract labour and the concept of value as a measurable quantity. Nevertheless, he agrees that Marx's theory of value is, in fact, the theory of distinctive social form of wealth and labour in capitalism, and that value is not fully realized in production, but requires commodity exchange in the market in order to be validated (Carchedi, 2009, p 155). As this brief overview of the current Marxian debate on value shows, more than one path leads to the recognition of unity of production and circulation founded on the centrality of money form. So it is possible to move forward in the empirical direction and zero in on the legal, technological, and other forms located in the sphere of circulation that play a role in the process of realization of value produced on digital platforms.

Because the sphere of circulation was, for obvious reasons, almost equated with the market, while the market was considered to be the essential grid of neoclassical, and later on, neoliberal economics, a curious dichotomy emerged, consisting of production on the one side and market forces, on the other. The value-form approach removed the unwritten obligation to put all explanatory weight on production and, thus, enabled the forces of competition and the social forms related to the sphere of circulation to gain proper analytical status. The development of Marxian research programme is dependent upon its ability to give an adequate account of financialized capitalism (Kincaid, 2007, p 146), which means it has to take seriously the forces of competition and monopoly and expand – to come back to Smith's discussion – the ordering of the social forms.

The dialectic of social forms, understood here as ordering of internally related social forms, can be indeed traced to Marx's exposition in the first volume of *Capital*. On the most elementary level, as Smith explains, commodity form and money form are the two determinations of value-form, and both are, as we move away from simple commodity production to fully developed capitalist accumulation, incorporated into capital form (Smith, 1997, p 178). Once the origin of capital form is accounted for through the ordering of social forms, we can proceed and analyse the movement of capital through different stages, from production to circulation and distribution (Smith, 1997, p 178). This is a familiar sequence for the students of Marx, to which Smith adds further clarification by introducing the notion of causal mechanism. It is clear that by itself, the ordering of social forms is not explanatory. It is simply a classification. However, for Marx, as Smith shrewdly notes, each determination of a social form comes with an elaboration of a mechanism operating in the capitalist mode of production, for example mechanism of exploitation, given the relation between capital and labour, or the mechanism of extraction of surplus profit given the introduction of new technology (Smith, 1997, p 181).

Without further specification of the causal relations lurking behind the ordering of social forms, our point here is that the unity of production and circulation, based on the analysis of social forms, depends, not only on the link between commodity form and money form, but crucially on the legal form as well. Thus, legal or juridical form should be inserted in the elementary ordering of social forms inasmuch as it can be shown that commodity form and legal form necessarily go hand in hand. Moreover, the introduction of legal form does more than conclude the examination of the aforementioned relation between commodity and money by adding an extra axis. It facilitates the empirical analysis of monopoly and its necessary legal form, which is essential for the political economy of digital monopoly and its intrinsic relatedness to intellectual property rights – we return to that in the Chapter 3. For now, it is important to emphasize that the legal form is a special kind of social form, one that enables economic determination of form as commodity on digital platforms.

Abstractions, social forms, and modes of production

One of the most important Marx's insights was that there is no such thing as a universal, natural way to produce. His understanding emphasized the social character of any production, focusing on both the social forms that elements engaged in production acquire – means of production become capital in the capitalist production – and on the resulting social relations, workers being exploited. Unlike the neoclassical mainstream economic thinking starting from the individual choice of consumption as the central principle that puts the whole economic system in motion, Marx extended classical economists' focus on both production and exchange (Murray, 2005, p 76). His expansion of the social character of the object of research, most importantly through the social and economic form determination, is perhaps the most important methodological aspect that differentiates his approach. Many authors, particularly Marxists, but also some heterodox economists (Hein, 2014, p 50), recognized that the analysis of social phenomena through forms can be deployed as a critique of the mainstream economics and its naturalizing approach.[2] Whereas mainstream is focused on 'a science of the reproduction of society within specific economic and political forms', Marx's 'critique of political economy must be conceived of as a science of these forms' (Elbe, 2013). Emphasizing further this key difference, Elbe points out how the overall method of Marx's critique 'can be described as the "development" or "analysis" of forms'.[3]

Scientific methodology of Marx's approach

It is common to use term goods and services to talk about economic outputs. Although this is an important classification of the two types of very different kinds of products (Parry et al, 2011), with a long history and disputed legal interpretations (Smith & Woods, 2005), it says nothing on the social character of outputs acquired through social and economic determination of form. Discussing platform capitalism outside of classical Marxian categories of commodity, labour, capital, and surplus value leads to such impoverished positions, as we explain in Chapter 4 discussing digital platforms. Scientific work, Murray claims developing from Marx, requires construction of determinate abstractions in order to grasp objects of inquiry in their actually existing forms, shaped by social processes.[4] General abstractions, such as production, or goods and services are not sufficient, since 'In their generality, they describe one object as well as the next, and do not allow the scientific thinker to touch on the specific differences of the object under scrutiny' (Murray, 1988, p 122). With this approach, Murray argues, 'economics pretends to do what cannot be done, to provide a scientific account of the production and distribution of wealth in utter abstraction from historically specific social forms' (Murray, 2000, p 28).

Instead of goods and services, general descriptions of production outputs, there is a more specific abstraction when it comes to capitalist production, commodity. Commodity however, does not cover outputs from non-capitalist production. Yet, nor do goods and services, or products, or outputs – all of them are general abstractions merely enabling us to express in short the following meaning: any sort of results, or outputs, from any kind of production. Murray calls such abstractions general. Science, however, he emphasizes, requires more than just general abstractions, it 'deals with understanding the actual, and since the actual is always determinate, general abstractions are in principle inadequate for scientific explanation' (Murray, 2000). In Marx's words, workers and means of production are general abstractions: 'whatever social form of production, workers and means of production always remain its factors' (1864/1978, p 120). Once they are connected, which has to occur for a production to take place, Marx continues, what matters is 'the particular form and mode in which this connection is effected' (Marx, 1864/1978, p 120). In other words, a production always occurs in a social setting, which determines the character of the elements, or factors, taking part in that production. When factors of production are captured by categories adequate to the particular form and mode of production, to their social setting, according to Murray we are dealing with determinate abstractions, 'appropriate to the specificities of its actual object' (1988, p 122).[5]

Production, Marx notes, is useful as a general abstraction since it 'emphasizes and defines the common aspects and thus spares us the need of repetition' (1857/1987, p 23). However, actually existing concrete productions differ. Although some of their features are shared across all, some across a few epochs (Marx, 1857/1987), it is essential, Marx emphasizes, to capture differences between the ways humans produce. Those differences are captured by what Murray calls determinate abstractions. Both types of abstractions are required, since without determinate ones, general abstractions have little scientific worth (Murray, 1988, p 126). Marx continues on how his approach differs from classical economists:

> For example, no production is possible without an instrument of production, even if this instrument is simply the hand. ... Consequently [modern economists say] capital is a universal and eternal relation given by nature – that is, provided one omits precisely those specific factors which turn the 'instrument of production' or 'accumulated labour' into capital. (1857/1987, p 23)

Parsed through Murray's terminology, Marx charges classical economists for not being able to differentiate a general abstraction, such as a tool, from a determinate one, such as capital, a tool used in a capitalist production. Hence, they fail to see how productions differ, leading them to treat capital and capitalist social relations as both eternal and natural features of production. In Marx's words: 'On the failure to perceive this difference rests, for instance, the entire wisdom of modern economists who are trying to prove the eternity and harmony of the existing social relations' (1857/1987, p 23). Their aim, Marx continues, criticizing Adam Smith and John Stuart Mill, is not to grasp particular features of the capitalist production, but rather 'to present production ... as encased in eternal natural laws independent of history, at which opportunity bourgeois relations are then quietly smuggled in as the inviolable natural laws on which society in the abstract is founded' (Marx, 1857/1987, p 25). Failure to grasp the need to construct abstractions adequate to the specific character of production, Murray develops, leads to 'illusion of the economic'. The illusion results from 'projecting certain perceived or real features of the capitalist production process onto the labour process in general', leading in turn to another mistake, imagining 'that the labour process in general can stand alone, that it can actually exist independently of all determinate social form' (2002a, p 257).[6] Given that the neoclassical vision of production and wealth is deeply embedded in the regulation and legal forms of the current liberal order, and that this is an issue of particular relevance for understanding the persistence of digital monopolies and the inability of most regulatory measures to curb their power, we utilize our Marxian approach to develop a more acute understanding of digital platforms. We will return to these issues throughout the book.

Development of determinate abstractions through social forms

To be able to grasp the specificities of digital monopolies, we have to develop both general abstractions, which denote what is common in different productions, and determinate abstractions, categories appropriate to the logic of the studied production, its element, and relations between them. Products, goods, and services will not do much for us, as they describe any output from any system of production. Similarly, production of commodities, traditional source of the capitalistic production of surpluses by which capital expands and accumulates cannot be applied to outputs free of monetary charge to consumers, such as Google web search, or Facebook and the set of social networking companies it acquired (Instagram, WhatsApp). If outputs are not commodities in a traditional Marxian sense, what are they?

Keeping in mind Murray's contributions on general and determinate abstractions, we notice from the very start of all drafts of *Capital* that use-value is a general abstraction, with determinate abstractions being the forms in which wealth and elements of production appear under the capitalist production.[7] The seemingly magical property of use-values when they become commodities, Marx notes, is that despite their differences in material attributes, they became quantitatively comparable through the value form they acquire in the exchange. The same happens with human labour. Becoming a commodity itself as an element of the capitalist production, 'the private labour which produces [commodities] acquires as a result a general social form, the form of equality with all other kinds of labour' (Marx, 1864/1978, p 159).

One of Marx's most vivid critiques of the classical political economists' naturalization of capitalist production, of their failure to grasp the character of objects under research and accompanying categories, is developed in the third volume of *Capital* in Chapter 48. The Trinity Formula is the name Marx coined for the three sources of revenue – capital, land, labour – appearing in the works of political economists he critiqued. Marx argues how capital, land, and labour cannot be deployed as categories in an analysis of a concrete, historically existing production such as the capitalist one. While capital belongs to a definite social form of production, land (or earth as Marx also called it) and labour are generic, universal elements of any form of production. When deployed in the capitalist mode of production, they acquire a social and economic character, which has to be captured by determinate abstractions adequate to the resulting determination of form (1864/2015, p 889). The grave error committed by political economists was mixing of different levels of abstractions in the same conceptual understanding.

Another manifestation of the naturalizing approach ignorant of the role of social forms is in the realm of distribution. The forms of distribution of social wealth – manifested as the division of revenue to owners of capital, land, and labour power – seem separate from the production process. They are, however, an elementary part of the capitalist form of production, Marx argues. Financialization inserts further divide in the realm of distribution between workers and the owners of capital, resulting in extreme forms of social and economic inequality. In the mainstream economics and political economy, and in 'the customary view', Marx notes, 'these relations of distribution appear to be natural relations, relations arising from the nature of all social production, from the laws of human production pure and simple' (Marx, 1865/1981, p 1017). Although societies have to produce surpluses (producing more than they consume to reproduce their populations) in order to advance, there is nothing natural about the form that production and distribution of surpluses acquire. As Marx highlights in the closing part of *Capital*, Volume 3, every production of surplus is a matter of social arrangement, resting on the separation between labour necessary for the reproduction of worker and her dependants, and surplus labour, labour in the excess of what workers gets in return (Marx, 1865/1981, p 1017).

While we return to the questions of social and economic forms on digital monopolies, it is worth mentioning here briefly some of the key issues raised by the methodological approach outlined in this section. Free Software and Open Source production and their outputs play an important role in the business models of digital monopoly platforms. This is especially the case for Apple and Google, whose core technologies are impossible to imagine without Free Software and Open Source products they utilized and developed further. A significant portion of such production occurs on a volunteer basis, with labour not directly taking the waged form. When it does take such a form, organizations paying the wages are often not-for-profit. When they are for-profit capitalist firms, performing work is in many cases not directed by the capitalist production process and workers are paid to do what they used to do voluntarily or within not-for-profit organizations prior to their entrance in the capitalist production process. Furthermore, resources and technology necessary for the production of software, such as computers, buildings, network equipment, are means of production that are frequently owned by workers or by public research and academic institutions.[8]

Modes and social forms of production

If human production is not a singular kind of naturally organized activity, what is it then and how do we conceptually understand its plurality? Using available natural resources humans developed multiple co-existing and nowadays largely interconnected forms of production. In our present historical epoch, a single form, the capitalist one, is capable of dominating all other forms. Marx called it the capitalist mode of production. Although this methodological approach is best to scientifically grasp the plurality of production, we are faced with two significant problems. Marx did not define the concept of the mode of production in one place, nor did he use it consistently across his texts, despite using it frequently (R. Jessop, 1990; Himmelweit, 1998; Olsen, 2009). In the broadest sense, we understand a mode of production to signify a social form of production with significant differences that mark it from other forms. The term modes of production serve two functions. It enables us to grasp multiple co-existing social forms of production, their categories, and laws of motion. It also enables us to conceptualize the capitalist mode of production as the dominant mode whose logic of surplus value extractions, in a strictly economic sense, drives the overall production of wealth, penetrating into and to a significant extent shaping other social forms and modes of production, with a tendency to turn them into capitalist production. Given the existence of various social forms of production as inputs in the production of digital platforms the approach enables us to develop insights into the structure and dynamic of their relationship. Furthermore, it also helps us to rethink (see the last chapter) how we understand these non-capitalist social forms of production in the light of their possible strengthening and broadening.

In the traditional Marxist sense, slavery, feudalism, and capitalism are all understood as modes of production developing throughout human history. In the more orthodox understandings, rarely present nowadays but dominant throughout much of older Marxist literature, this development occurs in succession, with more empirically grounded and conceptually subtle readings grasping those modes as intertwined and co-existing. Similar to the comments on lack of consistency in the usage of the concept, Banaji's reading of Marx's usage of the term reveals that Marx did not settle on a single concept. He used a whole array of concepts to signify modes of production: 'forms of production', 'forms of the social process of production', 'epochs in the economic development of society', 'epochs of production', 'periods of production', and 'historical organizations of production' (Banaji, 2010, p 52). From the variety of terms deployed by Marx, Banaji settles that for him the mode of production 'figures as a "social form of production" or "social form of the production process"' (Banaji, 2010, p 52). Judging by the choice of terms alone, Banaji's reading is in the direction of ours. However, a more detailed reading reveals that Banaji settles on modes of production as umbrella concepts covering long periods. For Banaji, the capitalist mode of production spans over centuries of capitalist development, leading him to see the history of capitalist development as configurations of the capitalist mode of production, rather than as a combination of various modes of production with the capitalist one growing towards the position of dominance.

From the social form perspective, with contemporary societies as the object of research in mind, the productive way to understand various forms of production is not to bundle them under a single umbrella concept but to grasp their specificities though the development of categories, laws of motion, causal mechanisms, and social relations adequate to their own character. If modes of production are reserved exclusively for epochs, for long historical periods, then what term do we use for non-capitalist production within those epochs? From the perspective of digital monopoly platforms operating under the capitalist mode of production, how do we account for the variety of other participants on which digital platforms rely on, such as NGO, self-employed, Free Software, or public sector producers? To what mode or social form of production do they belong? Given that in the entire second part of the first volume of *Capital* Marx discusses the transformation of money into capital, how do we understand and name the social and economic form determination of money in non-capitalist productions? Calling it money would be staying on the level of general abstractions, and such things cannot exist in the realm of production – there is no generic, or natural production, it always assumes forms that are socially and economically determined. Money is a general abstraction; its social character has to be grasped through a determinate abstraction adequate to its character in a specific social form of production.

In other words, if modes of production are reserved for epochs, then non-capitalist productions under the domination of the capitalist mode cannot be covered with the concept modes of production. At best, we could call them social forms of production, whose ascendance to dominance transforms them into a mode of production. In this understanding, we would be dealing with multiple social forms of production, with a single form becoming a mode through its rise to the dominant position. The other option is that we accept the existence of multiple co-existing modes of production, with a single dominant mode. Both options seem sensible as they allow expressing what is conceptually and analytically required: the presence of significantly different socially formed ways to produce wealth.[9]

Regardless of the terminology and the lack of definitional consistency, we are certain that there is a single dominant mode of production. For a mode to dominate, the first condition is that it has to dominate over others. Furthermore, the second condition is that for a mode of production to be historically specific, there has to be a historical period when either the mode did not exist or it was not dominant. During its ascendance to dominance, there must have been other modes, affirming the notion that multiple modes of production do co-exist. Without those two conditions Marx's understanding of the capitalist mode of production, which includes simultaneous existence of other types of production, would be rendered meaningless. An important question for grasping the diversity of productions that can be identified on digital platforms, a question that we keep open throughout the book, is how to conceptualize these other types of production: as social forms of production, or as modes of production, and what methods and criteria do we utilize for these distinctions.

Simple abstractions: determined, but not fully

Unlike Murray's work, focused on Marx's methodological approach that is interpreted through concepts such as general and determinates abstractions, Banaji starts his treatment of types of abstraction concluding how 'neither Marx nor Engels ever consciously reflected on the nature of their categories' (2010, p 53). His starting point differs, while the fragments of Marx's methodological writing such as those uncovered by Murray are lacking. Yet, Banaji ends up with a related, if not broadly speaking similar conclusion, albeit through different terms and with a loser, less tightly defined set of arguments. The differences between his and Murray's reading seem complementary. Banaji points out that Marx defined the term 'simple categories' to denote categories 'common to several epochs of production'. This meant that 'in this simple determination, "wage-labour", that is, the commodity labour–power, was known under various forms of social production before the capitalist epoch'.[10] In the capitalist mode of production, we are dealing with wage labour as 'historically determinate abstraction equivalent to the abstraction of "capital" and "commodity-fetishism"'. At this 'deeper level of abstraction', as a '"concrete" category, wage-labour was, for Marx, capital-positing, capital-creating labour'. Marx called this approach to categories to be 'in the strict economic sense' (Banaji, 2010, p 54).

If we, however, identify relations of production with 'particular forms of exploitation', historical specificity gets 'radically impoverished'. In such a line of argumentation, if 'what makes an economy "capitalist" is the statistical preponderance of the simple abstraction "labour–power as a commodity"', a simple category is confused for a historically determinate one when it becomes dominant in its quantity, when it dominates statistically as a form of labour, Banaji argues. What is missed by the reading Banaji assigns to Maurice Dobb, and what is the key method for Marx to grasp wage labour as capitalist, is to see wage labour on the same level of abstraction as Marx, 'in the strict economic sense', Banaji emphasizes. Such a labour has to be 'value-producing labour' (Banaji, 2010, p 55). More importantly, in many historically important schools of Marxist thinking, such as Stalinist 'pseudo-Marxism and the "critical" tendencies of modern Marxism', this mistaken use of simple determinations in place of determinate historical social forms led to mixing of separate levels of abstraction (Banaji, 2010, p 61). The addition of simple abstractions fills a theoretical gap, naming the type of abstractions between the general and determinate ones.

While Banaji does not utilize the term determinate abstractions, commenting Rubin, he seems to be on the same track as Murray, recognizing the importance of naming such specific type of categories with the term *concrete abstractions*: 'When simple abstractions are confused for concrete categories, when they are not yet subjected to a process of further abstraction which is a process of their concretization, the specific forms and functions which compose their historical content in any given situation are left "indeterminate"' (Banaji, 2010, p 98). This usage suggests an agreement with the logic behind Murray's choice of the term determinate for non-general abstractions that are fully determined. Rubin can be helpful here as the first author that interpreted Marx in a way that represents the diverse approaches banded under the New Marx Reading label. Rubin shows how Marx used the variety of terms to denote forms that 'do not reflect the properties of things', but properties of the 'social character ... inherent not in things as such, but in things ... through which people enter into certain production relations with each other' (Rubin, 1928/1973, p 39).[11]

Since in Marx, 'we are dealing with the basic distinction between the material process of production and its social forms ... with the social forms of the process of production, as opposed to its material-technical aspects' (Rubin, 1928/1973, p 40), Rubin concludes, this grasping through 'differences in form' is 'the completely new methodological formulation of economic problems' (Rubin, 1928/1973). Classical economists, Rubin continues, reduce 'social-economic forms ... to their material-technical content'. Looking over the horizon of the capitalist economy:

> Marx asked: why does labor assume the form of value, means of production the form of capital, means of workers' subsistence the form of wages, increased productivity of labor the form of increased surplus value? His attention was directed to the analysis of social forms of economy and the laws of their origin and development, and to 'the process of development of forms (Gestaltungsprozess) in their various phases'. (Rubin, 1928/1973, p 43)

Complementary to Murray's and Banaji's methodological insights, Rubin concludes how:

> the uniqueness of Marx's analytical method does not consist only of its historical, but also of it sociological character of the intense attention which it paid to social forms of economy [by which he] tried to explain the origin and

character of social forms which are assumed by the material processes of production. (Rubin, 1928/1973, p 43)

Rubin calls this new approach to political economy sociological (Rubin, 1928/1973, p 37). For Rubin, political economy 'deals with human working activity, not from the standpoint of its technical methods and instruments of labor, but from the standpoint of its social form' (Rubin, 1928/1973, p 31). What Rubin seems to have in mind, writing about political economy affirmatively, and not in the sense of Marx's critique of political economy, is that Marx's approach to the object of study covered by political economy, constructed through his critique, provides us with an improved approach. Put differently, there is an affirmative theory of the social and economic production of wealth in Marx's work that goes beyond the mere critique of political economy. This affirmative reading, however, differs significantly from the one that has been a hallmark of traditional Marxism, of what Reuten perceptively calls 'a "positive" theory of value', whereby Marx had a "labour theory of value" with ' "value" being a naturalistic concept, reckoned in a labour-time dimension' (Reuten, 2003, p 154). In our reading, close to Rubin's, such a methodological approach contains some of the key ingredients for improving our understanding of monopoly digital platforms. Extending Marx's underlying method to production through social and economic determination of forms allows us to start developing an understanding of non-capitalists forms of production that play an important part for the capitalist monopoly platforms, such as publicly financed research and Free Software production. Furthermore, the approach enables us to develop a more nuanced understanding of the operations of the capitalist mode of production as monopoly digital platforms.

Synthesis, categories, and levels of abstraction

From the left political perspectives, it is often correctly said that production has to overcome value as its driving force. This implies overcoming of the capitalist mode of production and its self-expanding pursuit of surplus value. Such statements are frequently followed up by the notion that an alternative should be production for the sake of use-value. However, use-value is a general abstraction denoting usefulness to humans. Given that outputs of a production have to take certain social form through the process of production, their form remains unspecified with the category use-value. The entire mainstream economic cannon, embedded in legal forms targeting monopolies such as antitrust, makes a related mistake with their understanding of utility. Being general abstractions, not only do utility and use-value have no unit of measure, they both lack any way of being captured on the level of appearances.[12] They are general abstractions, predominantly on the side of consumption. Murray summarizes this in his notion of 'use-value' romanticism, arguing that use-value, like production, lacks 'specific social form' and it is 'technological naiveté that technology develops free of specific social forms and purposes' (Murray, 2016, p 50).

Moving one level of abstraction down from the level of generalities such as products or outputs, we can say that products are mostly outputs exchanged for money, or what is commonly referred to as commodities. However, since we find both production and circulation of commodities in a broad array of modes of production and historical epochs, the level of this abstraction is still too general to capture the specificities of the capitalist mode of production. In Marx's words, this is as if we are 'acquainted with nothing but the abstract categories of circulation, which are common to all these modes of production, we cannot possibly know anything of the specific points of difference of those modes, nor pronounce any judgment upon them' (Marx, 1867/2010, p 124). Similarly, the mere presence of wage labour, as Banaji correctly insists, and as Marx also noted, cannot be the criteria for the capitalist mode of production, as we find wage labour in many modes of production and historical epochs. This type of abstraction, appearing in multiple modes of production, can be named simple, using Banaji's terminology. In that case, the term general remains reserved for abstractions that do not have an empirical instance and that are without a concrete, really existing social context, such as labour, production, and product.

The result is the hierarchy of types of abstractions. General abstractions, such as production, labour, product/output, goods, and services, are the highest level of abstractions, sparing us of repetition, shortening what we need to say yet without expressing anything on the social context or form. Simple abstractions, a level below the general ones, are socially formed abstractions shared across several historical epochs and modes of production, not being fully determined within a given mode of production. The examples are commodity and wage labour. They appear in pre-capitalist modes of production, such as feudalism, where the driving logic of production is not surplus value extraction. Hence, the determination of commodities that occurs in feudalism, including the commodification of labour as wage labour, remains limited qualitatively and quantitatively. Finally, dropping another level below, we find determinate or concrete abstractions, whose form is socially and economically determined by the mode of production they belong to, such as wage labour, commodity, and surplus value within the capitalist mode of production. Determinate abstraction are the most important ones. In order for the character of a mode of production to be properly understood, it is essential to grasp how determinate abstractions differ from single and general abstractions, along with specific tendencies, causal mechanisms, and laws of motion that bind elements of production together. We will come back to this methodology and apply it directly to digital monopolies later in this chapter.

Technological form and the experiential dimension

To complete the analytical framework necessary to understand digital monopolies we need to situate the experiential dimension of technology within the capitalist mode of production. This implies theorizing the role of internet users in order to understand how the realm of experience and the realm of commodification interact through technological forms. Pairing and combining economic processes with subjective dimensions of human experience is a long-standing theoretical puzzle for Marxian theorists: from Lukács, Frankfurt School, and Raymond Williams' cultural materialism, to Jodi Dean's communicative capitalism and many other approaches. However, technology can add to that complexity because of an entrenched Cartesian paradigm that distinguishes material objects from social relations of exchange (Hornborg, 2014).

For traditional political economy, technology is often understood as fixed capital, part of the means of production. Here we look at technologies not only as means of production and products of a given mode of production, but also as technological forms that, through technical objects, frame unequal social relations of monetary and non-monetary (that is, data) exchange. Whether the experiential dimension contains political participatory actions, consumption of advertising and cultural images or posting racist and xenophobic content on social media makes no difference to the system of capital reproduction. The dominant technological form frames all engagements instrumentally to commodify them and accumulate capital. Along the way, it produces consequences (or negative externalities in mainstream economic terms) to democratic processes through surveillance, privacy abuse and disinformation. To unpack this complex proposition let us start from theoretical roots of commodity fetishism, which will allow us to extend the concept of fetish and instrumental rationality to the critique of capitalist technological forms such as platforms and digital devices.

Commodity form, fetishism, and reification

For Marx (1996), commodities are results of the capitalist mode of production, products of human labour that have a use value but are shaped in capitalist society through their exchange for money. Yet commodity is not just the result of production inputs and exchange of outputs. It is also a social form. Marx differentiated between the natural form of a commodity, such as a chair, and its social form, which makes it a commodity in capitalist society (Heinrich, 2012, pp 40, 41). In a society, where the capitalist mode of production dominates, commodities acquire a fetish-like character in which the social foundation of their existence becomes obscured and in which a 'definite social relation between men assumes a fantastic form of the relation between things' (Marx, 1996, p 83). The act of exchange is the act in which fetishism occurs. Such a mystification of the underlying social relations is the core of the capitalist mode of production more broadly. With capital (profit and interest), land (rent), and labour (wages), a complete 'mystification of the capitalist mode of production' occurs, creating a 'conversion of social relations into things, the direct coalescence of the material production relations with their historical and social determination' (Marx, 1998, p 817). These mystifications do not arise out of the conscious manipulation of the ruling class, but from the structure of bourgeois society and the activity that constantly reproduces this structure. The subjects of the social processes cease to be people and instead become commodity, money, and capital (Heinrich, 2012, pp 181–4).

Among the earliest interpreters of fetishism was Lukács (1972) who played a crucial influence on the development of Frankfurt School's theory. Lukács famously developed the notion of reification and expanded it to include class-consciousness of the working class.[13] Yet, Lukács failed to distinguish between the total reification of pure capitalism, and the partial reification of existing capitalism which led him to excessive degrees of essentialism (Albritton, 2003, p 62). While focusing on the concept of totality, he overstated the degree to which reification takes hold at the level of historical reality. As a result, capitalism becomes impossible to transform, unless transformation becomes conceived as a total revolution in which the proletariat acquires knowledge of the whole (Albritton, 2003, p 74). Extending the reification concept towards pure dominance over consciousness also creates a danger of exaggerating control mechanisms in capitalist society, control mechanisms that are a direct result of the essential, economic, characteristics of a capitalist society. In the process of interpretation of the commodity form, Lukács lost much of Marx's critical edge, which was founded on a dialectical dynamic between the economy and social forms.

The decisive element of the Frankfurt School method was similar, geared to trace economic and social phenomena back to social relations between humans. This was done to 'unmask their fetishist objectification and conceive of them as being the acts of human beings themselves, which had somehow escaped human control' (Wiggershaus, 1995, p 55). Horkheimer and Adorno (2002), in their famous critique of the culture industry, provided an interpretation of the social irrationalities of the commodity form. Culture becomes a commodity completely subject to the law of exchange, which becomes its predominant logic. Advertising loses its function of orienting the buyer in the market and, in conditions of monopoly capitalism, 'strengthens the bond which shackles consumers to big combines' (Horkheimer and Adorno, 2002, p 131). Similarly, Marcuse (2007) viewed culture and mass communications as structural elements that enact the widespread logic of the commodity form: 'If mass communications blend together harmoniously, and often unnoticeably, art, politics, religion, and philosophy with commercials, they bring these realms of culture to their common denominator – the commodity form. The music of the soul is also the music of the salesmanship. Exchange value, not truth value counts' (Marcuse, 2007, pp 60, 61).[14]

While opening up the 'commodity form' to social irrationalities resulting from commodity exchange unfolding in the background, most Frankfurt School theorists remain disconnected from the original formulation by Marx and from considerations of the underlying political economy, value, and the unity of production and circulation. Reasons for it can be located in the general disillusionment with the historical role of the working class and the struggle between labour and capital for bringing social change in mid-twentieth century. They are simultaneously fateful to Marx, and divergent from him. According to Lotz (2018, p 977), Adorno and Horkheimer present nicely how a specific ideological and psychic structure is produced as empty wishes by the culture industry. However, they rarely trace this structure back to the fact that it depends upon the structure of production by media corporations and the structure of distribution and consumption. The theoretical apparatus of the Frankfurt School is inspired by the notion of the commodity, yet it expands this concept into other areas that disconnect it from its roots in the critique of political economy (Postone, 1996).

However, instead of criticizing their lack of faithfulness to Marx, let us consider the Frankfurt School critique as an extension of the critique of political economy towards an 'expansive critical theory of society' (Murray, 2018, p 779). Corporate platforms and their technologies are produced within a capitalist mode of production with their value realized in circulation either through direct sales or through a share of surplus value from advertised products. Platforms steer and frame certain types of online actions, controlling, processing and commodifying data as a business strategy along the way. The lack of a direct monetary exchange in the usage of some services contributes to their reified existence, strengthened by desires for autonomous systems, and legitimized by digital mythologies (Mosco, 2004). The Frankfurt School theory helps shift our focus away from technical appearances of platforms, and moves it towards uncovering economic processes behind these systems. However, in our approach, commodification and the commodity form is not the starting point nor do we argue that the internet user is a dominated subject whose dystopian experiential dimension she cannot possibly escape. Our approach reverses the logic of the Frankfurt School and looks at how the experiential and economic dimensions reinforce each other. Nonetheless, it is glaringly obvious that this relation is asymmetrical and that only corporate actors hold the keys to framing the technical structure of possible behavioural and experiential responses online. Before we move on to our understanding of the technological form, let us briefly examine another theoretical element that will allow us to precisely situate technological forms within the capitalist mode of production: instrumental rationality.

Rationalization and the technological form

That the commodity form and commodity exchange govern many aspects of society is a far-reaching premise. The way in which this premise was connected with the impact and distortion of the totality of human relations in capitalism was through a 'rational critique of reason'. In sociological terms, such an approach was evident in the re-interpretation of the rationalization concept developed by Max Weber. Weber argued that modern society was increasingly bureaucratized and rationalized as it moved away from traditional society in the early 20th century. The driving force behind this transformation was not capitalism or industrialization, it was the underlying cultural values found within the Protestant ethic in Europe that decisively separated modern from traditional society. Yet for the Frankfurt School, it was not the unique system of cultural values, but bourgeois society, commodity form, and market exchange that imprint a totalizing rationality on society.

Marcuse (2009) directly opposes Weber's understanding of value-free[15] science, neutrality, and value-free rationality as drivers of social change within modernity. Weber's reason is, according to Marcuse, an abstraction that renders possible the universally calculable efficiency of the capitalist apparatus. Rationality with the aim of calculable efficiency organizes and controls things and humans, factory and bureaucracy, work, and leisure. Yet, for Weber, it remains only formal because it does not specify the purpose of scientific-technical constructions nor their subjects and objects (Marcuse, 2009, p 154). Critique of Weberian concepts was the foundation for Marcuse's most famous works and one of his main theses – that technology is not neutral, and that it always implies a system of instrumental purposes. Advanced industrial society becomes a political project of dominance over nature, and technological rationality becomes a political rationality: 'in the medium of technology, culture, politics, and the economy merge into an omnipresent system that swallows up or repulses all alternatives. The productivity and growth potential of this system stabilize society and contain technical progress within the framework of domination' (Marcuse, 2007, p xlvii).

Marcuse (1998) also made a crucial distinction between technology and technics. Technics, on the one hand, implies the technical apparatus of industry, transportation, and communication. Technics is just a partial factor. Technology, on the other hand, is a 'mode of organizing and perpetuating (or changing) social relationships, a manifestation of prevalent thought and behaviour patterns, an instrument for control and domination. Technics by itself can promote authoritarianism as well as liberty, scarcity as well as abundance, the extension as well as the abolition of toil' (Marcuse, 1998, p 41). It is the social form that technics acquires in the capitalist mode of production that makes it a technological form, and within a capitalist society, a tool for control and dominance. The relation between technology and technics allows for broad conceptualizations of the role of technical systems in society. While technics can be understood as a system in which society can be successful in achieving certain ends, technology should be understood as potentially being validated by criteria other than efficiency and pure instrumental reason (Gandesha, 2018, p 657).

Marcuse argued that a true transformation of capitalism must also take into account the transformation of the dominating social and economic form of technics and technical solutions and the potential for transforming science and technology towards serving human needs better (Marcuse, 1971).[16] Such an approach was expanded by Feenberg (1996) in his critical theory of technology. He developed the so-called design critique by arguing that social interests always influence the implementation of technical principles. Technical creation therefore involves interaction between reason and experience: '[k]nowledge of nature is required to make a working device. This is the element of technical activity we think of as rational. But the device must function in a social world, and the lessons of experience in that world influence design' (Feenberg, 2010, p xvii).

The process of software production can be described as a dynamic between programmable solutions to given problems on the one hand, and experience of service users analysed through usage data on the other hand. In that sense, there can never be a single, all-encompassing, rationality governing all social relations. There are always multiple and competing rationalities at play (Feenberg, 2017). Therein lies the political dimension of how technical systems are deployed and constructed and how design features allow and promote certain behavioural responses while reducing and constraining other types of responses. The dialectical method of the Frankfurt School allowed Marcuse to observe the existence of a distorted technological form of capitalism in its totality, of the social impact of its specific character emanating from the dominant commodity form and production for profits he called one-dimensional society. However, his ideas should not be dismissed as a dystopian critique of consumer society.[17] Such a broad conceptualization can still be useful if we consider the multiplicity of potential rationalities instead of a single one-dimensional rationality for how certain online solutions are created. The key is to understand the social form of technology. Focusing solely on the appearance of algorithms, or technics, over-emphasizes the novelty of new technical discoveries, while missing basic characteristics that enable their widespread use for the purpose of capital accumulation and reproduction. The introduction of algorithms in many areas of contemporary economy, politics, and society is a continuation of the drive towards implementing various automation techniques to increase efficiency ensure optimization, calculability, and predictability. Automation is always found in the adoption of new tools that, taken together, result in new technological forms.

Technological form is, therefore, the result of a given mode of production, whether capitalist or not. Humans have always produced useful tools and pragmatic solutions for given problems: from spears and axes to algorithms and platforms. The mode of production, which produces technological forms, shapes the range of experiential possibilities of the technological form. We could imagine that a mobile phone produced outside of the capitalist mode of production would not be constrained by 'planned obsolescence' of purposefully limiting its durability in order to sell new devices as soon as the old ones become obsolete.[18] In the case of Free and Open Source (FLOSS) production, sitting to a degree outside of the capitalist mode of production, the resulting social form of production and its technological forms are socially and economically determined as non-commodities, allowing for the widest possible range of experiential possibilities. Production under public investments usually does not take the form of a commodity, although legal interventions since the 1970s and 1980s have allowed public investment and production to result in commercialization and marketization through intellectual property rights. In the case of free online services such as Google's web search and Facebook's social networking service, the technological form is socially and economically determined as a 'pre-commodity'. There is no direct monetary exchange for the usage of these services. Nonetheless, users' experiences aid data commodification and capital accumulation, simultaneously influencing design choices, optimizing them for profit-making goals. Legal forms protect competing commercial uses of these technologies, allowing monopolies and surplus profits to remain unchallenged. In the case of other services offered under a direct monetary charge, the technological form is socio-economically determined as a commodity. This is the case with, for example, Apple's iPhone or Microsoft's Windows OS and Office. The legal form allows these products to attain commodity status, and companies producing them to keep surplus profits and monopoly power.

We will expand on the complex commodification process in the next section, focusing on the theoretically most difficult part – extraction of surplus value through free-of-charge Google and Facebook products. For now, it is important to conclude that this unusual discrepancy between the technological form and the commodity form is the reason behind many difficulties in Marxian conceptualizations of value creation and extraction on digital platforms. It is often difficult to pinpoint what is the commodity through which monetary exchange occurs in different data-driven business models. Another issue that makes it difficult is the struggle to theorize technology and its users. Important considerations such as exchange, exploitation, commodification, and capital accumulation often push the study of technology into the background. The result is that the complex co-articulations between the technological form, commodity form and the given mode of production through a science of social forms are frequently omitted. The technological form serves as a theoretical link between the experiential dimension and the socioeconomic dimension of the mode of production that gives it its social existence. Similar to commodities, the experiential dimension of the technological form is defined by its use value: technologies are useful for some purposes or not. However, unlike commodities their experiential dimension can also be shaped by their status as a pre-commodity or a product with a different social and economic determination of form (which, for a lack of better term, we call non-commodity), implying social relations sitting outside of monetary exchange. Technological form is determined by the socio-economic form and partially determining in the experiential realm of its users as it frames the range of possible uses and purposes. Throughout the book, we will argue that issues such as surveillance, privacy abuse, and disinformation are the result of the capitalist mode of production geared towards creating technological forms that optimize and streamline extraction of surplus value at the expense of a wider, democratic experiential range of its use. Different technological forms, produced and constructed outside of the capitalist mode of production, are necessary to attain such goals.

Production on digital platforms

Free Software and the production of public wealth

It would be difficult to imagine development of Google, Amazon, Facebook, and, to a significant extent, Apple, without public investments in technology and infrastructure development (Abbate, 1999; Leslie, 2000; Mazzucato, 2013; Greenstein, 2015) and without their use of Free Software and Open Source software (FLOSS) at the core of their products. Both public investment and FLOSS are productions whose character differs significantly from the capitalist mode of production. Free Software and Open Source are two separate, yet closely related movements and concepts of production of software. Their goal was to formalize existing practices of software production by utilizing copyright for a specific types of licences that either ban software being turned into commodities (Free Software Copyleft types of strict licences), or that makes commodification optional under certain conditions (Open Source permissive licences). Both came out of a long history of software production that differed from the capitalist production of commodities. Initially, since the late 1950s, software was written collaboratively with engineers exchanging code and documentation across organizational boundaries, often calling themselves hackers (Levy, 2010). Final outputs, software binaries, source code, and documentation were also shared. There was no commodification of outputs. Other than production scattered across organizational boundaries, production was not directed by capital, nor was its goal extraction of surplus value. Typically, producers either were volunteers working on software in their spare time or employed within non-profit organizations, such as academia, research centres, military, or civil sector.[19] Since profit, valorization, and extraction of surplus value was not the goal, there was no direct economic determination of the elements of production, at least not in the sense in which capitalist commodity production determines them. Competition was not the dominant relationship between the producers. Instead, cooperation among producers was the default relationship.[20]

Free Software is a movement created to protect such production by legal means, by defining Copyleft licences through the use of copyright in order to subvert it. The purpose of copyright was to legally assign ownership and thereby give the owner control over consumption and distribution of copyrighted material. Copyleft licences used the same mechanism for the opposite: to limit a certain kind of re-use of copyrighted material by mandating that if the modified versions get distributed they have to be made available under the licence of the original.[21] In the case of production of Free Software under Copyleft licences, where profit is not the goal of production, and where current and future public availability of the product is prescribed through its legal form, we use the concept of public wealth.[22] The concept has been already deployed from the perspective of the mainstream economics, arguing for the state behaving like a private producer of commodities, revaluing its assets at current market prices and treating them as capital, shifting them to more profitable uses by extracting profits (Detter & Fölster, 2018).

From our social form perspective, such an approach attempts to do the opposite of what we are trying to establish. It places an obstacle to recognizing specificities of non-commodity producers, utilizing the term 'public' to refer to all forms of wealth regardless of their social and economic forms, while also assuming that their best productive use comes from deployment within the capitalist production.[23] A broad category of public wealth can help us as a simple abstraction, to start capturing those specificities, drawing the initial line between public and private wealth. The final determinations of the forms of public wealth, their social and perhaps legal and economic formation, occurs in various ways, depending on the social form of production by which public wealth is produced. Due to our focus on advertising-funded digital platforms, in relation to other forms of production in this book we stay mostly on methodology and the broad simple abstraction of public wealth. However, further categories can be developed to capture forms, their ordering and causal mechanisms adequate to the character of fully determined instances of public wealth and its production.[24]

In the case of Free Software, production has the following specific properties that differentiate it from capitalist commodity production: the goal of production is not extraction of surplus value, consumption of outputs carries no direct price for consumers, and outputs can be consumed by anyone regardless of their personal wealth. These aspects give such outputs their 'publicness', and a certain egalitarian character due to their availability to all consumers regardless of their personal income or wealth. Contrary to commodities, whose distribution according to individual purchasing power introduces inequality in consumption due to different levels of individual income and wealth, availability of public wealth tends to increase equality due to far weaker dependence of consumption on individual income and wealth.

Open Source as a bridge to capitalist production

The production of public wealth in software is both beneficial and problematic for the dominant commodity production. When an output is effectively prevented from taking the social form of commodity, labour expended in its production cannot be the source of surplus value, nor can its production be the direct source of profit for a capitalist producer. Thus, Copyleft style strict licensing was an obstacle to investments and expansion of capital. Sections of hacker and engineering communities saw this as a major problem, disagreeing with Free Software's strict approach of mandating sharing of outputs, preferring instead a more fine-grained approach, making sharing optional under certain conditions. The Open Source movement was created to attract investment by creating and promoting use of such more permissive, Open Source, licences. Open Source licences are a legal form that allowed new modifications of software to be closed down. Source code did not have to be shared, and the final product could be shaped through application of legal forms into two distinct elements of the capitalist of production: software could be sold as a commodity or its modifications could be kept within the company utilizing it as capital and thus enabling a competitive advantage.

This move enabled the merger of the capitalist mode of production with the misfit early software production, formalized through Free Software movements and its Copyleft licences. The merger was not easy as the character of public wealth, the output of Free Software Copyleft production, and its most influential advocates, did not fit easily in the requirements imposed by the capitalist production, by the logic of the valorization of capital.[25] Something had to give somewhere. Commodity form had to be connected with and imposed onto the existing Free Software production without destroying it, and money had to be allowed to take its dominant form as capital. Richard P. Gabriel, one of the earliest Free Software engineers who was trying to combine commercial enterprise and free software in 1980s, a decade before Open Source was created, describes this tension: 'There is in general a trade-off between doing things in the commons, where innovation is easy because of the large number of diverse people and unfamiliar ideas, and doing things behind closed doors, where it is easy to keep a competitive advantage through secrecy and intellectual property laws' (Goldman et al, 2005, p 5).

While the authors state in passing that working on projects in the commons is 'about working on things for the public good' (Goldman et al, 2005, p 15), the concept public good is neither theorized nor defined, with the book written 'to help business executives understand' open source communities and to 'help them achieve their company's business goals' (Goldman et al, 2005, p 12). Similarly, many Open Source advocates saw integration of Free Software into business, through both Open Source permissive licences and the different overall conceptual approach, as commoditization, as they often called it. 'The forces of commoditization, being natural market forces, cannot be beaten' (I. Murdock, 2005, p 91); 'All the world's a commodity ... Open Source is simply the software world's mechanism for becoming like everything else ... Open Source accelerates the natural progress of software toward commodification, or standardization' (Asay, 2005, pp 103–4). There was no conceptual space left for the different social form of output and a different overall social and economic character of production that Free Software represented. Instead, the capitalist commodity production was naturalized.

In our understanding, both Free Software production and public investment in technology and infrastructure are different social forms of production whose outputs are not commodities and whose goal is to construct a new kind of wealth, public wealth we call it, without profit as the necessary measure of success. Open Source business models could not have existed without those two social forms of production, without these two types of public wealth serving as its inputs. In the case of Free Software, one of the central aims of Open Source companies has been what they called community building, community self-governance, and related issues.[26] Their primary aim was to keep the inputs flowing while minimizing the cost. What they effectively do with the processes associated with the 'community', is steer, structure, and support production that serves as cost-free input for their own production of Open Source commodities.[27] This often involves employing the so-called community managers and the most prominent developers of those Free Software products their results crucially depends on.[28]

By doing so, companies insert money acting as capital in the production of public wealth, steering, and, to an extent, changing the character of production towards commodification and realization of surplus value. The extent to which this occurs cannot be judged without empirical studies that would investigate whether the production of public wealth changed, and how. If the process of production of public wealth changed significantly by the introduction of Open Source capital, by its purpose being redirected to extraction of surplus value, we can be talking about partial or full transformation of production from one social form to another. In many Open Source cases, however, the software retains certain aspects of public wealth, with new services offering deployment, maintenance, further development, and education sold for a price as commodities (Krishnamurthy, 2005).

The overall goal of production of Open Source companies is surplus value extraction. Two social forms of production interact. While non-profit institutions that produce Free Software, such as NGOs, academic and research institutions, peer-to-peer networks of volunteers, or as it is often the case, the mix of all this, are not capitalist producers, but producers of public wealth, Open Source for-profit companies are. It is entirely correct that all those actors are often part of the same large community of producers, as Open Source advocates like to emphasize. The two social forms of production, one producing public wealth as its end goal, and other commodities, produce improved FLOSS together. However, it is a matter of scientific correctness to recognize their different social forms of production and to capture theoretically how elements of production are shaped, how their forms get determined, socially, and often economically and legally, within their respective production processes.

Pre-, intermediate, and final commodities

When GAFAM utilize public wealth as input in their production, they deploy it as capital, as means of production in their capitalist production process. Furthermore, advertising-funded products such as Google's web search, Gmail, Google Maps, or Facebook's social networking services and communication apps offer their key functionality free of charge to consumers. However, unlike Free Software or many public research outputs, they are produced with the purpose to extract surplus value and accumulate capital. Their free-of-monetary-charge availability serves only as a step in the overall chain of valorization and surplus extraction. They are produced within the capitalist mode of production and their specific character is an essential element in advertising-funded business model, initially constructed decades ago by free newspapers, radio, and TV stations. The central product in such a business model is not a commodity, yet advertised commodities are crucial, as the overall aim of production cannot be met without them. The social and economic determination of form is thus shaped by the character of the overall capitalist production process with valorization of commodity and realization of surplus value as the driving goal. Hence, regardless of their peculiar free-of-monetary-charge character, such outputs are determined abstractions when produced within advertising-funded business models, determined by the character of the overall production process geared to extract surplus value. For all these reasons, we call such products pre-commodities.

Using standard Marx's symbols (M for money capital, C for commodities, Mp for means of production, L for labour power, P for productive capital), we are adding the symbol pC for pre-commodity. This results in the following representation of Google's production of its web search engine: Money capital (M) buys means of production and labour power as commodities (means of production and labour power have a grey background to mark that they are general abstractions), deploying them in the production process as productive capital, resulting in output of pre-commodities. Marx develops this schema in detail in the first chapter of the second volume of *Capital*, and the major difference is that the production process results with production of commodities, with the symbol C instead of pC. In the advertising-funded business model, revenue and profits for digital platforms are derived from selling advertising space. However, advertising is not the final goal of production and valorization process; its value is contained in advertised commodities, final objects for sale. To underscore the

Figure 2.1: Pre- and final commodities

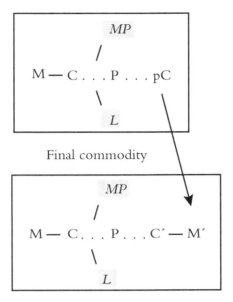

Pre-commodity

$$MP$$
$$/$$
$$M - C \ldots P \ldots pC$$
$$\backslash$$
$$L$$

Final commodity

$$MP$$
$$/$$
$$M - C \ldots P \ldots C' - M'$$
$$\backslash$$
$$L$$

finality of the process and the place where value and surplus value reside, we call such products final commodities (Figure 2.1).

There is a long history of debates on the advertising-funded business model in the national accounting literature (L. Nakamura et al, 2017, p 8) with the recently re-calculated historical data showing its success: 'the average content share of advertising-supported media [that] grew from 45 percent in 1929 to 70 percent in 2016' (L. Nakamura et al, 2017, p 11). While newspapers required physical distribution, radio and TV channels eased those limits, remaining, however, limited in their reach and subject to many national regulatory laws. By building a nearly global (China escaped its reach by blocking Google and Facebook access and building its own platforms) digital platforms on the basis of what used to be a geographically localized advertising-based business model, Google inserted itself as perhaps the most important mediator for the global commodity production. Taking a slice of value of each commodity advertised on its platform and being available for the vast majority of the planet, Google inserted itself between the commodity producers and consumers worldwide, mostly eluding regulation thus far.

Google's key products – web search, Google Maps and Gmail – are pre-commodities, and, as such, they contain no surplus value. Instead, they enable contractual relationship with other commodity producers, whose advertising on Google platforms provides the company with revenue. In other words, Google's pre-commodities are inserted at the centre of the global capitalist mode of production as its chief advertising platform, for which they reap enormous financial rewards in the form of sold advertising space.[29] Having a different relationship with the geographical location where advertised products are sold, Google is able to avoid paying taxes in those localities, thus breaking the logic of taxation laws and their broader social purpose as the main source of funding for government activities. Paradoxically, while Google and similar companies could not have developed without vast investment in production of public wealth in the form of infrastructure, scientific, and applied R&D, their evasion of taxes reduces funds available for future production of public wealth. We develop this more in Chapters 5, 6, and 7.

The next step in a more accurate representation chain of Google production is to add the advertising as a commodity itself. However, advertising on its own does not create any new value; its value is a deduction from the value of the advertised product. For the producer of the advertised commodity, the cost of advertising is a part of costs of circulation, a necessary expense in order to realize the surplus value potential of its product, the advertised final commodity. Hence, we call advertising *intermediate commodity*, a commodity with a specific social form, which adds no new value in itself, but whose value is already included in the value of the final commodity, whose sale it helps to realize. With the exception of transport and warehousing for Marx,[30] in his work, and in the national accounting standards, we find that value is not produced during circulation, in activities occurring after the production of final commodities in order to realize their value through sales.[31] For this reason, the addition of predicate final to advertised commodities signifies the last step in valorization, the specific social form of output necessary to fulfil the aim of the capitalist mode of production.

Including the advert as intermediate commodity, along with the inclusion of consumer and associated activities, we get a more complete picture (see Figure 2.2). Google's revenue comes from adverts, but their value comes from final commodities. The whole chain is driven by the aim of the producers of final commodities to extract surplus value. Every reduction of the costs of circulation increases the surplus value and its portion that stays with the producer. This simple calculation is

Figure 2.2: Full production in advertising-funded business models: Google web search

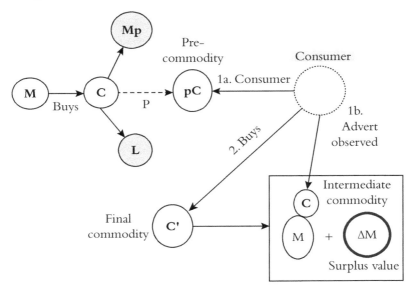

the central reason behind the rise of Google as the ultimate advertising platform dominating internet advertising spending in the largest markets, reaching potential consumers far more cheaply and with more precise matching of consumer preferences than radio, TV or newspapers are able to do.[32] Advertising-funded digital platforms, such as Google's web search and Facebook's social network, extract profits from the sphere of circulation of commodities. An important element still missing is consumer preferences for final commodities. During their use of Google's pre-commodity, consumers' on-line behaviour is captured by Google and the data are used as input, as the raw material for the production of targeted adverts, the key intermediate commodities linking Google's pre-commodity with final commodities.

There are two sets of outputs, or useful objects, that consumers desire. Some of them take the social form of pre-commodity and others are final commodities. No consumer desires adverts as such, intermediate commodities only link to the final ones. During the consumption of pre-commodities, their producer obtains a massive amount of consumer behaviour data on the web. Initially, this was done through small technological objects called cookies, stored in consumers' browsers. Nowadays, Google uses over two hundred signals, obtained in various ways, for extracting consumer preferences from the data. This enables digital platforms to offer more fine-grained targeted advertising, using preferences as raw material input in the production of more effective adverts in the form of intermediate commodity.

While pre-commodities are being consumed, adverts matching consumer preferences are being displayed. Once a consumer of a pre-commodity clicks on an advert and buys a final commodity, or if the producer of an advertised final commodity can observe growth in sales linked to such adverts, the full circle is closed. The value of a final commodity is realized. A portion of the producer's costs of circulation allocated to advertising ends up as the revenue of the digital platform in the form of payment for the intermediate commodity, the advert. This revenue funds the production of both pre- and intermediate commodities. Although no value exchange takes place between the consumer and producer of pre-commodity, between the Google web search and its users, gathering and processing data on users' on-line behaviour is how data enter the production of adverts as raw material, and how the resulting consumer preferences enable more precise selection of adverts for the products consumer may desire.

The business model as a whole and its abstractions

Adding three special kinds of commodities to our conceptual understanding points toward an extra step in form-determination. Simple abstractions such as commodity and wage labour denote categories that are shared by various social forms of production and whose form may not be yet fully shaped. They become determined within a definite social and economic form of production. We know that commodities become fully determined within the capitalist mode of production. Yet, considering that each determination is marked by its functional uniqueness within a process of production, our new understanding of the three additional determinate abstractions (pre-, intermediate, final commodity) points to further development of forms. Commodity as a category, it turns out, does not have to be the final determination of form for outputs within the capitalist mode of production. Within certain types of capitalist business models on peculiar technological forms, commodity gets additionally determined.

This is how we may summarize the business model of advertising-funded digital platforms through the lens of these new determinations of commodity-form: the goal of the production on such platforms is profit from the sales of advertising space, purchased by the sellers of advertised (final) commodities. Adverts are (intermediate) commodities with specific features of having no value on their own and no intrinsic purpose for consumers. Their value is an expense contained in the value realized from the sale of advertised (final) commodities. Typically, and correctly, both adverts and advertised products are considered commodities, as they are both outputs of capitalist production aimed for markets. Yet, with the single category, their differences are lost. We capture those differences with the determinate abstractions *intermediate and final commodity*.

Finally, the most difficult element to capture theoretically are free-of-monetary-charge services on digital platforms. Users' on-line behaviour captured through usage of these services is the key raw material input into digital platforms' production of adverts as intermediate commodities. When platforms' free-of-monetary-charge services achieve near-monopoly status, adverts (whose production and sale is enabled by these proxy products) become both cheaper and more tailored to consumer preferences than in the 'old' media advertisings. In turn, such adverts enable the virtuous cycle by which platforms capture vast portions of marketing budgets globally, leading to singular points where vast amounts of capital accumulate. We capture the specificities of such free-of-monetary-charge products that lead (via intermediate commodities) to sales of final commodities with the determinate abstraction *pre-commodity*. Despite of their free-of-monetary-charge availability, which distinguishes them from commodities, their entire purpose is to lead to sales of commodities through more efficient advertising, through shortening of circulation time of capital.

3

Marxian Perspectives on Monopolies

There are various Marxian approaches towards understanding monopoly. The most direct and sustained is the monopoly capitalism perspective (for example, Baran & Sweezy, 1968; Magdoff & Sweezy, 1987; Foster, 2014a), tied to the *Monthly Review* magazine. This uniquely American school of thought takes monopoly as the latest developmental stage in the capitalist mode of production. Its main authors argue that the 19th-century capitalism was shaped by similar-sized producers in an environment of intense industrial competition. The main argument is that, since the 1970s, capital increasingly escapes production and enters a speculative domain of financialization. This results in monopoly-finance capitalism, a specific regime of capital accumulation benefitting a tiny minority of capital lenders and shareholders, transnational companies, and corporate owners and managers (Magdoff & Sweezy, 1987; Sweezy, 1994; Foster, 2016). According to these authors, capitalism has now entered a stage of increasing concentration of capital in the hands of fewer and fewer companies and owners.

While this thesis holds some weight towards describing the contemporary snapshot of GAFAM's oligopoly, it cannot explain the specificities of the platform business model, commodity chains on digital platforms we described in Chapter 2, or legal forms necessary for the reproduction of capital through platforms. Moreover, it does not engage in theorizing value, surplus value, and money but, instead, replaces it with the concept of the economic surplus (Baran, 1956/1973; Barclay et al, 1975), thus severing ties with some of Marx's central concepts. Hence, monopoly as a stage in capitalist development does not explain how the platform economy went through its successive stages of competition, financial collapse, current oligopoly, and regulatory challenges, nor does it take sufficient account of the legal forms necessary to establish monopoly over technical discoveries through copyright and patents. From our perspective, there are three approaches grounded in Marxian theories that are useful for the analysis of digital platforms. First, understanding that monopoly is not a stage in capitalist development but a dynamic process enabled and/or constrained by a specific regulatory regime. Second, understanding that monopoly is a process of concentration and centralization of capital visible in mergers and acquisitions across the history of capitalism. And third, that monopoly is not just related to economic processes, but to how private property is shaped by the politics of the bourgeois state in the form of intellectual monopoly.

Revisiting competition and monopoly

To explore and properly understand the implications of monopoly in platform capitalism, that is, to understand what is behind the notion of digital monopoly we first need to consider monopoly in itself. This, as it turns out, has not been an easy or straightforward task for Marxian theory for reasons we will expound shortly using *Monopoly Capital*, seminal work by Paul Baran and Paul Sweezy, as our entry point. Our objective in this part of the discussion is twofold. We start by listing the fundamentals of Marx's theory of competition and monopoly in the interest of removing the concept of perfect competition that had mystified the investigation of capitalist production and exchange for too long. That effort should put us in a better position in the course of evaluation of platform capitalism. Even a cursory view of these contributions thus far reveals that an overwhelming explanatory burden has been placed on the concept of monopoly. Monopoly pricing surfaces as a theoretical *deus ex machina* and resolves the plot in the drama of contemporary capitalism, carrying on its shoulders far-reaching conclusions about the anatomy of latest stage of capitalist development.

Originally published in 1966, *Monopoly Capital* is by no means the first Marxian investigation into the nature and scope of monopoly under capitalism.[1] However, we start with *Monopoly Capital* because it encapsulates certain failings and drawbacks in understanding competition and monopoly that are still very much present in the contemporary mind-set, particularly in various approaches to digital platforms in the context of capitalist production. What it comes down to is the internalization of perfect competition as the benchmark against which market structure is assessed and measured. The neoclassical concept of perfect competition is well known and notorious for its unrealistic set of assumptions. In the neoclassical tradition, perfect competition had been depicted in terms of utility-maximizing behaviour of consumers and profit-maximizing behaviour of businesses. Furthermore, it is assumed that all actors are instrumentally rational and have full knowledge of all relevant circumstances that can be obtained only under conditions of stationary economy (Stigler, 1957). Importantly, under perfect competition business firms are described as passive price-takers, that is, there are by definition many business firms on the production side, each of them too insignificant to influence the market price and therefore faced with horizontal demand curve. These features are necessary for the neoclassical model of general equilibrium to make sense, and the critiques on the grounds of internal inconsistencies and untenable assumptions have been made elsewhere (Keen, 2011; King, 2012).

The point we stress here is related to the fact that if one accepts perfect competition as the benchmark, that is to say, if the neoclassical notion of competition turns into an analytical anchor, a number of controversial consequences follow. First, monopoly and other forms of the so-called imperfect competition can appear only as forms of deviations from the norm. Perfect competition and monopoly emerge as a discrete polar opposite with the former leading the way as a regulatory ideal, while the latter is positioned at the other end of the spectrum as the extreme form of defective market. Moreover, the exclusive focus on the antithesis between perfect competition and monopoly means that one is concerned only with market relations, so reasoning and judgement about inner workings of the economy are being reduced to the analysis of market structure, leaving the sphere of production as a separate and, presumably, less important issue. Finally, as the perfect competition versus monopoly framework is set firmly in the background, on the policy level one becomes completely embroiled in the controversy between protection of property rights and implementation of antitrust laws.

Baran and Sweezy, for their part, start by describing the rise of new institutional form, namely 'Giant Corporation' that has replaced small-scale firms, at least in the most advanced capitalist countries.

> Today, the typical economic unit in the capitalist world is not the small firm producing a negligible fraction of homogeneous output for an anonymous market but a large-scale enterprise producing a significant share of the output of an industry, or even several industries, and able to control

its prices, the volume of its production, and the types and amount of its investments. The typical economic unit has the attributes, which were once thought to be possessed only by monopolies. (Baran & Sweezy, 1968, p 6)

Thus, monopoly capitalism is explained as process of gradual spread or generalization of monopoly, an insignificant phenomenon in Marx's time, pushed and sustained through the new institutional forms and practice of governance. As their argument unfolds, one can see that the attempt to describe the new economic and institutional reality of the mid-20th century capitalism is explicitly based on neoclassical distinction between small-scale economic units best understood in terms of price-taking behaviour and Giant Corporation dominating the market in terms of its price-setting agenda. The theoretical opposition between perfect competition and monopoly is then translated into historical opposition between vibrant 19th-century capitalism where allegedly competition reigned supreme and the stable but stagnant monopoly capitalism of the 20th century.

Baran and Sweezy have presented their explanation of monopoly capital not by outright rejection of the Marxian theory of value, but through a series of modifications. In the first step, the notion of surplus value has been replaced by the new concept of economic surplus. The traditional Marxian notion of surplus value is understood to be equal to the sum of profits, interest and rent. Economic surplus, as defined by Baran and Sweezy, includes capitalist consumption and investment, expenditures of all levels of government, military spending, and costs of unproductive activities such as advertising. In a footnote they explain that Marx in *Capital* and in *Theories of Surplus Value* demonstrated that revenues of state and church, wages of unproductive works, and so on, also come to comprise surplus value (Baran & Sweezy, 1968, p 10). However, no coherent account of the relationship between surplus value and economic surplus had been put forward, only a replacement of the tendency of the rate of profit to fall with a new tendency related to the stabilization of monopoly capital of the economic surplus to rise.[2] Once monopoly-pricing process under the neoclassical mantle is put in place, market prices appear to be detached from the production process, subjected only to the discretionary decisions of monopoly corporations in the pursuit of their long-term strategy. The general conundrum for monopoly capitalism can in turn be reduced to the search for channel through which accumulated economic surplus can be absorbed.

The confusion about the status of competition is not exclusively related to the original approach of Baran and Sweezy in *Monopoly Capital*, but it goes all the way to the present, as exemplified by the notion of the 'ambiguity of competition' put forward by Bellamy Foster, McCheseny, and Jamil Jonna (2011). Ambiguity of competition refers to 'the opposite ways in which the concept of competition is employed in economics and in more colloquial language, including the language of business itself' (Foster et al, 2011, p xx). To underscore this ambiguity, they rely on the commentary given by Milton Friedman in his classical pamphlet *Capitalism and Freedom*. Friedman ponders upon the baffling fact that competition in ordinary discourse means rivalry in the sense that competitors strive to outdo each other, whereas in the competitive market, given that all businesses are passive price-takers, there is no competition in terms of rivalry (Friedman, 1982, p 119). Monopoly, on the other hand, exists when individuals or businesses are able to determine terms of access for a particular good or service, and Friedman notes that inasmuch as monopoly does include rivalry in some sense, it comes closer to the ordinary notion of competition (Friedman, 1982, p 120). Taking Friedman's observation on board, Bellamy Foster et al insert the ambiguity of competition with the underlying note that most cases of 'competition and competitive strategy that dominate economic news are in fact rivalrous struggles between quasi-monopolies (or oligopolies) for greater monopoly power. Hence, to the extent to which we speak of competition today, it is more likely to be oligopolistic rivalry, that is, battles between monopoly-capitalist firms' (Foster et al, 2011, p 20). The way out of this ambiguity can be stated in simple terms: the neoclassical notion of 'perfect' that needs to be retired and the ordinary concept of 'competition' commonly found in the tradition of classical political economy must be elaborated further. Moving this debate toward the field of digital platforms, how much competition and how much monopoly is allowed within the economy, is ultimately sanctioned by the state(s) and their regulatory regimes within the field of political struggle of competing interests.

Marx on competition and monopoly

Marx developed his formulation picking up the cues put out by classical political economists, and that is the reason why it is possible to group them under the label of 'real competition'. The key moment of Marxian understanding of competition revolves around its association with the sphere of production. Analysis of competition does not enjoy much prominence in the first volume of *Capital* and Marx does not allow his reader to chew over the reasons for such treatment. He writes:

> It is not our intention to consider, here, the way in which the laws, immanent in capitalist production, manifest themselves in the movements of individual masses of capital, where they assert themselves as coercive laws of competition, and are brought home to the mind and consciousness of the individual capitalist as the directing motives of his operations. But this much is clear; a scientific analysis of competition is not possible, before we have a conception of the inner nature of capital, just as the apparent motions of the heavenly bodies are not intelligible to any but him, who is acquainted with their real motions, motions which are not directly perceptible by the senses. (Marx, 1996, p 321)

Methodologically, Marx moves in an opposite direction relative to the one we are accustomed to from the neoclassical treatment of the matter. Hence, there can be no question of making an inference based on market structure. The first necessary step consists in acquiring a conception of the inner nature of capital, that is, the analysis of production and the creation of value and surplus value in production. In other words, Marx first wants to show that surplus value is an unpaid portion of the working day whose magnitude depends on the rate of exploitation. After that he moves on to question accumulation of capital enabled by the absolute and relative production of surplus value, and only then do the forces of competition come into the picture. Generally, 'individual capitals can compete on the product market only on the basis of prior commodification of labour power, and the existence of "free" class of wage workers who can, in principle, be employed by any capital' (Chattopadhyay, 2012, p 73). Competition in the product market, once wage labour is expended and output produced, acts as 'a coercive law of competition' – an important formulation with which Marx points to the link between production and exchange. Coercive law of competition is nothing less than the extension of the law of value in the market sphere (Marx, 1996, p 324). Extra-surplus value may arise because of adoption of a new method of production, but it disappears as soon as this new method generalizes across industry, courtesy of coercive law of competition.

In the third volume of *Capital*, Marx introduces prices of production and finally shifts ground to arrive at a concrete level where the inquiry into relations between capitals becomes pertinent. Marx is careful to separate internal and external moments of the capitalist accumulation process and to make sure that different elements get the appropriate explanatory role in the overall account. Thus, on many occasions in the third volume of *Capital*, he highlights the function of competition with regard to the prices of production and the rate of profit.

> Competition can influence the rate of profit only to the extent that it affects the prices of commodities. ... In order to equalise unequal rates of profit, profit must exist as an element in the price of commodities. Competition does not create it. It lowers or raises its level, but does not create the level which is established when equalisation has been achieved. (Marx, 1998, p 851)

The inner nature of capital and the rules and logic of capital accumulation cannot be explained through competition simply because the analysis of the exploitation of labour in connection to the creation of surplus value and profit had already accomplished that task. Hence, the explanatory closure had been attained as far as the internal moment of accumulation is concerned. It is by virtue of capital's ceaseless search for new routes of expanding the magnitude of surplus value and securing ever-higher profits that competition as a form of external enforcement kicks in. In competition of many capitals, where one particular capital ventures, by incorporating new method of production or otherwise, others must follow. In that sense, the search for new technologies that raise productivity or secure higher profit rate in some other way is not a matter of choice or preference for innovation but socially mediated drive enforced by coercive law of competition.

If we accept the explanation of the connection between law of value and competition, what about the place of monopoly in Marx's theory of accumulation? If we were to begin with the conclusion, we would say that competition and monopoly in capitalism, to use David Harvey's formulation, operate based on a contradictory unity as exemplified throughout the history of capitalism (Harvey, 2014, p 134). What is this contradictory unity in this case, and how should one interpret that dictum? The point of entry is somewhat similar to the one we had on the issue of competition. Just as competition should be thought of as an intricate process rather than a state, so does monopoly entail more than a simple definition of a product market with a single seller. First, monopoly is already present at the outset of the capitalist process of production in the form of the monopoly over the means of production. Harvey sums this point up clearly when he reminds us that 'the monopoly power inherent in the private property forms the basis for exchange and by extension for competition'. Thus, it should be recognized that the power of capital rests on 'the assemblage of all of these individual monopolistic property rights into a social order where the capitalist class can be defined vis-à-vis labour by its collective monopoly over the means of production (or, in the updated version, the means of financing)' (Harvey, 2014, p 135). Just as firms are not powerless price-takers in the market, neither are they powerless entities in the realm of property rights.

What about the production process itself, where does it leave us in terms of monopoly under the assumption that the necessary property rights are secured? In the analysis of the production process proper, again we find monopoly, or more precisely, the tendency toward monopoly, analytically separated by Marx into two distinct categories: concentration and centralization of capital. On the one hand, given that 'every individual capital is a larger or a smaller concentration of means of production, with a corresponding command over a larger or a smaller army of labour' (Marx, 1996, p 621) the concentration of individual capital grows as the process of accumulation moves forward from one cycle to the next. Concentration, therefore, always accompanies accumulation of capital and comes to signify the amassment of social wealth in the hands of individual capitalist (Marx, 1996). Centralization, on the other hand, amounts to the inimical rivalry between many capitals and the realization of monopoly power by few:

> The cheapness of commodities depends, *ceteris paribus*, on the productiveness of labour, and this again on the scale of production. Therefore, the larger capitals beat the smaller ... It always ends in the ruin of many small capitalists, whose capitals partly pass into the hands of their conquerors, partly vanish. (Marx, 1996, p 620)

The centralization of capital is enabled by competition between capitals and it is further propelled by the credit system, which at one point, as Marx argues, is 'transformed into an enormous social mechanism for the centralisation of capitals' (Marx, 1967, p 626). The limit of this process and the limit of capital in any branch of industry would come about if 'all the individual capital invested were fused into a single capital' (Marx, 1967, p 627). Therefore, the centralization of capital at the limit corresponds to elimination of all competition and attainment of absolute monopoly power by a single economic unit. This position is certainly possible, at least in theory, and it implies, not just monopoly power over price and quality of the product, but, quite likely, monopsony power over labour force in a given industry. In any case, it should be clear that competition and monopoly do not function as discrete and exclusive points but are situated on a continuum set up by the logic of capitalist accumulation. Whatever the root cause of centralization, that is, monopoly power may be rising labour productivity, economies of scale, or network effects, it cannot be separated from the prevailing logic of capital accumulation or contradictions that arise. Competition tends to monopoly power, which, in turn, is usually located within an industry and never completely secured from the technological, institutional, and political changes of capitalism at large. We will expand on this in Chapter 5 where we discuss financialization and regulation.

Property form determination and intellectual monopoly

So far, we have argued that there is a need to understand the relation between competition and monopoly as a dynamic interplay, and that the market structure and the movement in the sphere of exchange must be traced back to production of commodities and the process of capital accumulation. However, it would be wrong to think that it is a matter of simple reduction. Although it may appear that the vocabulary of political economy is self-sufficient and capable of delivering more or less full explanation, it is well understood that it is not the case. This is particularly pronounced in the case of digital monopolies where the forces and capacities that are shaping the competitive dynamics and enabling the leading companies to preserve their monopoly power are not just economic or reducible to objects of political economy. These non-economic layers are technological, organizational, even cultural, but most importantly legal. The realm of digital monopolies is notoriously stratified, hence the need to talk about how the legal dimension that is encapsulated in the regime of intellectual property rights (IPRs) has been the decisive instrument of stratification, which we will explain further in Chapter 6.

Christophers (2016) takes on the very same issues as does the value-form theory, centred around the question of how does the sphere of exchange, under Marx's assumption that value creation does not take place there, still format the developments in production. Christophers takes as self-evident the point that 'capitalism cannot reproduce itself even in the short-term, much less the long-term, in the absence of a stable, market-based regime of value realization. The products and services provided by capitalists must be monetized in exchange, and value thus realized, otherwise capital circulation grinds to a halt' (Christophers, 2016, p 71). From that it follows that the analysis of competition and monopoly – their structure, interrelatedness, and legal form – is crucial for understanding the workings of capitalist accumulation in a given historical period and segment of the economy. However, before we get into the more concrete analysis of digital platforms and intellectual property rights, let us come back to the more abstract level of theorizing the commodity and legal form, starting from Pashukanis' (2001) attempt to develop a materialist theory of law in which we find the first articulation of intrinsic relation between commodity and legal form.

The first strategic goal of Pashukanis' theory was to avoid reductive explanations of law as a purely ideological phenomenon, that is, an ideological fiction that simply serves as the instrument of the ruling classes. For Pashukanis, legal regulation is, prima facie, the necessary component of commodity production and exchange. As he explains, 'whereas the commodity acquires its value independently of the will of the producing subject', in the realization of value 'a conscious act of will on the part of commodity owners' is presupposed (Pashukanis, 2001, p 112) because commodities cannot, as Marx noted, go to the market themselves and perform exchange in their own right (Marx, 1872/1976, p 178). The claim here is, not just that commodity form and legal form are two sides of the same coin, but also, more controversially, that at the same time that '[t]he product of labour becomes a commodity and a bearer of value, man acquires the capacity to be a legal subject and a bearer of rights' (Pashukanis & Milovanovic, 2001, p 112). Just as value cannot but appear in the form of money, so the relation between commodity owners cannot but take the legal form.

If contestation and conflict are enshrined in the commodity form – contestation and conflict between legal persons, that is, bearers of right as opposed to bearers of customary privileges – then there must be an impersonal arbiter in the form of the bourgeois state. The state makes sure that 'property ceases to be unstable, precarious, purely factual property which may at any moment be contested and have to be defended, weapon in hand' (Pashukanis & Milovanovic, 2001, p 115). Jessop summarizes Pashukanis' definite position well when he writes that '[t]he legal form of the *Rechtstaat* (or constitutional state based on the rule of law) characteristic of bourgeois societies is required by the nature of market relations among free, equal individuals'. Moreover, 'although the state authority introduces clarity and stability into the structure of law and underwrites the operation of juridical relations, the material basis of the specific form of bourgeois law and legal subject is still rooted in capitalist relations of production' (B. Jessop, 1990, p 53). Without going further into the state theory debate, the question that concerns us here is whether Pashukanis' commodity form theory of law provides the grounds to intrinsically link legal form with other social forms of Marxian value theory. Furthermore, how is one to conceptualize and possibly extend commodity form theory of law to be fit for analysis of digital monopolies and contemporary capitalism?

For our purposes, then, Pashukanis' examination of the legal form[3] represents a natural extension of value-form theory we discussed in Chapter 2 into the realm of law. For many legal theorists working outside of the Marxian framework the relation of capital and law can be put in deceptively simple terms: law creates capital. The theoretical incentive behind this claim can be found in the need to tackle the problem of intellectual property rights. For instance, Drahos starts with the notion of abstract objects, which can be viewed as ideas and intellectual concepts that make 'the core structure that is integral to the identity of concrete objects' and that in contemporary capitalism stand behind many capital assets, production patterns, goods, and services (Drahos, 2016, p 181). Because of their peculiar ontology, Drahos concludes that IPRs at the same time constitutes abstract objects as form of capital and determines its ownership (Drahos, 2016, p 186). Law, then, has the capacity to constitute abstract objects, which can in turn, under the right social conditions, enter the circuit of capital and augment the process of capital accumulation. Brands, copyrights, patents, and trade secrets become essential legal forms for the rise of data-driven business models.

This line of reasoning can be pushed a bit further by posing the question of the relation of capital form to legal form in general. Following Marx, we argue that, just as commodities cannot enter the market by themselves, capital cannot enter the process of production by itself, nor does it move by itself into the capital and money markets. Legal form is, therefore, no less constitutive for movement and operations of capital than for exchange of commodities. Furthermore, legal form is responsible for formatting capital, endowing it with certain features that enable the creation of wealth under capitalist conditions. Pistor (2019) asserts that, despite proliferation of different forms of capital since the beginning of the 1970s, including finance capital and data capital, on the most basic level capital can be defined quite simply as an asset – physical object, financial claim, or abstract object – clothed in legal code (Pistor, 2019, p 2). Pistor's argument that capital cannot exist without law is important because it clears the pathway for bringing capital form into the theory of legal form, expanding it and making it more comprehensive. The reason why there cannot be capital without law has to do with the features that only law can bestow on capital, namely priority, durability, universality, and convertibility (Pistor, 2019, p 3ff). Legal code protects the asset holder or the owner of capital from competitors and other rivals, as well as from uncertainties (up to a point) that plague the capitalist economy. Priority ranks the competing claims, durability and universality extend priority claims in time and space, respectively, while convertibility enable the conversion of private claims and, thus, the protection of their nominal value (Pistor, 2019).

Occasionally, Pistor gives the impression that it is enough to legally code an asset in order to generate wealth, a claim that would be dubious even for assets such as financial claims or software code, which as assets exist only through legal form. On the other hand, it is clear that she takes legal coding of capital to be the necessary preparatory action for the generation of wealth, a procedure that, if done right, turns 'an asset into capital and thereby increase its propensity to create wealth for its holder(s)' (Pistor, 2019, p 2). In other words, the labour process and the process of accumulation of capital are not theorized, but it is tacitly assumed that they are there. Legal form permeates the capitalist mode of production, whether one observes it from the standpoint of capital or the standpoint of commodity exchange (including labour power commodity).

The main argument that Pistor tries to push through is simple but striking: 'Law is the cloth from which capital is cut'; legal form makes capital not just economically intelligible, but 'it allows capital to rule not by force, but by law' (Pistor, 2019, p 209). And yet, even fictitious capital (M-M') – which ontologically cannot be separated from its legal form (in stark contrast to productive capital (M-C-M')), and which is construed as the investment debt instruments or shares, depends in the last instance on anticipated revenues that logically must come from other value producing activities. Now, the distinction between productive and fictitious capital can still carry a lot of weight in analysing contemporary capitalist dynamics. Nevertheless, it needs to be supplemented by taking on board analytically important difference between tangible and intangible capital.

The appropriateness of the latter rests on the nature of intellectual property regime, that is to say, on the strength and scope of intellectual property rights (Boyle 2003). When put in place, IPRs tend to generate what Pagano and Rossi call intellectual monopoly (Pagano & Rossi, 2009) and, given the extent to which IPRs have become key to the capital accumulation, one can even use the label intellectual monopoly capitalism (Pagano, 2014). Depending on the dimension one is interested in, the introduction of IPRs results in a series of ramifications. Economically, they enhance commodification, boost the forces of monopolization and prepare the ground for secular stagnation (Orhangazi, 2008; Haskel & Westlake, 2018). Politically, they are at the forefront of the second enclosure movement (Boyle, 2003) that makes class conflict more fierce and volatile as income and wealth inequality becomes more pronounced. They are the legal background behind commercialization of the internet and the rise of many Silicon Valley companies that dominate the global internet.

Historically, IPRs are one component of the regime of accumulation that has been in the making since late 1970s. This regime of accumulation should be seen as an outcome of the rise of financialization, proliferation of intangible capital facilitated by IPRs, and the disintegration of production through global value chains. What we term digital monopolies is but one layer of this regime of accumulation (Durand & Gueuder, 2018; Montalban et al, 2019). We will sharpen the focus on the operational modes of tech giants sitting at its centre in the following chapters. For now, we only indicate the legal form as constitutive part of Marxian theory of social forms and the profound changes that have unfolded in the relation between capital and law in the post-1970s regime of accumulation. Because digital platforms are all about software, artificial intelligence, databases, design, and so on, they would not be able to operate, as they do now, and rise to power, as some of them have, without the proper legal form, namely intellectual property rights.

Powerful global companies get to choose the jurisdictions in which their interests are served best, profiting from decentralized nature of private law (Pistor, 2019, p 9). In each scenario the state remains, as Pashukanis explained, an impersonal body, a regulatory apparatus standing above the conflict driven region of private interests. Alternatively, private actors can unite and use their lobbying muscle and tacit political influence to create an international property regime that guarantees priority, durability, universality, and convertibility for the owners of capital. The latter case is, in fact, the story of the Agreement on Trade-Related Aspects of Intellectual Property Rights (TRIPS), an international agreement signed by all members of the World Trade Organization in 1994, an agreement that can be described as 'a dramatic expansion of the rights of IP owners and a significant instance of the exercise of private power' (Sell, 2003, p 7). To put it somewhat bluntly, capitalism has to find the right kind of legal form in order to balance the contradictions and tensions, which are inherent to it as a mode of production. Given the dynamism of capitalism that 'cannot exist without constantly revolutionising the instruments of production', it is clear that the legal form must follow and readjust to the internal dynamics of the economic order.[4]

Therefore, as much as TRIPS has been rightfully seen as an important milestone in the history of property rights, the rise of digital monopolies opens new challenges from the standpoint of capital, especially concerning the legal status of algorithms and data. Some legal scholars, such as Julie Cohen, have argued that 'the law for the platform economy is already being written', not by the public authorities and from the perspective of the common good, but by 'uncoordinated but self-interested efforts of the information–economy participants and the lawyers and lobbyist they employ' (Cohen, 2017, p 136). Since data flows became the raw material for platform capitalism (Srnicek, 2017), the race is on not just to extract and collect data but bring about juridical enclosure that will, at the very least, guarantee the control over data for the platform that extracted it.

Cohen places access-for-data model of interaction between platforms and its users at the centre insofar as the by-product of that arrangement is nothing less than 'a quiet revolution in the legal status of data as (*de facto* if not *de jure*) proprietary informational property' (Cohen, 2017, p 154). What is happening in these enclosure attempts can be described as terms-of-use agreements (contracts) doing the work that formal property rights cannot do at this point, 'the combination of asserted contractual control and technical control becomes the vehicle through which platform imposes its own logics on the encounters it mediates' (Cohen, 2017, p 155). If the leading digital platforms are working on mechanisms and procedures that will enable them to secure data as input for their business operations, and if the logic of datafication forces them to reconfigure and update the current intellectual property regime, then the next question concerns the conditions that platforms have to meet in order to turn data accumulation into capital accumulation.

So what is unique about digital monopolies of GAFAM? On the one hand, digital monopolies are just a reiteration of a long-term historical dynamic between competition and monopoly driven by capital accumulation and the quest for the expansion of surplus value and profit (Christophers, 2016). In order for capital to expand in such conditions, a legal environment needs to exist allowing commodification of platform usage data in the form of permissive antitrust regulation and intellectual property rights. Once these legal forms are in place, capital can reproduce in line with Marx's production scheme we outlined in Chapter 2 and in line with the extended commodity chain that includes pre-commodities, intermediate commodities, and final commodities in the case of Google and Facebook. As capital accumulates and these companies expand their global share on valorization and extraction of surplus value from advertising, they attain monopoly position affecting production and innovation in the tech industry on the one hand, and the dynamics of competition in advertising markets on the other hand. Digital monopolies are monopolies on capital, technical knowledge, and platform usage data. The two latter dimensions create a set of unique contradictions in the capitalist mode of production, as we have argued through the analysis of technological and legal forms.

4

Platforms, Advertising, and Users

Digital platforms have expanded their scope from venture capital supported projects, towards global operations and multi-billion dollar oligopolies. However, the platform model is not entirely new. It was a common business model for newspapers, radio, and television. Before increasing commercialization through cable and satellite television, broadcasting was, for the most part, a state-supported monopoly only partially commercialized and privatized in many European countries. Production either relied on state subsidies through mandatory subscription payments in the public service model, or on advertising in the market oriented model. For example, audiences could freely listen to radio stations, while the state or the advertising industry provided funding for content production. Similarly, some digital corporations derive profits by providing advertising space for boosting sales and creating demand through the increase of consumption of products produced in other parts of the economy, obtaining their revenue from the circulation of commodities and capital in the economy as a whole. Additionally, they also produce their own means of production, such as software systems, algorithms, and AI, whose sales serve as an additional source of income and profits.

What is new about the digital platform model, compared to traditional media, is the scope and scale of gathered data, along with automated and improved analysis. Analysing big data requires technical assistance because manual analysis is not possible, or even conceivable, in any reasonable or economically viable amount of time. While the traditional media model required separate firms and an entire industry for audience and market analysis (for example, Nielsen, PwC), platforms developed entirely new markets on their own, along with the tools for analysing those same markets. The scale of their operations and the accumulated background data on consumer preferences provide them with a comparative advantage that is difficult to match in the data-driven business. In this chapter, we focus on platforms, advertising, and users as elements of the specific business model within the capitalist mode of production. These elements occupy the centre of many mainstream and critical analyses. Focusing on platforms, advertising, and users allows us to connect the theoretical approach outlined in the discussion about social forms in Chapter 2 with the more empirically oriented Chapters 5, and 6.

Platforms and zero-price markets

The term platforms entered widespread use after the 2000 dot-com crash in what the managerial ideology called the Web 2.0 (O'Reilly, 2005). It was simply an updated version of 'internet exceptionalism', or the belief that new business models defy standard economic rules and result in profitable businesses with frictionless ease (Greenstein, 2015, p 341). The discourse was filled with unrestrained optimism and technological determinism. Networked software infrastructures of the Web 2.0 will escape the confines of personal computers with their proprietary models and enter a free realm that will allow more creativity and opportunity for development. New companies will establish socioeconomic models that allow businesses to flourish and users to interact, collaborate, and search information freely. New business models will provide horizontal organizational structures, which will challenge the 'old', vertical integration model. Network technologies will create an open, participatory, and democratic internet culture. So the story went.

Undeniably, new web platforms contained a set of technical affordances conducive to specific types of activities (van Dijck, 2013). But they also contained a set of discursive strategies 'to sell, convince, persuade, protect, triumph, or condemn' as well as 'to make claims about what these technologies are and are not, and what should and should not be expected of them' (Gillespie, 2010, p 359). Put differently, a widespread digital discourse was put into place in order to legitimize new capitalist business models (Fisher, 2010).

Mainstream economics provided some of the earliest analyses of digital platforms. The initial subject were industries such as software, portals and media, video games consoles, and payment systems, conceptualized as multi-sided markets (Rochet & Tirole, 2003). A complex set of arguments developed by theorists proposing the notion of multi-sided markets relies on the existence of two distinct groups of agents, as they call users and customers on either side of the platform, both benefiting from increased usage of the platform. Credit card customers, for instance, the most typical case study, benefit more with the growth of number of retailers accepting the cards, and vice versa. Theorists call this positive effect – 'when consumers in one market provide a benefit to consumers in another related market' – reciprocal inter-side network externalities (Luchetta, 2014, p 191). A credit card company is the creator of the platform enabling customers and retailers to interact. However, the logic that does hold for this particular example breaks down with the inclusion of advertising financed platforms such as Google web search. The advertisers do benefit from more users, but it cannot be claimed that users of web search benefit from additional adverts (Luchetta, 2014, p 195). Luchetta rejects the thesis on two-sided markets for advertising financed web search platforms concluding how 'externalities flow only from the numerosity of searchers to advertisers, and not the other way around' (Luchetta, 2014, p 207), pointing out how users never desire adverts, while digital platforms do seek to gather users' data.

Platform capitalism and imperialism

Mainstream approaches studied platforms from a neoclassical benchmark of competition and efficiency in two-sided and multisided markets. Marxian approaches focused on contradictions and tensions within widespread usage of platforms in contemporary society and economy. In both mainstream and Marxian approaches, platforms are usually considered 'digital infrastructures that enable two or more groups to interact' (Srnicek, 2017). Platforms rely on data as their main economic resource. They rely on bundles of algorithms to process data input and provide profitable data output. Platform intermediaries bring together customers, advertisers, service providers, producers, suppliers, and physical objects. Platforms come with a series of tools that enable their users to build their own products, services, and marketplaces (Srnicek, 2017, p 32). Srnicek raises this intermediary role to the centre of a new logic of capitalism, which he calls platform capitalism. Moreover, he proposes a far-reaching thesis arguing with broad strokes that 'with a long decline in manufacturing profitability, capitalism has turned to data as one way to maintain economic growth and vitality in the face of a sluggish production sector' (Srnicek, 2017, p 11).

Data as a resource does not just mean that it is simply taken from the users. Data must be cleaned and organized into standardized outputs for it to be useful: 'data are a material to be extracted, refined and used in a variety of ways. The more data one has, the more uses one can make of them' (Srnicek, 2017, pp 30, 31). Data performs many important functions to capitalism, Srnicek explains. These include educating and giving a competitive advantage to algorithms; enabling coordination and outsourcing of workers; allowing for optimization and flexibility of productive processes; transforming low-margin goods into high-margin services; and so on. Platforms are business models that build upon data and that find different ways to handle, monopolize, extract, analyse, and use large amounts of data (Srnicek, 2017, p 32).

Acting as intermediaries between different groups provides platforms with a key competitive advantage over traditional business models. Platforms take advantage of 'network effects', which means that the more numerous the users who use a platform, the more valuable the platform becomes for everyone else: 'this generates a cycle whereby more users beget more users, which leads to platforms having a natural tendency towards monopolisation. It also lends platforms a dynamic of ever-increasing access to more activities, and therefore to more data' (Srnicek, 2017, p 33). Finally, platforms embody a politics which means that the rules of product and service development, as well as marketplace interactions, are set by the platform owner. The owner gains access not only to more data but also control and governance over the rules of the game (Srnicek, 2017, p 34). Srnicek finds the application of the platform business model in an impressive range of industries which includes advertising platforms (for example, Google, Facebook), cloud platforms (for example, AWS, Salesforce), industrial platforms (for example, GE, Siemens), product platforms (for example, Rolls Royce, Spotify), and lean platforms (for example, Uber, Airbnb).

However, while widely accepted and referenced, Srnicek's approach also leaves much to be desired. For example, there are no theoretical arguments for understanding digital monopolies other than simply claiming that platforms rely on network effects that lead to monopolies (Srnicek, 2017, 2018). Such interpretations leave little room for understanding histories of corporate development as many platforms regularly use a number of strategies to increase their user base and extract more data. Examples include signing strategic contractual relationships or simply acquiring competing companies. Relying solely on network effects naturalizes both technologies and markets as phenomena with their endogenous development dynamics. It does not explain mechanisms and social forms necessary for the extraction of surplus value from data, legal forms necessary for the reproduction of capital or socially, economically, and politically biased technological forms. We will deal with these issues more closely in Chapters 5, and 6.

Jin (2015) provides a more empirically elaborate and theoretically grounded analysis of platforms. He studies platforms such as social network sites (SNS) (for example, Facebook and Twitter), search engines (for example, Google), and smartphones (for example, iPhone and Galaxy) with their operating systems. Their ubiquitous usage, particularly in the mid-2010s gave rise to an ideology of worldwide universality. However, as he convincingly demonstrated, platforms point toward a continued dominance of the United States in the digital economy and culture, despite the fact that countries such as Korea and China invented and advanced their own platforms (Jin, 2015, p 6). The use of non-Western platforms is still mainly limited to their own national territory and diaspora, despite some strong exceptions such as the Chinese platform TikTok. Regulation in the European Union is a counter-balance to the US dominance. This legal battle is undecided and we will return to it again in Chapters 5, 6, and 7.

The hegemonic power of American companies, Jin argues, is the result of their advancements in integrating various digital services which allows them to gather information from users, commercialize and commodify that information and accumulate capital for the owners of platforms and countries in which they are based. 'The U.S. which had traditionally controlled non-Western countries with its military power, capital, and later, cultural products, now seems to dominate the world with platforms in terms of both capital accumulation and spreading symbolic ideologies and cultures' (Jin, 2015, p 7). The platform, as a concept, consists of three interconnected layers. First, it consists of a layer of hardware architecture and software frameworks that allow other programmes to run. Second, platforms allow communication, interaction, and monetary exchanges: 'platforms themselves are economic entities with both a direct economic role as creators of surplus value through commodity production and exchange and an indirect economic role, through advertising' (Jin, 2015, p 9). Finally, platforms' cultural biases and preferences are embedded in their technical design. This is the point that closely resembles our understanding of the technological form we discussed in Chapter 2.

As Jin continues, 'platforms are deeply involved in political culture, not only as corporate strategies in developing close relations with the nation-state in the pursuit of favourable government policies for their businesses, but also as delicate corporate policies in avoiding any particular responsibilities'. This is perhaps most strongly reflected in the rise of intellectual property rights that protect various aspects of platforms' technological design and allow monopoly profits to rise from unique industrial application of technical solutions for managing and processing data. The majority of industrial patents are held by highly developed countries such as the United States further reinforcing Jin's understanding of the politics of platforms in which intellectual property is 'not only about technology transfer or the protection of creativity, but also the asymmetrical power relations between a few IP holder countries and corporations and the majority of IP users' (Jin, 2015, p 103).

For Jin, digital monopoly platforms constitute the new stage of American imperialism, which he refers to as 'an asymmetrical relationship of interdependence in platform technologies and political culture between the West, primarily the U.S., and many developing countries, including two great powers – both nation-states and transnational corporations' (Jin, 2015, p 12). Platforms are, therefore, decisively commercial while also being supported by the state-industry complex. His approach is closely related to ours, particularly with regard to the importance of nation-states and the increasingly important role of intellectual property rights for the reproduction of capital we discussed in Chapter 3. However, we also depart from Jin as he does not engage in untangling the social forms of the capitalist mode of production on platforms. While offering a strong critique of platform imperialism, he focuses on the current appearance of platform capitalism, leaving out the analysis of how value is created and distributed and how monopolies are created and challenged.

Contributions and limits of legal critical theory to understanding platforms

Critical legal theory has been one of the most productive fields for understanding digital monopolies. In the past few years, Google and Facebook have come under some scrutiny in the US and the EU. Legal scholars have been among the loudest voices asking for regulation of the dominant firms, pointing out the glaring omissions of regulators to act adequately in acquisitions of competitors (Khan, 2016; Wu, 2018; Newman, 2019; Paul, 2019). We will engage more directly with some of the key scholars such as Timothy Wu and Lina Khan in Chapter 5 since their work engages with the history and changing dynamics of antitrust regulation in the United States. Other legal scholars, however, deal more directly with the specificities of the platform business model in general. They postulate that understanding transactions such as data exchange and extraction regularly occurring on platforms requires 'identifying exchanged nonmonetary costs', with information and attentions costs being the two distinct types of cost for the user (Newman, 2015, p 165). The attention cost is higher for the free-of-charge products, since in hybrid models where users pay for the product, quantity of advertising is reduced, or entirely removed (Newman, 2015, p 169).

This approach has consequences on how regulators understand Google and similar platforms. One of the main arguments in Google's defence has been that their products are free, there is no monetary exchange and therefore we cannot talk about a monopoly where there is no price and no market (Bork & Sidak, 2012). Newman points out that if there is a single supplier in web search, users can 'pay' for the transaction with 'inefficiently high information or attention cost', leading to the same problems such as monopolies in priced markets (Newman, 2015, p 174). The author assigns the problem to neoclassical economics and its excessive focus on prices that leads to oversight of zero-price markets. He calls for antitrust institutions to conduct analyses from zero-price markets perspective instead. For instance, through such an approach Facebook's acquisition of Instagram would have been seen as 'designed to eliminate competition in zero-price markets for users', instead of being allowed without much commentary from antitrust theorists (Newman, 2015, p 194).

Absence of prices for consumed outputs poses a problem for regulators. Antitrust regulations and interpretations are anchored in the idea that competition leads to lowering of prices, which through cheaper products leads to higher consumer welfare. From this perspective, monopolies are seen as negative as they prevent competition and keep the prices – that would be reduced through competition – unnecessarily high. Since modern antitrust law is 'firmly grounded in neoclassical economics, which is in turn centred on price theory', absence of positive prices posed a challenge for traditional regulatory theories and analytical frameworks (Newman, 2015, p 149). The logic of prices as the ultimate measure of consumer welfare, Newman highlights, leads to the conclusion 'that courts and enforcement agencies ought to be extremely cautious when applying antitrust law to suppliers of zero-price products' (Newman, 2015, p 201). Google utilized this logic of argumentation as a support for their practice, pointing out how since competition laws are primarily concerned with what is best for consumers, free products should not be seen as a reduction of consumer welfare (Newman, 2015). Named free products in legal jargon, digital products of this kind have been frequently exempt by the US courts from adhering to their terms of service with their users. The underlying logic has been that users cannot expect a strict adherence to the terms of service in return for something offered for free (Newman, 2018, pp 575–7).

This myth of free, as Newman named the story of providers of zero-price digital services, has its roots in both idealization of the boom of the dot.com IT 'new economy' and associated business models, and in mistaken understanding of the economics of the new models. Focusing on zero prices, mainstream economists failed to see that this does not mean zero-cost for the consumers, Newman argues. In return for zero-cost services, consumers do not pay with fiat currencies. Instead, they are exposed to targeted advertising, paying with their attention or personal information. Free providers monetize what they get in return for zero-price services. While consumers have a long history and ability of judging the value of products they desire based on price, they have very little means of judging the value of what they give up in return for zero-price services. In other words, unlike with price-based transactions, the cost of zero-price transactions is unclear to consumers.

Zero-price market approach is helpful in several aspects for Marxian approaches. It breaks up with seeing free-of-monetary-charge services as exceptions outside of the capitalist mode of production by acknowledging the exchange of users' data in exchange for free services. It understands producers of free services as typical capitalist firms engaged in profit seeking. Finally, it argues for restoring prices in production to the analysis. The last two points are broadly in agreement with Marxian interpretations, which require monetary flows to be operational. However, Newman's critique falls short on three accounts. First, in a different way than the neoclassical economics it criticizes, it ends up naturalizing competition and capitalist markets. Second, it does not extend the logic of capitalist production on digital platforms to the whole circuit of capital, omitting the advertising and final commodities carrying value from the conceptual framework. This is critical, since without seeing the whole circuit of valorization, it is difficult to get to grips with both the logic of individual producers, such as advertising-funded digital platforms that dominate in the production of 'free' products that are central objects of Newman's analysis, and with the capitalist mode of production as a whole. Finally, without a methodological approach that can grasp social and economic determination of forms, Newman's account is deprived of ability to capture differences in form that elements of production, especially products, in his object of study, acquire. This goes both on the input side, as forms of public wealth (Free Software Copyleft, publicly financed research outputs), and within the production process as different types of commodities.[1]

The role of advertising in production and circulation

Critique of advertising is a vast field of study. We will not present all of the possible approaches for studying the role of media advertising in capitalism.[2] Instead, we will focus on three approaches that deserve special attention from the perspective of advertising-funded platforms. First, we will look at how the originators of monopoly capitalism thesis defined the systemic role of advertising. Second, we will look at how authors within the critique of political economy of communication and media attempted to provide a materialist understanding of communication and audiences. Finally, we will look at how some authors analyse advertising as the process of circulation of capital relying for the most part on the reading of Marx's *Capital*, Volume 2. Understanding advertising from the perspective of media economics is rather simple. Advertising is defined as a form of competitive behaviour as firms use advertising to compete in attracting consumers to switch to their own product rather than that of their rivals (Doyle, 2002, p 41). However, in oligopolistic conditions competitive behaviour acquires a different form with multiple political and social implications. The 'alliance' between the media and advertising has become more complex. Traditionally, the mass media sold products to consumers on the one hand, and audiences to advertisers on the other hand. With the rise of monopolistic players capturing internet advertising, the role of the media changed.

Advertising as a sales effort

Advertising is not an irrational whim of the monopolistic corporation or oligopolistic industry. It is a structural necessity of monopoly capitalism and it represents one of its 'nerve centres' (Baran & Sweezy, 1968, p 115). The sales effort is meant to increase demand in over-productive monopolistic industries that seek expanding markets to realize their produced surplus. The sales effort increases in importance where price competition stops being the determining factor in attracting consumers. Corporations increasingly engage in product variation, 'planned obsolescence', model changes, offering various credit schemes to boost their sales, and so on (Baran & Sweezy, 1968, p 115). The impact of the sales effort on the income and output structure of the economy is similar to government spending financed by tax revenue (Baran & Sweezy, 1968, p 125). It expands aggregate income and output and is associated with higher employment of workers in advertising agencies, advertising media, and so on. Additionally, advertising plays a role similar to the one assigned by innovations (Baran & Sweezy, 1968, p 126). It creates demand for a product and encourages investment in plant and equipment which otherwise would not take place.

The sales effort downplays the importance of savings and stimulates increasing consumption:

> [a]nd the principal means of carrying out this task are to induce changes in fashion, create new wants, set new standards of status, enforce new forms of propriety. The unquestioned success of advertising in achieving these aims has greatly strengthened its role as a force counteracting monopoly capitalism's tendency to stagnation. (Baran & Sweezy, 1968, p 128)

The actual use of new products is not an important issue in this process as it is driven primarily by capital accumulation and not by satisfying already existing or newly discovered needs that improve the way in which humans reproduce and advance. For this reason, Baran and Sweezy argued that the sales effort essentially represents a waste of economic resources. In monopoly capitalism, the sales effort is no longer an adjunct to production. It increasingly dictates what is to be produced and under which criteria. This changes the notion of the socially necessary costs of production and the nature of the social product itself (Baran & Sweezy, 1968, pp 131, 132).

In reaching potential consumers, the rising role of the electronic media in the 1960s played an enormous role. The volume of advertising and the price charged for space and time was determined by the media's access to the public (Baran et al, 2013b, p 39). Increasing reliance on advertising revenue also led the media towards explicit or implicit pressures towards promoting specific types of editorial policies. Since advertisers seek to reach the largest audiences, they are inclined towards avoiding antagonizing and controversial media content. On the other hand, the public is attracted by programmes that contain tensions, debates, contests, and rivalries. The media solution is to promote programmes such as quiz shows, sports, and less controversial public issues (Baran et al, 2013b, p 39). At the point of analysis of culture and communication the position by Baran and Sweezy in their published and unpublished material (Baran & Sweezy, 1968; Baran et al, 2013b, 2013a) is close to the classical culture industry position[3] of the manipulative entertainment industry and the decline of standards and quality in culture (Horkheimer & Adorno, 2002). For example, they state that '[t]he trouble with advertising is *not* that it promotes conformity to certain norms of life and behaviour. The trouble is that advertising of necessity promotes conformity to norms that, by any rational standard, are worthless or humanly destructive' (Baran et al, 2013b, p 41). They see an increase in the quantity of cultural goods in print, drama, music, and cinema available in conditions of monopoly capitalism. However, they also point out that it has been accompanied by an equally impressive change in quality – 'a change in general for the worse' as 'we witness the diminution of the mind, the debasement of tastes and the brutalization of manners' (Baran et al, 2013a, pp 44, 45).

The impact of advertising on commercially funded media is certainly not as straightforward and mechanic, nor is the end media product an inevitable diminution of standards. In order to gauge the decline of standards, it would be necessary to pre-define certain standards that might serve as benchmarks. Yet this is extremely difficult, if not impossible, to determine. Ultimately, a position implying a directly negative impact of advertising potentially leads towards an elitist understanding of culture and offers a theoretical cul-de-sac, which allows little room for interpretation. It grants no agency to audiences and the public. The connection between the economic conditions of commercially supported industries and their cultural output can best be described as a structural tendency, or a constraint, that has a potential influence on media production (G. Murdock & Golding, 2016). The conditions under which this tendency might be displayed are the matter of empirical research, and the understanding of specific historical conditions under which it develops. Before we turn to the complex issue of the relations between the economic factors and cultural output, we will provide a position developed within the field of the political economy of communication during the 1970s. Baran and Sweezy focused on monopolistic industries that aimed to sell an abundance of commodities in search for new and expanding markets for their excess productive capacity. The media played a secondary role in their analysis. For the political economy of communication, the media plays a central role.

Consumption of advertising as commodity production

Mediated communication provides the public with access to politics, economy, culture, and entertainment. The media are the gateway for individuals and social groups aiming to understand broader societal issues deemed important for the news agenda by media professionals, editors, producers, and media owners. As recipients of mass media content audiences' understanding of society is framed by what the media present as relevant. This provided a strong impetus in critical thinking towards understanding the media as a societal superstructure or a sphere of ideological manipulation, false consciousness, and conformity (for example, Althusser, 2014). A well-known reference from the early works of Marx and Engels is often used to support such an understanding: '[t]he ideas of the ruling class are in every epoch the ruling ideas, i.e. the class which is the ruling material force of society, is at the same time its ruling intellectual force' (Marx & Engels, 1974, p 64).

Dallas Smythe (1977, 1981/2005) provided a materialist approach to media and communication, countering then-dominant tendencies of looking at the media from the perspective of symbols and meanings that deceive audiences in the interest of media owners and ruling classes. Smythe aimed to answer the essential political economy question by determining what the commodity produced by the media industries is. The dominant answer from the perspective of Western Marxism at the time was that the produced commodity is the 'message', 'information', 'image', 'meaning', 'manipulation', and so on. Smythe's response was that the main commodity produced by the media is audiences and readership:

> of the off-the-job work time, the largest single block is time of the audiences which is sold to advertisers. It is not sold by the workers but by the mass media of communications. Who produces this commodity? The mass media of communications do by the mix of explicit and hidden advertising and 'programme' material. (Smythe, 1977, p 3)

To support this position Smythe (1977) puts forward eight theses. First, with their advertising expenditures the advertisers buy the services of audiences who pay attention in predictable numbers and at particular times to particular communications. Second, a sub-industry of audience and marketing research checks whether the advertisers are getting what they pay for. Third, owners of TV and radio networks, newspapers, and magazines are the principal institutions producing these commodities. Fourth, mass media content aims to recruit audiences and maintain their loyal attention. Fifth, the audiences perform the work of learning to buy consumer goods: 'they work to create demand for advertised goods which is the purpose of the monopoly capitalist advertisers' (Smythe, 1977, p 6). Sixth, the principal aspect of capitalist production has become the alienation of workers from the means of producing and reproducing themselves. Seventh, advertising has become a productive activity under monopoly capitalism conditions. Eighth, mass media institutions developed the equipment, workers, and organization to produce audiences for the system.

Smythe's provocative approach sparked a widespread debate on the role of media and audiences in capitalist society (for example, Jhally & Livant, 1986; Livant, 1979; Meehan, 1984; G. Murdock, 1978/1997) and attempted to shift the focus of political economy towards a more central understanding of the role of the media in supporting demand and driving up consumption. Yet, Smythe's argument also contained some crucial errors. For example, while attempting to counter the 'media manipulation thesis', he essentially granted the manipulation aspect to the economic dimension.[4] In other words, the audience in Smythe's approach 'works' in its leisure time to produce commodities while being unpaid and while being un-coerced by the manipulative strategies of the media. This is hardly a starting point for alienation and exploitation of labour along the lines outlined by Marx. As Hardy argues with reference to contemporary applications of Smythe's approach, alienation and social reproduction do not describe the totality of user engagement with social media, nor do they describe the media literacies involved in navigating 'free' services and benefits, albeit in structurally disadvantaged ways (2014, p 143). In addition, as Murdock (1997, p 470) argued 'it is not a question of choosing between theories of ideology and theories of political economy, but of finding ways of integrating these two into a more adequate and complete account.'

The problem of combining two approaches to media and communication remains one of the central occupations for all critically informed analyses of capitalist society. Further in this chapter we will deal with how Smythe's thesis was extended to understand commodification of audience activities on the internet (for example, Fisher, 2012; Fuchs, 2015). While acknowledging the reasoning behind such an extension, we will also describe some theoretical problems that it creates in conceptualizing the division between work and leisure, production, consumption, and circulation. Smythe provided theoretical inspiration for answering the question of what the material role of communication is, and what the commodity produced by media industries is. We now turn to an understanding of advertising that does away with some of the problems of determining what productive and unproductive labour is and if audiences labour and end up being exploited and alienated. We will focus on advertising as part of the process of circulation of capital in the economy as a whole. Such an approach manages to avoid some of the theoretical pitfalls present in the original argument by Smythe and provides ways of interpreting the role of advertising and algorithms in speeding up the capital reproduction process.

Advertising as circulation

The rise of the internet and algorithmic solutions provides a close connection between consumers and producers of commodities based on widespread background data analyses offering insights into consumer needs and wants. In the mass media era, this process was dependent, as Smythe noticed, on a range of actors and institutions such as the mass media, which had access to audiences on the one hand; and audience and marketing research agencies that provided data on socio-demographic trends of audience behaviour on the other hand. With the rise of global platforms, the mass media lose their privileged position of providing access to audiences and consumers. This function now belongs to major digital platforms such as Google and Facebook. The role of marketing and audience research agencies is also declining since companies such as Google and Facebook rely on their superior data capture and data analysis strategies to analyse audience and consumer behaviour. As Lee (2011) puts it, Google vertically integrates the search engine, advertising agency and the rating system so that advertisers have no need for intermediary organizations that specialize in advertising, market research and rating. Theoretically, this process can also be described as the process of circulation of capital, which, due to algorithmic solutions, becomes ever faster, and, in theory, more precise or, at least, more optimized.

The circulation process from the Marxian perspective describes the social reproduction of the capitalist system and the interaction between different economic units. The transformation of produced commodities into money requires an effective demand for those commodities and, on a larger scale, the transformation of money into the elements of production such as the means of production and labour power (Mattick, 1998). The function of Marx's reproduction schemes 'is to demonstrate how the economic forms of value (and so surplus value) condition the reproduction of society as the organisation of the human production and consumption of use-values' (Mattick, 1998, p 29). Circulation of capital involves different changes and flows of forms from capital to money to the elements of production to commodities and back to money (Murray, 1998, p 37). The process of circulation is the process of realization of capital. In the development of capitalism, the tendency has become to increase the pace of capital realization. The role of advertising, the media, and now the internet and algorithms, are essential in speeding up the process of realization and accumulation. Capital circulation can be shortened, according to Murray, in many areas. By shortening turnover time of fixed capital. Reducing the expenses associated with storage of commodities. Reducing the costs involved with money and accounting. By developing new production technologies and introducing new labour management policies (Murray, 1998, p 54).

Many of these functions are often attributed to changes in capitalist production from Fordism towards post-Fordism or lean production, which reduces production costs and responds to consumer demands more quickly with adapted products and services. Here, the role of technologies that gather information about consumers and their desires is sometimes celebrated as bringing forward consumer sovereignty and putting more power in the hands of consumers. Yet, as Smith (1998) argues, this is hardly the case as capital accumulation remains the driving force of lean production and the driving force behind shortening capital circulation time. Lean production incorporates a continuous feedback loop between capitalist enterprises and consumers. The loop is designed to help capital proceed through the realization stage of the capital circuit as rapidly as possible (Smith, 1998, p 73). The feedback process connects consumer responses and manufacturers through information gathering. Information gathering measures the level of customer satisfaction, determines whether the complexity of product design matches the competence levels of consumers, and then feeds back into production, which allows a shift in product mix and product design re-starting the new capital circulation cycle (Smith, 1998, p 78).

Integrating consumers into the design process is not the ultimate corporate goal as the goal of expanding capital accumulation remains unchanged: 'the integration is a strategy undertaken by capital in the hope that it will increase the rate of consumption' (Smith, 1998, p 81). Hence, the use of information technologies to track consumer responses can be seen as an 'objectification of the consumer's subjectivity and self-understanding'. Once objectified, this information can be appropriated by manufacturers and distributors who are then able to tailor marketing messages: 'Messages that are addressed to an anonymous mass are less effective than those directed to you personally' (Smith, 1998, pp 85, 86).

Google and Facebook are companies that provide such advanced information gathering functionalities to commodity producers and advertisers as they are at the forefront of information technology development for consumer tracking and surveillance. As Robinson (2015, p 44) argues, it is the relationship with other capitals together with the loyalty of their users that are crucial factors in their ability to accumulate capital. They 'act as a mediating channel between advertisers seeking to realize surplus value and users attracted by the use value of free services. They effectively levy a charge on advertisers' surplus value for improving and accelerating their ability to make sales' (Robinson, 2015, p 46). Expressed through the categories we developed in the book, free-of-charge pre-commodities attract users who then also consume adverts as intermediate commodities purchased by the producers, or resellers, of final commodities in order to enhance sales and realize value and surplus value. User data collected by Google and Facebook, Robinson continues, reduces advertisers' costs of circulation with more accurate advertising, disaggregation of advertising expenditures into smaller chunks and access to smaller or niche markets. The degree of the reduction of costs of circulation is determined by the effectiveness of advertising in enabling sales (Robinson, 2015, p 47). Since platforms have no control over what users do, or how long they use the platform, they directly appropriate user-generated content backed up by legal and technological assurances. Simultaneously, the technological aspect of software and algorithmic affordances 'does not merely implement the appropriation of content. It enables the display of advertising alongside this content and the control of these users by means of changing what is possible or permissible on the platform' (Robinson, 2015, p 47).

Having looked at different ways of conceptualizing the role of advertising in capitalism (sales effort, audience commodity, circulation of capital) we only touched upon an important issue of the influence of advertising on editorial policies in the media. In the context of the internet and algorithmic solutions, a similar claim can be made about the influence of advertising on the types of technical decisions that go into algorithmic changes that promote, or support, distribution of specific content to its users. What the political economy of communication literature shows is that advertising dependent businesses have a structural tendency to favour specific types of media production and/or distribution.[5] It is, therefore, difficult to justify the ideology of neutral carriers of information and free flow of information taken on by companies such as Facebook and Google. Looking at advertising from the perspective of circulation of capital and from the perspective of the critique of the political economy of communication helps to pinpoint where different pressures towards updating technological forms based on commercial interests come from.

User activities in capitalist production

In this section, we critically evaluate some of the Marxist approaches to digital platforms. The role of non-paid activities, such as the use of digital objects and creation of content by individuals, has occupied many writers in Marxist tradition, leading to concepts, such as immaterial labour (Lazzarato, 1996), free labour (Terranova, 2000), and digital labour (for example, Scholz, 2013; Fuchs, 2014b). One of the key aspects that caught their attention was what seemed like blurring between production and consumption. The explosive growth of on-line activity exposed, rendered visible, and in the process altered the socialization of humans. The seemingly palpable emancipatory potential arising from decentralization of communication and from a huge array of useful objects suddenly available free of charge was initially idealized[6] and critiqued (Barbrook & Cameron, 1996). The approach taken by the authors in the *Postoperaismo* tradition was to point out the inclusion of human activity in the process of capitalist production, and to offer a glimpse of emancipatory potential.

A similar seeming mixture of production and consumption was first noticed with the rise of traditional mass electronic media, radio, and television. Accepting what he understood as Baran's and Sweezy's demonstration that 'monopoly rather than competition rules contemporary capitalism', Smythe accused Marxism of having a blind spot for mass communication systems, stretching the argument by claiming that 'audiences are commodities', and proposing that 'all non-sleeping time under capitalism is work time' (Smythe, 1977, p 3). Key claims utilizing Smythe – audience performing unpaid labour and being constituted as a commodity – in combination with post-autonomist Marxism make important insights into capital accumulation mechanisms occurring on digital media. However, we will argue that it is not necessary to conflate production and consumption to analyse and criticize capital accumulation on digital platforms. In fact, keeping these two departments separate and understanding their interaction in the process of reproduction of capital allows us to get a broader and more accurate picture of the role data-driven business models in the capitalist mode of production.

Many authors participating in the audience commodity and digital labour debates present a critique of the way capitalist production misuses human activities that are not rewarded for their contribution. As a counterpoint, Hesmondhalgh asks whether Smythe is demanding payment for the unpaid labour of audiences and poses a provocative question: 'it is unclear to me why he [Smythe] does not include payment for sleep in his demands, given that this too seems to involve the reproduction of labour power' (Hesmondhalgh, 2010, p 280). While extreme, the example of sleep points to the limits of collapsing the distinction between production and consumption. Fisher acknowledges this, stating that 'the political economy of SNS [social networking sites] is unique in allowing the integration and conflation of previously distinct processes of production, circulation and consumption' (Fisher, 2012, p 181). However, by conflating those spheres, categories constructed by Marx to grasp the capitalist mode of production, such as labour power, capital, exploitation, and surplus value, lose their meaning and explanatory power for the entire mode of production.

Caraway (2011) argued that by conflating leisure time and time sold for a wage, Smythe effectively removed the purpose for the existence of labour power and its appearance as a commodity in capitalist production. The status of people who are legally free to sell their labour power is thus erased, since all of their time becomes 'exploited', according to Smythe. If the category of labour power is relativized, if the special social form that labour power acquires under capitalist production as a commodity cannot be differentiated from other human activities, Marx's concepts of capitalist production of surplus value and exploitation of the workers are rendered inoperable. For Caraway, Smythe '[d]ismissed the fruits of the struggle for reduction in the workweek by claiming that the time saved was merely fantasy, since all time is now productive. Hence, no real gains were achieved by workers' struggles' (Caraway, 2011, p 703).

Caraway's key point, that Smythe's version of history is blind to workers, their struggles and demands, is due to Smythe's adoption of the reading of history present in Baran and Sweezy, where social changes are 'a matter of the inner dynamic laws of capitalism' (Caraway, 2011, p 704). This line of critique, correct or not in terms of its extension to Baran and Sweezy, is an important point to keep in mind for two reasons. Strict functionalism that explains everything through the needs of capital leaves no space for a different way of producing outputs, both within the world dominated by capitalist production of commodities and in general. When no conceptual space is left for other production and distribution logics to co-exist with the dominant capitalist one, when economies are not mixed, when social forms of production are not seen to co-exist, successions of various modes of production are not possible, since transition from one dominant mode of production to another implies co-existence during the transition period. Additionally, how can the dominance of the capitalist mode of production be superseded if no alternative ways of producing can be present simultaneously, albeit in a subservient role? The second major problem with Symthe's theory is the agency of the workers' movement, which is erased from our understanding of history if leisure time and shorter working week, what they fought for, cannot be understood to exist outside of the logic of capitalist production. Critics of Smythe do not refer to anything Smythe did in his lifetime or to any of his engagements from a leftist perspective.[7] They refer to the analytical consequence of Smythe's postulate, to how it alters our understanding of history.

From Smythe's audience labour to digital labour

Fuchs (2014a, 2014b, 2015) argues that there is a common denominator between the human activity that involves the usage of digital platforms and wage labour. In this understanding, consumption of digital platforms performed voluntarily, mostly in leisure time, for pleasure, produces the same thing, value, such as labour performed under the control of management, in specific time determined by the legal contract, in return for a wage. Since the first activity does not involve money, as consumption is free of charge, money cannot be the commonality that relates to value. Time spent in consumption for pleasure is equated with the time spent in waged labour for pay. Both produce value. This conceptual understanding is packed under a broader name, Marx's labour theory of value. However, we will argue that once time is taken as the source of value on digital platforms it becomes difficult to understand other important aspects of Marx's theory. For example, the centrality of money, the importance of exchange, social, and economic form-determination of production and its elements, and labour power as a specific social form of labour that under capitalist production becomes a source of surplus value. Let us present some of the main arguments Fuchs puts forward in order to position our own understanding of the contribution of user activities to capital accumulation on digital monopoly platforms.

Fuchs coins the term 'digital labour theory of value', which he considers feasible and necessary. This involves utilizing, and perhaps modifying 'Marx's labour theory of value'. This theory of Marx, according to Fuchs, 'argues that the value of a commodity measured as the average number of hours it takes to produce it is a crucial economic category for the critical analysis of capitalism' (Fuchs, 2017, p 44). Some authors, Fuchs continues, dispute the validity of Marx's labour theory of value, postulating that value depends on utility. He is concerned, since 'the claims that the labour theory of value is no longer valid implies that time plays no role in the contemporary capitalist economy' (Fuchs, 2017, p 45). The category of time plays the central role in Fuchs's understanding of Marx's theory of value. Defending his position from those who point out that labour without a price cannot have value, Fuchs argues how they confuse price and value and that such criticism is 'based on a lack of knowledge of Marx' (Fuchs, 2015, p 587).

Value can be understood as labour measured in time:

> If 500 million people use a corporate platform that is funded by targeted advertising for an average of 90 hours a year (which is on average 15 minutes a day), then the value created is 45 billion hours of digital labour ... 45 billion hours of work are therefore exploited. (Fuchs, 2015, p 587)

In the case of commodities not being sold, Fuchs concludes, nothing changes, since 'workers are also exploited if the commodities they create are not sold because value and surplus value of a commodity is created before it is sold', and 'exploitation is based in the sphere of commodity production' (Fuchs, 2015, p 587). It is clear that Fuchs' understanding of value as presented in the quotes we selected here cuts out some of the central features of Marx's explanatory framework. For Fuchs, commodity exchange seems to play a lesser role. If exchange was not an important element for the realization of value, then the dot-com market crash of 2000/01 would never have happened. The reason behind the crash was the development of digital business models, which were unable to sell their products and services and, hence, were not realizing value at the point of exchange, nor extracting surplus value. In our reading, exchange provides a moment of socialization, and it is impossible to conceptualize Marx's theory of value, or the unity of production and circulation without it.

For Fuchs, the transformation problem, or more precisely 'transformation of commodity values into prices of production', as Marx puts it, does not exist. Not for the reasons put forward by interpreters of Marx's work that do not consider value to be an empirical category (Milios et al, 2002, pp vii–x, 127–8; Wei & Heinrich, 2011), but due to the identity of labour time and value. This identity, if true, cannot conceptualize the entire capitalist mode of production driven by the race for profits, for expansion of monetary inputs, or for surplus value in Marx's categories. Since how could a capitalist, driven by the logic of selling the outputs for more money than the cost of inputs, be simultaneously interested in increasing the value of the output of a production cycle, and in lengthening of labour time, which, according to Fuchs, adds value to output? Hudis provides a useful insight in the incompatibility of labour time-based theory of value with the reality of capitalist production:

> If value were based on the actual hours of labour, commodities that take longer to produce would have a greater value. Since capitalism is based on augmenting value, that would mean that capitalists would try to get workers to work slower rather than faster. This is, of course, clearly not the case. (Hudis, 2013, p 96)

Fuchs' assertion and his theoretical apparatus resemble the view held by some Marxists, inheriting Engels' reading, according to which 'the value of commodity is determined consciously by labour, measured in time, of individual producers' (Elbe, 2013). The reading was important for socialist political projects as it held the promise that wealth that is chaotically and unjustly distributed in capitalism can be brought under the control, 'managed and applied according to plan'. Postone's extensive reading of 20th century political economists and Marxists finds the commonality between traditional Marxist interpretations as they all 'imply that overcoming capitalism would involve' that 'labour could ... realise its social character directly', once the mediation imposed by the capitalist production would be overcome. Another commonality is an interpretation of Marx's theory as an extension, or a refined version, of classical political economy, where labour is understood, as far back as in John Locke's writing, and in both Ricardo and Smith, as the source of all wealth (Postone, 1996, p 53). Marx's theory of surplus value and exploitation, Postone summarizes, is taken to be the major difference from classical political economists, with the main problem being exploitation occurring through markets, in the realm of distribution, enabled by the private ownership of the means of production.

In the background of Postone's reading is the idea that traditional Marxist understanding provided a basis for socialist and communist political forces to take over the capitalist state without drastically changing the social form of production that includes waged and supervised labour in a manner very close to what is found in capitalism. In other words, such an understanding provided a foundation for political interventions in the realm of distribution, keeping the realm of production to a significant extent similar to the capitalist one. In Postone's words, while Marx 'uncovers unexamined, historically specific social basis' of the categories of political economy, 'classical political economy, then, based itself on the transhistorical form of appearance of a historically determinate social forms'. Marx develops this in detail in Chapter 48 of *Capital*, Volume 3, the Trinity Formula. As paraphrased by Postone: ' "the productive activity of human beings in general" is a mere phantom, an abstraction that, taken by itself, does not exist at all' (Postone, 1996, p 56). In contrast to Marx's insight on social form of labour under capitalist production, 'the traditional interpretation takes "labour" to be the transhistorical source of social wealth' (Postone, 1996, p 59).

Fuchs' concept of (digital) labour does not engage in understanding the social form of digital labour, since he equates human activity in consumption to be the same sort of activity as that of wage labourers employed in capitalist production, working on digital platforms, producing commodities.[8] If outputs of any activity that end up as inputs in capitalist commodity production do produce value and are therefore exploited, it follows that there is no monetary aspect involved between the 'worker' and capitalist producer. That is, value cannot appear in the form of money. The only way this type of activity could count as 'labour time', and add value to the commodity produced by digital platform producers, is under the condition that any labour, regardless of its social form, in a transhistorical conception, can be a source of value when combined with capitalist production which utilizes some aspect of such activities as inputs.

However, if this type of consumption is labour, as Fuchs claims, then what is the social form this labour takes, since it is not under the control of capitalist production? These labourers, that is, consumers, act on their own will, in their own time, with no control over when and how their activity proceeds. Caraway noted the issue of control over labour, reminding us that for Marx, worker in capitalist production works under control and supervision of capitalist (Caraway, 2011, p 697). Furthermore, he notes, 'there is no formal contract, negotiation, or discussion of terms between audience and advertiser', an aspect otherwise present in all wage labour under capitalist production. Fuchs and many other critical authors find the solution in ideological coercion in which social media are presented as a form of participatory new democracy while masking exploitation as play (Fuchs, 2014b, p 122).

Let us return to the broader question of the role of audience and user activities on digital platforms. While Fuchs blames ideological manipulation for the widespread usage of social media, we argue that the specific technological form we explained in Chapter 2 – consisting of social and economic form (pre-commodity) obtained by a useful technological product (Google web search, Facebook social networking) within the advertising-funded monopoly digital platform, aided by legal forms, all of it under the capitalist mode of production – is the ultimate source of corporate control and dominance. The ideological discourse always plays an important part in convincing people to buy commodities and use new technologies. Offering new technologies free of charge certainly aids that purpose. However, the final decision on the act of data or monetary exchange through engagement with digital platforms is still in the hands of individuals. They are not physically coerced or contractually obligated to use Google's web search, Facebook's social networking, or Netflix's streaming service. The focal point of dominance lies in the inability of individual users, regulators, nation states, or transnational entities such as the European Union to change corporate control and influence or even alter technological forms in oligopolistic conditions.

At the same time, we do not argue that user activity does not contribute to capital accumulation, nor that their activity cannot be conceptualized as commodified. We argue that there is a series of mediations, obtaining definite social and economic forms that allow leisure activities to become commodified as inputs contributing to the wider business model of surplus value extraction. Digital labour debates were pointing in the right direction. However, while sharpening our ability to understand how user activity becomes commodified, it also lost some of the Marxian critical edge by conflating production and consumption. It remained trapped in the social factory metaphor (for example, Scholz, 2013) and thus accepted a productivist approach to social media by interpreting Marx's theory of value as a labour-time based theory of value. Focusing on time as the crucial element for value creation loses sight of commodity exchange as a point where value and surplus value are realized and where productive acts of labour are finally socialized. By adopting the mainstream logic of prosumer capitalism this distinction became even more blurred making it difficult to theorize production, consumption, wage labour, value, and surplus value. Digital labour is perhaps best conceived as a metaphor grasping some difficulties of directly applying the Marxian critique of the capitalist mode of production to digital platforms. However, in the end, conflating production and consumption might create more problems than it solves, as it is unable to make a distinction between general, simple, and determinate abstractions within the capitalist mode of production.

Financialization and Regulation

Accumulation of capital based on commodification of user data leads to privatization of many aspects of social and political life, previously outside of the process of commodification. Yet, regardless of widespread public outrage, major companies end up being largely unscathed in their economic, and especially financial, performance for three different reasons. First, concentrated and centralized capital creates high entry barriers (investment costs) for newcomers who could potentially challenge their power by providing alternative outputs. GAFAM invests substantial capital in research and development as well as in mergers and acquisitions putting innovation within the industry under their control. Moreover, accumulated data on web search history, social networking, and online purchases puts all newcomers at a significant disadvantage in providing alternative outputs. This is especially the case for the advertising financed digital platforms such as Google and Facebook: software and algorithms extract consumption preferences from the accumulated background data (obtained from the usage of pre-commodities), enabling production of higher quality targeted adverts (intermediate commodities).

Second, legal forms of financial regulation and financial profits enable scaling up and growth of tech business models and provide support for their international expansion, creating enormous personal wealth to shareholders and top executives, and sharpening economic inequality. We will provide evidence of how Google forged a path of trust building among shareholders and investors by acquiring new companies, and by entering legal struggles throughout its corporate development. Finally, the US regulation favours the growth of single large companies under current interpretations of antitrust legislation, and in merger and acquisition approvals. Companies use their economic strength to influence political decisions through lobbying and other practices that capture the political and regulatory processes, further strengthening their ongoing business operations.

Labour, financial profits, and technological forms

Developing algorithms for recognizing patterns in gathered data allow GAFAM to secure intellectual property rights and to lock-in future profits coming from updated technical solutions. Google provides advertising on their properties such as Google Search, YouTube, Google Play, Gmail, Google Maps, as well as on third party websites within the so-called Google Network Members programme. Facebook relies even more on direct ads within their platform properties (Table 5.1). Apple attracts the majority of its revenue through iPhone, Mac, and iPad sales, although it is attracting revenue in more data-driven areas such as the Apple Store, Apple TV, and Apple Watch. Amazon attracts the majority of its revenue from online stores. Online sales are streamlined through data analysis. The most profitable segment is Amazon Web Services (AWS), which includes cloud-computing platforms and services. Major corporate customers for AWS include Netflix, LinkedIn, Facebook, BBC, Baidu, ESPN, and others. Microsoft is, much like Apple, a more traditional tech company, which relies on proprietary technologies such as Windows OS and Microsoft Office. The company is quickly expanding into the cloud computing area with products such as Microsoft Azure. It also attracts advertising revenue through its search engine Bing, although it remains too weak to compete with Google in web search.

Technological forms provided by GAFAM enable high-speed and ubiquitous exchange of data between interconnected computers, servers, and, increasingly, physical and biological objects (that is, digital assistants, cars, smart cities, wearables, implants, and so on). Data passing through interconnected nodes allows these companies to search for patterns, commodify data, and secure intellectual property over functionality and pattern recognition mechanisms. According to estimates from May 2018, there was 2.5 quintillion bytes of data produced every day with 90 per cent of all world data being generated between 2016 and 2018 (Marr, 2018). *The Economist* announced on its May 2017 cover that 'the world's most valuable resource is no longer oil but data' (The Economist, 2017). While *The Economist* was celebrating new rules of competition, in reality, the majority of data gathering and analysing practices unfold within the closely protected, oligopolistic organizational confines of GAFAM. For example, Google has the potential to collate a file on an individual user with the equivalent of

Table 5.1: Core business and major corporate segments for GAFAM

Company	Core business	Corporate segments (2019) % of revenue	Number of employees (2019)
Alphabet Inc.	Internet content and information	- Advertising on Google properties (Google search, YouTube, other) – 69.9% - Advertising on Google Network Members' sites – 13.25% - Google cloud – 5.5% - Other bets – 0.4% - Other products and services – 10.95%	118,899
Apple Inc.	Consumer electronics	- iPhone sales – 54.7% - Mac sales – 9.9% - iPad sales – 8.2% - Wearables, Home, and accessories (AirPods, Apple TV, Apple Watch, Beats products, HomePod, iPod touch, and so on) – 9.4% - Services (digital content stores and streaming services, AppleCare, licensing, and other services) – 17.8%	137,000
Facebook Inc.	Internet content and information	- Facebook ads – 98.5% - Payments and other fees – 1.5%	44,942
Amazon Inc.	Specialty retail	- Sales in North America – 60.9% - International sales – 26.6% - Amazon Web Services – 12.5%	798,000
Microsoft Corporation	Software infrastructure	- Productivity and business processes (LinkedIn, Office 365, Dynamics 365) – 32.7% - Intelligent cloud (Azure, Windows Servers, Microsoft SQL) – 31% - More personal computing (Windows, Xbox, Bing, Phone) – 36.3%	148,465

Sources: Company Form 10-K reports and corporate websites

1.5 million documents. If stacked upon each other, these documents would be more than 150 metres high which, according to UK legislation, qualifies as a skyscraper (TruePublica, 2019).

Research and development expenditures

GAFAM engages in commercialization and privatization of technology, largely through data-dependent outputs protected by patents, brands, copyright, and other legal forms. Concentrated and centralized capital allows them to keep their dominant position by investing capital in new means of production, the development of existing technological forms and in research of new technical solutions. In 2019, GAFAM spent $67.7 billion on R&D. Amazon was the biggest spender ($35.9 billion) with 12.8 per cent of its annual revenue. The percentage of R&D expenditure as part of the revenue has been rising steadily for Amazon since 2011. The increase coincides with the development and profitability of the Amazon Web Services subsidiary. The lowest total ($13.6 billion) was spent by Facebook, although it represents as much as 19.2 per cent of its $70.69 billion revenue in 2019. Facebook continuously invests the largest percentage of its revenue, although it also shows high yearly fluctuations.

Microsoft is the most consistent as its percentage fluctuated very little between 2005 and 2019. It spent $16.88 billion or 13.4 per cent in 2019. Google has increased its percentage since 2005, although it shows a steady trend between 2015 and 2019. Apple spends the smallest revenue share on research and development (between the lowest 2.2 per cent in 2011 and the highest 6.4 per cent in 2012). The 6.2 per cent of revenue in 2019 represented a $16.22 billion investment. Small spending percentage is the result of its specific management decisions. Apple is a clear case of catering towards shareholders and investors, which affects its research investment strategy. Apple is focused on integrating existing components through innovative designs (Mazzucato, 2013). Product integration and design also include a strategy of built-in-obsolescence where iPhones, for example, can be charged a limited number of times to ensure there is constant need for replacement technology (Miller & Maxwell, 2017). Moreover, the assembly of many of their products is outsourced to countries providing cheap labour such as the infamous Foxconn company in Taiwan where worker exploitation rates and working conditions resemble those of the early industrial age (Qiu, 2016).

GAFAM's oligopoly is a double-sided phenomenon. First, GAFAM pay extraordinarily low taxes, which allows them to keep larger share of revenue, monopolizing further capital available for investment in the high tech industry. Second, monopoly on technical discoveries for analysing data forecloses the possibility of realizing high future profits for competing companies. Realization of monopoly profits creates high entry barriers for actors trying to collect capital needed to compete by providing alternative products. Software solutions are legally protected in the form of patents that add to the stock of intangible assets and, if commodified, increase future profitability for data monopolies. Capital invested in production leads to production of intermediate, advertising based data commodities and their valorization in the case of Google and Facebook. Capital invested in research and development, which precedes or follows production, achieves valorization only in the degree to which labour leads to the production and sales of new commodities.

However, since in a market economy it is never certain from the outset that it will be possible to apply new discoveries and inventions, 'the profit risk of capital invested in the sphere of research is higher than the average. This is one of the main reasons for the preponderance of large companies in this sphere' (Mandel, 1976, p 254). Monopolies have an interest in perfecting existing products, or in bringing new products in order to keep their competition at bay. The threat of a falling rate of monopoly profits is averted by constant product differentiation and constant market expansion (Mandel, 1976, p 539). This is also one of the reasons for short-term thinking and avoidance of risky investments with lower chance of commercial success. However, even if there is an investment in a risky product line, GAFAM can absorb losses in one corporate segment as it achieves high profitability in other segments.

Composition and division of tech labour

Value-producing labour is the source of value from the perspective of value form theory we outlined in Chapter 2. However, the causal relationship between labour embedded in commodities and market prices is abandoned in the approach. Therefore, abstract labour has to be validated and rendered socially necessary in commodity circulation. Such a reading of Marx allows for a wide range of implications for understanding digital monopolies: from understanding the peculiar character of free-of-charge products as pre-commodities in the capitalist mode of production, through the role of labour in their production, to the ordering of social forms (productive capital, wage labour) in platform production. Validation of labour for advertising-funded platforms is enabled in the dynamic balance between the pre-commodity, the intermediate commodity, and the final commodity that allows surplus value to be extracted and shared between the producers. While technical labour and platform production in general differ from typical, industrial commodity production, contradictions between capital and labour remain the same, along with strategies by which capital aims to exploit labour, cut down expenses, and increase profit rates.

Introducing labour-saving machinery is a typical long-term strategy for maintaining growth and high profit rates. Given the processes of concentration and centralization of capital, the problem of managing companies in monopoly conditions also increases in importance. In industrial capitalism, Taylorism was a way of controlling the workforce and searching for surplus populations that provide cheap, low-skilled labour (Braverman, 1998). In the 1970s labour management was transformed through increasing transnational mobility of capital; complex value chains for supply and distribution of labour and commodities; pressures to reduce labour costs due to increasing size of transnational corporations, intensification of competition, and financialization (Huws, 2019, pp 66, 69). Starting from the 1990s, employment patterns in most Western countries were marked by deregulation that favoured unhindered flow of capital, intellectual property, and information. Following the 2007–8 crisis employment patterns of 'virtual work' emerged in which fixed boundaries between home and work were eroded (Huws, 2013, p 4), followed by further flexibilization and casualization of labour based on short-term contracts, project-based work, longer working hours, less social security, and weak trade unions.

While stories of brilliant programmers and entrepreneurs still dominate the public debate about the tech industry, even in face of increasing regulatory scrutiny and negative publicity surrounding many social harms the industry causes, the tech industry is notoriously stratified (Dyer-Witheford, 2015; Prado, 2018). At the bottom are service workers hired through vendors. They maintain tech campuses and serve the needs of other tech workers. Contingent workers are hired 'on contract' through staffing agencies and include roles such as quality assurance testing, content strategies, on trial design, policy enforcements, and so on. Non-productive workers are full-time employees working on creating products that do not generate revenue. These roles include receptionists, admins, salespersons, facilities managers, and others. They have similar benefits as productive workers but not as much prestige. Finally, productive workers build products that produce revenue and are rewarded with best wages and benefits. The usual software development roles include software engineers, user interface designers, and product managers (Prado, 2018). On top of the tech industry are the billionaire hacker entrepreneurs whose innovations stemming from university grants, and funded by venture capital, became brand names of digital culture (Dyer-Witheford, 2015, p 65). The techno-utopian visions of society promoted by major companies only focus on the top layer of computer programming and promote the 'rags-to-riches' stories of brilliant programmers who scaled their ideas towards worldwide usage and enormous personal wealth (Dyer-Witheford, 2015, p 65).

Financialization plays an important role in fostering such divisions of labour and extreme wage inequalities. The shareholder logic offers stock awards and bonuses to ownership, management, and skilled labour. Institutional shareholders gain ownership and equity over tech companies by investing their capital. However, once their initial loan and risk premium is repaid, they 'retain a claim on the firm's future income, that is the fruits of others' labour *in perpetuity* (or until the firm dissolves, or they sell their shares, and so on). And the mere legal ownership of a firm is *sufficient* to lay claim on its profit' (Wright, 2018). At the same time, stock bonuses, table tennis in the workplace, in-office baristas, and even indoor rainforests (Surette, 2018) are offered as perks to productive workers. However, what is missing from these notions is an understanding that these perks are not free but are instead paid for by those same workers who are told they are using free gifts and unique benefits of working for tech companies. At the same time as stock bonuses and job perks keep the tech elite in check, financialization drives continual restructuring and outsourcing, which disperses production in search for optimal combination of skill and cost with the help of ICT systems and service level agreements (Thompson, 2013, p 482).

Underneath the algorithms and artificial intelligence (AI) systems are armies of temporary, precarious, mostly work-at-home, part-time wage labourers of the gig economy (Woodcock & Graham, 2020) who perform repetitive, micro-tasks that enable smooth running of computer interfaces and global content flows. GAFAM is particularly active in seeking cheap labour to improve its technical systems. Search engine evaluation has been widely used to test if algorithms retrieve useful information in different cultural, geographic, and linguistic contexts. These types of work activities are usually performed via third-party companies that specialize in product localization (Bilić, 2016). Local 'raters' are hired to provide scores on the usefulness of search results in their own locations and are remunerated on a first-come-first-serve basis. In the United States, raters, or web search evaluators, are paid an average of $13.70 an hour for a total of 20 hours a week. They deliver search engine ratings, through localization companies, on to Google's engineers who improve and train complex algorithms. Improving search through human input has direct economic consequences and provides better connection between consumers and advertisers.

Similarly, work performed by Amazon Mechanical Turk (AMT) is used across the tech industry to improve software systems and to simulate autonomous AI systems. As Irani (2015, p 724) argues, 'the dreams of AI have become more urgent as Web 2.0 businesses attempt to amass and extract value from increasing volumes of people's data'. Even when machine-learning algorithms work, they require training based on datasets classified by humans: 'AMT promises ways to weed out porn, attach relevant advertisements, and quickly integrate breaking news into algorithmic indexes' (Irani, 2015, p 724). In addition to search evaluation and AMT there is widespread use of so-called commercial content moderation (CCM) (Roberts, 2016, 2018) on social media platforms. CCM workers are dispersed globally, and work for low wages on a temporary task basis to review digital content that passes through commercial online platforms. The curation process includes reviewing and removing content that is often racist, homophobic, misogynist, and includes explicit language or extreme violence: 'CCM workers are arbiters and adjudicators of which content violates taste, rules, or sociocultural norms, and which content should be kept up on a site' (Roberts, 2016, p 1). AMT, search evaluation, and commercial content moderation make the workers invisible behind smooth technical interfaces and ideologies of autonomous machines and AI systems. In fact, work performed for AMT is often framed as a computational problem, not a labour management problem (Irani, 2015).

There are increasing cracks and fissures in new divisions of labour as controversial practices surface and occupy public debates (for example, Amazon Workers and Supporters, 2018) in order to make the global labour supply chains visible and platforms more accountable. There is a widespread lack of ability to collectively bargain due to the fragmentation of the work process; and the asymmetry of information between workers and platforms (Graham & Woodcok, 2018). Engineers and computer programmers were traditionally kept silent with high salaries and benefits. However, they are also overworked and surveyed, which leaves long-term consequences on their quality of life. Increasing dissatisfaction among tech workers includes traditional workplace issues such as bad management, long working hours, and salary disparities; issues of diversity, racism, and sexism; ethical and political issues of how their companies engage in business cooperation with radical politicians, governments, and regimes (Tech Workers Coalition, 2018).

Shareholder value and financial profits

Recent research shows that CEO compensation has grown 940 per cent since 1978, while typical workers compensation has risen only 12 per cent during that time in the United States (Mischel & Wolfe, 2019). Much of the personal wealth for tech company owners and CEOs is accumulated through various types of stock options, awards, and financial profits (Table 5.2). Tech sector is increasingly being overvalued as shareholders seek quick returns. In terms of production, the creation of technologically driven commodities comes at high risk since capital and labour investments are significant, while the initial product that results from such investments often takes the form of an intangible asset. Only after it becomes successfully commoditized and marketed can tech businesses ensure profits in production and high valuation of their assets.

These risks are multiplied from the perspective of capital. They create a highly volatile situation in which lenders of capital seek short-term profits, while tech companies require long-term investments before new technical discoveries are successfully commodified. Public accountability towards creating socially responsible technologies sits outside of this circle of competitive pressures and profit-seeking interests of shareholders. The risk and reward nexus in contemporary capitalism has therefore intensified the contradictions between technological innovation and inequality (Lazonick & Mazzucato, 2013; Mazzucato, 2018a). Personal value extraction occurs when actors gain control over allocation of substantial business organizations that generate value, and then use product or financial markets on which the enterprise does business to extract value (Lazonick & Mazzucato, 2013, p 1097).

The stock market allows corporations to use stock options as a form of compensation for attracting, retaining, and motivating employees. Awarding stock-based compensations often comes with a vested period for exercising stock awards. Managers and/or high-tech workers closely align their interests with the (stock) performance of the company since this brings immediate monetary benefits. This leads to uneven distribution of resources, which is slowly becoming a source of dissatisfaction for tech workers (Prado, 2018; Tech Workers Coalition, 2018). Among GAFAM companies, Facebook has the highest stock-based compensation as percentage of revenue. In 2019, it was 6.8 per cent, which amounts to $4.86 billion. It was as high

Table 5.2: Reported salaries and personal wealth

Company	Key executives	Title	Reported salary $ million 2018*	Personal net worth $ billion 2019**
Alphabet Inc.	Lawrence Edward Page	Co-Founder, CEO & Director	1	53.1
	Sergey Brin	Co-Founder, Pres & Director	1	51.8
	Ruth Porat	Sr VP & CFO	679.36	N/A
	David C. Drummond	Sr VP of Corp. Development, Chief Legal Officer & Sec.	669.59	0.122
	Sundar Pichai	Director	1.88	0.916
Apple Inc.	Timothy Cook	CEO & Director	15.68	0.284
	Luca Maestri	CFO & Sr VP	5.02	0.101
	Jeffrey E. Williams	Chief Operating Officer	5.05	0.115
	Katherine L. Adams	Sr VP, Gen Counsel & Sec	5.31	0.070
	Chris Kondo	Director of Corporate Accounting	N/A	N/A
Facebook Inc.	Mark Elliot Zuckerberg	Founder, Chairman, and CEO	22.55	75.5
	David W. Wehner	Chief Financial Officer	1.26	0.078
	Sheryl Kara Sandberg	COO & Director	5.3	2.25
	Michael T. Schroepfer	Chief Technology Officer	1.33	0.556
	Susan J.S. Taylor	Chief Accounting Officer	N/A	N/A
Amazon Inc.	Jeffrey P. Bezos	Founder, Chairman, Pres & CEO	1.68	165.6
	Brian T. Olsavsky	Sr VP & CFO	0.163	0.012
	Jeffrey M. Blackburn	Sr VP of Bus. Devel.	0.178	0.165
	Jeffrey A. Wilke	CEO of Worldwide Consumer	0.255	0.165
	Andrew R. Jassy	CEO of Amazon Web Services Inc.	0.266	0.240

Table 5.2: Reported salaries and personal wealth (continued)

Company	Key executives	Title	Reported salary $ million 2018*	Personal net worth $ billion 2019**
Microsoft Corporation	Satya Nadella	CEO & Director	9.04	0.322
	Bradford L. Smith	Pres & Chief Legal Officer	4.48	0.158
	William Henry Gates III	Co-Founder, Technology Advisor & Non-Independent Director	N/A	103.8
			4.69	0.101
	Amy E. Hood	Exec. VP & CFO	3.98	0.102
	Jean-Philippe Courtois	Exec. VP and Pres of Microsoft Global Sales, Marketing and Operations		

Sources: * Yahoo finance (includes salary and bonuses); ** Forbes, Wallmine

as 30.8 per cent ($1.56 billion) of their revenue in 2012, the year Facebook made the initial public offering. The second in the group in 2019 was Google, which spent 6.7 per cent of the 2019 revenue on stock-based compensations or $10.79 billion of its revenue. Microsoft comes in third with 3.7 per cent ($4.65 billion), Amazon with 2.4 per cent ($6.86 billion), and Apple with 2.3 per cent ($6.06 billion).

Stock buybacks have become the main mechanism for manipulating stock prices and increasing average earnings per share for select shareholders. Companies buy their own stock and create artificial demand in open markets. US regulation does not require companies to announce the exact timing of the repurchasing programme. Companies usually announce the buyback strategy but the timing is only known to corporate insiders. Prime beneficiaries are executives who decide on the timing and amount of buybacks (Lazonick, 2014). Between 2003 and 2012, 449 S&P 500 companies dispensed 54 per cent of earnings, equal to $2.4 trillion, buying back their own stock, mostly through open market transaction (Lazonick, 2014, p 2).

Among GAFAM companies, Microsoft has constantly been repurchasing its own stock. For example, in 2019 it bought $18.4 billion. Apple is the absolute leader, especially after the death of Steve Jobs in 2012 and the instalment of the new executive board. In 2018, the company purchased $72 billion and in 2019 an additional $66 billion, an amount that could have been invested in jobs, salaries, and the development of new products. The buyback strategy shows how financialized companies increasingly move towards extracting value, rather than creating value (Lazonick et al, 2013). Since 2015, Google has started an aggressive buyback strategy. In 2019 it amounted to more than $18.1 billion. In 2018, Facebook bought back $12.8 billion and in 2019 $4.2 billion. These newly found allocation strategies coincide with increasing regulatory and public scrutiny, which results in pressure from investors to increase their return on invested capital. Amazon is the only company in the group that had a limited buyback strategies of under $1 billion between 2005 and 2017.

Risks and rewards in Google's path to monopoly

Public innovation was essential in providing knowledge, telecommunications infrastructure and labour prior to privatization and commercialization of the internet (Abbate, 1999; Leslie, 2000; Lazonick & Mazzucato, 2013; Mazzucato, 2013; Greenstein, 2015). As Lee (2019) points out, popular histories of companies such as Google regularly fail to emphasize how the company capitalized on the infrastructures, web developers, and content producers that preceded it. Instead, what is usually taken as a starting point is the gift and intellect of its founders: '[i]gnoring the history of the Internet and search engines naturalizes why Google is such a dominant force in multiple facets of society' (Lee, 2019, p 7). There are two broad arguments to be made from Google's corporate development. First, global expansion of its business model would not have been possible without public investments in the development of internet infrastructure and household investment in internet access worldwide. Public investments are not sufficiently recognized, and the public did not reap sufficient rewards from it (Lazonick & Mazzucato, 2013; Mazzucato, 2013, 2018b; Bilić & Prug, 2020). Instead, it is faced with covering the costs of minimizing negative effects of data-driven business models through regulation and legal action.

Second, once sufficient concentration and centralization of capital was attained, the shareholder perspective took hold and created wealth disparities and economic inequalities (Wright, 2018). Corporate interests become entrenched and regulatory actions are increasingly captured through lobbying and other forms of political influence. To unpack this we will look at what Google (Alphabet Inc.) reported as corporate risks to its business model in mandatory, audited, annual market reports between 2005 and 2019. According to the Securities and Exchange Commission (SEC) regulation, risk reporting is a mandatory section (Item 1A: Risk factors) within annual market reports (10-K) for all publicly listed companies. Analysing risk reporting allows us to understand how corporate development was shaped by the prominence and disappearance of certain risks at different points in time. As risk reporting is directed at shareholders and investors, it points toward reward allocation strategies stemming from risk-avoiding business operations.

Scaling technical infrastructure

Google's business model is highly dependent on the scale of operations and broad adoption of search technology, or network effects as some platform theorists argue (Luchetta, 2014; Srnicek, 2017). The more internet users engage with Google, the more data they provide for analysis and commodification. Consequently, advertisers, which provide the bulk of Google's revenue, reach more consumers and buyers. Scaling the infrastructure was always a technical obsession for the founders. Google's ambition was not just to be born on the web, but to scale with the web (Arthur, 2012, p 74). At the same time, clear separation between the 'organic' and 'paid' search became difficult because access to scale and scope creates strong incentives to organize search results in self-serving ways (Rieder & Sire, 2014). As a technology company, Google is highly successful in shifting interactions and negotiations with other actors onto the technological level of engineering problems, which include information crawlers, self-service interfaces, automated price setting, quantified ranking, and so on (Rieder & Sire, 2014, p 198). Technology obscures background economic processes.

A close look at the technological risks discussed by the company between 2005 and 2019 reveals that the early period of post-IPO growth included concerns about the pace of internet infrastructure growth, scaling and adapting Google's infrastructures of servers and data centres, infrastructure providers, malicious third-party applications, and index spammers. All of them relate in one way or another to the problem of reaching sufficient scale and scope. The reliance of web search technologies on the telecommunications infrastructure was outside of the control of the company.

Corporate growth and organizational changes

The idea behind the PageRank algorithm was developed by Larry Page and Sergei Brin, computer science PhD students working on the Stanford University's National Science Foundation (NSF) funded

Integrated Digital Library Project. The company was incorporated in 1998 and, in August 2004, it made the initial public offering (IPO), selling 19 million shares and raising $1.67 billion in capital, which set the company market value at over $20 billion. Stanford was the initial owner of the PageRank patent and Google was paying annual royalties for patent usage.[1] Stanford also had an equity in Google, which they sold in 2005 for $336 million, following own rules about not owning equity in publicly traded companies due to possible conflict of interest with other university research. Post-IPO, corporate development passed through three different stages. First, the initial period of growth, competition, and expansion (2005–2008). Second, the period of growth management and investment diversification (2009–2013). Third, the period of increasing legal costs and regulatory scrutiny (2014–2019).

Early organizational risks were tied to collective decisions by the founders and the CEO as well as new costs of managing the company in accordance with legislative rules for publicly traded companies. Promotion of management principles of flexibility, creativity, and innovation was evident in reported risks to corporate culture. Formal organizational risks include outsourced payment processing and payments to Google Network members. These non-Google websites show ads supported by Google's advertising technologies such as AdSense. In the initial period of post-IPO corporate development, it was essential for the company to establish widespread usage of its advertising-based model across the World Wide Web. It developed a broad network of sites using Google's technologies and set up a mechanism for splitting advertising revenues with sites showing Google supported ads. As the company grew in market strength, it became less reliant on advertising generated from Google Network members and more reliant on advertising generated directly on its properties (for example, search, YouTube). In 2005, the company generated 44 per cent of its revenue from ads displayed on Google Network members' sites. In 2019, these revenues dropped to only 13 per cent.

Growth management was also considered a risk to corporate development between 2005 and 2011. In 2011 Google acquired Motorola for a reported $12.5 billion. In 2014, it sold the company to Chinese Lenovo for $2.91 billion. Although it seemed like a major loss, Google paid only $1 billion for patents owned by Motorola, instead of the valued $5.5 billion if patents were bought separately. It used the acquired patents to strengthen its position in the mobile operating system market by further developing Android OS for smartphones (Su,

2014). The acquisition also resulted in a sharp increase of research and development staff in 2012. In the years following the IPO, sales and marketing staff outnumbered research and development staff in line with the corporate strategy of developing data-dependent advertising technologies such as AdWords and AdSense. In the period following 2011, R&D staff outnumbers other organizational units. R&D staff was now perfecting and updating already existing technologies, which created new risks for manufacturing and supply chains. A major organizational restructuring occurred in 2015 when Google Inc. was reorganized into the holding company Alphabet Inc. with Google representing one of its major subsidiaries. The restructured company was registered in the state of Delaware due to lower corporate income taxes (Bogenschneider & Heilmeier, 2016).[2]

Post-IPO competition with Microsoft, Yahoo, and traditional media

In official reports, Google addressed a number of competitive risks to its business model. Yet the prominence and disappearance of individual risks over time shows how they started as being specific and oriented towards individual companies, and then changed to risks that are more general in recent times as they gained increasing market strength. Perhaps most prominently, Microsoft and Yahoo were mentioned as two main competitors to Google between 2005 and 2008. The following citation for 2008 shows how Google was catching up with these companies, which, at the time, had superior capital, labour, and technology resources for conducting web search at their disposal:

> Microsoft has developed features that make web search a more integrated part of its Windows operating system and other desktop software products. We expect that Microsoft will increasingly use its financial and engineering resources to compete with us. Microsoft has more employees and cash resources than we do. Also, both Microsoft and Yahoo have longer operating histories and more established relationships with customers and end users. They can use their experience and resources against us in a variety of competitive ways, including by making acquisitions, investing more aggressively in research and development and competing more aggressively for advertisers and web sites. (Google Inc., 2009)

After 2008, Yahoo and Microsoft were no longer highlighted as risks. Instead, they were mentioned under a broader category of general 'competition for the company', a risk reported in all market reports between 2005 and 2019. In 2003, Google started offering auction-based advertisements after the purchase of Applied Semantics, a California-based company producing software applications for online advertising (Google Inc., 2003). After the purchase, Google renamed its newly acquired advertising technology AdSense. The purchase was also important because Applied Semantics worked closely with Yahoo. After Google's purchase, Yahoo had no alternative partnership for providing auction-based advertising (Greenstein, 2015, p 385). Once the model became entrenched, the infatuation with data-driven, targeted, precision advertising became the new norm for the internet advertising industry. Targeting users based on their location, search history, time spent on specific websites, and a vast number of other proxies became the rule. The intermediate commodities now matched a plethora of consumer attributes with possible product preferences. The business model rested on the unmatched quality of Google's free-of-charge web search, which started the production process as a pre-commodity, attracting users and enabling monetization of data through provision of an endless stream of consumer insight to interested advertisers.

Acquisition of DoubleClick for $3.1 billion in 2007 weakened Google's competition further. DoubleClick was a company specializing in online display advertising, a more traditional form of advertising similar to the printed press. Most common display advertising formats are banners. DoubleClick, a company founded in 1996 and one of the rare companies that survived the dot-com crash, provided Google with access to its advertisement software and its relationship with web publishers, advertisers, and advertising agencies (Story & Helft, 2007). The acquisition was a major corporate boost for Google, as Microsoft was also bidding to buy DoubleClick for $2 billion in order to strengthen its online presence. In addition, the purchase weakened attempts by Yahoo to move up the internet advertising market due to its collaboration with DoubleClick. The purchase directed the attention of advertising agencies towards Google and away from traditional media and their online outlets. As reported in 2006:

> In addition to Internet companies, we face competition from companies that offer traditional media advertising opportunities. Most large advertisers have set advertising budgets, a very small portion of which is allocated to Internet advertising. We expect that large advertisers will

continue to focus most of their advertising efforts on traditional media. If we fail to convince these companies to spend a portion of their advertising budgets with us, or if our existing advertisers reduce the amount they spend on our programs, our operating results would be harmed. (Google Inc., 2006)

The purchase of DoubleClick set the stage for Google's dominance in the internet advertising market by displacing competing products entirely and by controlling future innovation in the market (Devine, 2008). Internet advertising was now building on newly found optimism in profitability of digital business models after the dot com crash. As Figure 5.1 shows, internet advertising surpassed radio advertising in 2007, daily newspapers in 2010, and television in 2016 as the main medium for advertising investments in the United States with a total investment of $72.5 billion.[3] In the fourth quarter of 2017, search advertising represented a total of 44 per cent of the internet advertising market, banners 32 per cent, video 14 per cent, and other formats 9 per cent (PricewaterhouseCoopers, 2018). In October 2018, Google was the biggest US digital media property with 245 million unique

Figure 5.1: Advertising revenue per media type in the US ($ billion)

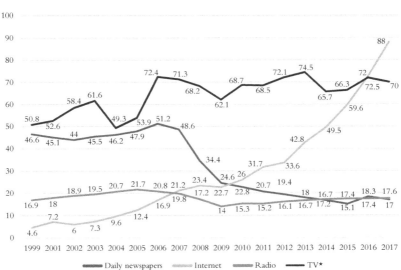

Source: Authors' analysis based on IAB Internet Advertising Revenue Reports (1999–2017)

visitors on all Google sites. Facebook was second with 212 million, and Microsoft third with 208 million (Neustar, 2018). In February 2019, Google held a 92.9 per cent share of the worldwide search engine market across all platforms (desktop, mobile, tablet). Microsoft's Bing was second with 2.4 per cent, Yahoo third with 1.8 per cent (StatCounter, 2020b).

Advertising risks between 2005 and 2019

Advertising represents a major source of revenue for Alphabet Inc. (Google), although the share in total revenue declined from 99 per cent in 2004 to 83 per cent in 2019. As company founders argued in the earliest presentations discussing the PageRank algorithm: 'we expect that advertising funded search engines will be inherently biased towards the advertisers and away from the needs of the consumers' (Brin & Page, 1998). Google separated so-called 'organic' search results from paid results, which was one of the reasons for the adoption of its solution to the problem of web search. It also provided a clean, clutter-free interface with no aggressive advertisements or other types of intrusive content. Paid search results were clearly labelled as sponsored ads. Internet users could simply skip over these results if they chose to. Separation of 'organic' and 'paid' search results, is the cornerstone of its corporate ideology of neutrality and objectivity (Hillis et al, 2013), a position increasingly scrutinized due to privacy abuse, surveillance, and distribution of content detrimental to democratic processes.

Google did not meet immediate success with this strategy in the 1990s and early 2000s. At that time, there were many competing business models. The dominant one was the web portal model provided by companies such as Yahoo, AOL, MSN, and others. Google was more interested in perfecting the technical characteristics of PageRank since web search was considered an auxiliary service for the broader business model of the web portal. The portal model promised better measurement of results for advertising agencies and more precision for targeting specific audiences. Yet it did not realize these promises by the late 1990s (Greenstein, 2015, p 372). Simultaneously, Google was signing contracts with other companies to rent their search service in attempts to provide its own profitable business model. One of the first major deals was a contract providing search for Yahoo in June 2000: Yahoo sent queries to Google, and Google provided the results (Greenstein, 2015, p 375). The contract accomplished three different goals. First, it saved Yahoo from investing in search services. Second, the deal gave Google revenue and legitimacy. Third, it directed a large number of search queries to Google, which they used to refine their algorithms (Greenstein, 2015, p 377). By 2002, Google signed 130 deals with other companies creating a vast Google Network of websites.

Google-supported advertising relies on direct clicks instead of impressions as with traditional media. Fraudulent clicks, which were not intended by users/consumers, create artificial revenues and losses to Google. Major risks that are reported in the entire period between 2005 and 2019 are the loss of advertisers and brand management. AdWords provide ads on desktops, laptops, tablets, and mobiles when people use the Google search engine. Ads are placed above organic results. The ad buying mechanism targets by region and shows how many people click on the ad, the percentage that click through to visit the website, and so on. 'Successful AdWords campaigns are based on the degree to which advertisers can predict the search terms users will employ' (McStay, 2016, p 28). In 2018, AdWords technology was rebranded to Google Ads. AdSense, on the other hand, works by web publishers making ad space available. Ad space is then auctioned by Google to the highest and most relevant bidder and then the payment is made to the publisher: 'Google's algorithms decide the winner on the basis of relevance of ad to customer and the type of site the customer is visiting'. The scope and reach of Google allows publishers to access a large number of advertisers (McStay, 2016, pp 28, 29). Currently, there are very little alternatives for Google's search-based advertising technologies. In 2019, Google was the world's second most valuable brand, behind Apple, with an estimated value of $167.7 billion (Forbes, 2019).

Reward distribution through stock performance

As it was growing its international user base, and international advertising revenue, it was concerned over exchange rates for income generated in different markets worldwide. In the more recent period, there were reported concerns in corporate reports over the investment portfolio market: negative impacts of liquidity, credit deterioration or losses, financial results, changes in interest rates, and other factors that affect domestic and international investments (Alphabet Inc., 2018). Ultimately, risk aversion as a competitive strategy for maintaining monopoly is aimed at securing appropriate reward distribution from corporate performance. Allocation of awards is concentrated at the top level of ownership and management, as well as at the level of institutional investors. Alphabet Inc. trades in three classes of stock: Class A and Class B common stock as well as Class C capital stock. Class A stock has one vote per share and Class B stock has ten votes per share. Class C stock holds no voting rights. Alphabet Inc. concentrates voting powers with its founders: Larry Page and Sergei Brin. As of 31 December 2019, they beneficially owned approximately 84.3 per cent of the outstanding Class B common stock, which represented approximately 51.2 per cent of the voting power of the outstanding stock (Alphabet Inc., 2020). However, the company is majority owned by institutional investors.[4] Stock-related risks are some of the most detailed risks in annual reports and relate to concerns over the ability of stock repurchasing programmes to create value for shareholders, increasing volatility of stock prices, and diminishing cash reserves (Alphabet Inc., 2020).

Legal and regulatory risks between 2005 and 2019

An overview of legal risks shows a clear tendency towards specific issues that appear and disappear in the early stages of post-IPO growth, as well as corporate concerns that appear in recent times. Some legal risks remain consistently reported and are closely related to the business model of the company, privatization, and commercialization of algorithms and other technical solutions. Core legal risks include protection of corporate intellectual property rights and protection against intellectual property rights claims by third parties. Among the early reported risks are changes in accounting rules, commercial disputes, insurance risks, and proprietary document formats. Proprietary document formats clashed directly with Google's business model as visible in the report for 2005:

> [a] large amount of information on the Internet is provided in proprietary document formats such as Microsoft Word. The providers of the software application used to create these documents could engineer the document format to prevent or interfere with our ability to access the document contents with our search technology. This would mean that the document contents would not be included in our search results even if the contents were directly relevant to a search. These types of activities could assist our competitors or diminish the value of our search results. The software providers may also seek to require us to pay them royalties in exchange for giving us the ability to search documents in their format. If the software provider also competes with us in the search business, they may give their search

technology a preferential ability to search documents in their proprietary format. Any of these results could harm our brand and our operating results. (Google Inc., 2006)

Pushing the limits of existing legislation was built into the corporate expansion of Google, especially in areas such as fair use of online text, a legal doctrine that permits writers to quote copyrighted material for criticism, news, teaching, research, and so on (Greenstein, 2015, p 387). Not asking for permission eliminated the need for endless transactions with content originators. This created a tense relationship with those same originators and producers.

Google could move considerable traffic to those sites by making their content visible in its search engine. Yet a simple statement within the organic listing – a sports score of a recent event, a phone number for a business, or an address for a store, for example – could satisfy a user and obviate the need to check through to the original site. (Greenstein, 2015, pp 377, 378)

Such tensions opened a broad conflict line in other areas. Google was engaged in fending off intellectual property claims such as trademark infringement on the display of ads in response to user queries that include trademark terms (Google Inc., 2008). This issue was taken before the European Court of Justice. In the case of Google France and Google Inc. et al v Louis Vuitton Malletier et al, the Court decided that Google did not infringe trade mark law by allowing advertisers to purchase keywords corresponding to their competitors' trademarks (Court of Justice of the European Union, 2010). Similar cases were brought before courts in the US, Australia, Brazil, China, France, Germany, Israel, and Italy in 2007. Copyright claims were filed against the company on grounds that Google Web Search, Google News, Google Video, Google Image Search, Google Book Search, and YouTube infringe authors' rights (Google Inc., 2008). Other claims in the early period include claims of patent infringement and demands for licence fees. The same vigour in minimizing intellectual property rights' claims by content producers and other actors in order to streamline web search and expand advertising technology revenue, was used to maximize the protection of that same technology between 2005 and 2019: '[o]ur patents, trademarks, trade secrets, copyrights, and other intellectual property rights are important assets for us. Various events outside of our control pose a threat to our intellectual property rights, as well as to our products, services and technologies' (Alphabet Inc., 2018).

In the most recent period of corporate development, further legal risks include security measures, legal proceedings, legal liability, claims and government investigations, regulation, and new and existing laws. Claims, suits, and government investigations that appear between 2012 and 2019 involve competition, privacy, consumer protection, tax, labour and employment, commercial disputes, content generated by users, goods and services offered by advertisers, and so on. According to the 2017 report: 'Regardless of the outcome, any of these types of legal proceedings can have an adverse effect on us because of legal costs, diversion of management resources, and other factors' (Alphabet Inc., 2017). Other risks engage in listing legislation that Alphabet needs to comply with[5] as well as the expansion of regulatory measures worldwide.

The European Commission fined Alphabet Inc. €2.42 billion in 2017 for giving prominent placement of its own comparison shopping service in search results, while demoting rival services (European Commission, 2017a). In 2018, the Commission issued an additional €4.34 billion fine for illegal practices regarding Android mobile devices that strengthen Google's search engine dominance (European Commission, 2018a). Finally, in 2019 the Commission issued a €1.49 billion fine for abusive practices in online advertising. Contracts with AdSense partners included clauses that prohibit publishers from placing any search adverts from competitors on their results pages. This prevented competitors from placing their search adverts in the most visible and clicked on parts of the websites' search results page. Specific clauses required publishers to seek written approval from Google before making changes to the way in which any rival adverts were displayed (European Commission, 2019). In October 2020, the US Department of Justice (2020) also launched an antitrust case against Google accusing the company of unlawfully maintaining monopolies in search and search advertising.[6]

As legislators and regulators are paying closer attention to Google and other tech giants, lobbying in Washington and Brussels is ramping up. GAFAM has collectively spent $582 million lobbying the United States Congress between 2005 and 2018 (vpnMentor, 2019). The most frequently occurring words across all submitted lobbying reports were 'privacy', 'tax', 'online', 'data', and 'security'. Privacy was the number one issue for Facebook and Google. For Amazon, Apple, and Microsoft 'tax' was the number one issue (vpnMentor, 2019). In 2018, Apple benefited from corporate income tax reductions introduced by the Trump administration. The company paid $38 billion in taxes to the US Treasury for bringing cash back to the country. This was a steep discount to the $78.6 billion the company would have owed if it repatriated that money sooner. The CEO of Apple, Tim Cook, received a 'thank you' note from the President while saving $40 billion in tax obligations (Dellinger, 2019). In 2019 alone, Google spent €8 million on lobbying in Brussels. Together with Amazon, Facebook, and Apple, big tech collective lobbying budgets in the European Union have increased by 510 per cent since 2014 (Cavallone, 2020).

The role of state(s) and regulation in the expansion of GAFAM

The long-term outcomes of antitrust fines from the European Commission leave much to be desired. They simply fix 'market failures' to restore competition and protect European companies and the Digital Single Market (European Commission, 2015) against outside competition. Even though fines issued to Google are substantial, they are dwarfed by the size of Google's annual revenue and net income. The US Department of Justice case will likely have a similar effect as it takes perfect competition as its normative benchmark. While it will likely put a pause on Google's expansion into other data-driven industry branches, it will do nothing to alleviate inherent contradictions of capitalism within a continuous dynamic between competition and monopoly. Antitrust legislation in the US and the European Union does not see a problem with monopoly and market dominance per se, only if competition and consumer welfare are hampered by abusive behaviour from the position of dominance (Kolasky, 2004; Niels & ten Kate, 2004; Scott Morton et al, 2019). Marxian approaches to monopoly power share concerns over price, output, market entry, and innovation in monopolistic industries (for example, Baran & Sweezy, 1968; Mandel, 1976; Foster, 2016). However, Marxian approaches also outline social forms and conditions that create monopolies and result from monopolies. There is, however, fundamental disagreement as to what leads to monopolies.

For mainstream economics, monopolies are distortions and aberrations in the economic equilibrium. Antitrust legislation, particularly in the US, protects competition, not competitors, in order to promote consumer welfare (Bork, 1993; Kolasky, 2004; Niels & ten Kate, 2004). Monopolies do not occur unexpectedly. They are outcomes of power relations and legal forms that allow, or restrict, certain types of behaviour over a longer period. Regulators globally have taken a blind eye to digital markets due to the opacity of data collection, misunderstanding of intermediate commodities in digital value chains, inability to regulate free of monetary charge pre-commodities in zero-price markets, and general expectation that digital markets will self-correct. Furthermore, despite the long history of antitrust laws, it suits the US to have domestic companies assuming the position of global monopolies. That, however, has to be achieved while preserving innovation and a certain level of competition, which requires a balancing act on the part of regulators and judges.

Pitfalls and interpretations of antitrust regulation

Antitrust is enshrined in the American and European liberal order of free market competition. What we are interested in here is the rationale behind antitrust regulation, not specific legal nuances, or detailed implementation in case law. At the level of European Union, competition law was built into articles 85 and 86 of the 1957 Treaty of Rome, establishing the European Economic Community. It is now enshrined in articles 101 and 102 of the Treaty on the Functioning of the European Union (TFEU). Nation-states still maintain country specific regulatory frameworks but the European Union provides a level of coordination in order to protect the European single market and competition between Member States. The main principle of the EU competition regime monitors the existence of market power. If market power is high it indicates weak competition and the need to protect companies against abusive behaviour such as predatory pricing, excessive pricing, discounts in markets with high-entry barriers, and so on (Niels & ten Kate, 2004).

In the United States, antitrust legislation was first enshrined in 1890 by the Sherman Act. The goal was to impose limits to trusts such as Standard Oil and its concentrated economic and political power. In 1914, it was supplemented by the Federal Trade Commission Act and the Clayton Act creating the foundation for contemporary antitrust regulation. Starting from the 1970s, antitrust legislation has taken a neoliberal, laissez-faire turn. Six main principles of US antitrust include an understanding that the ultimate objective is consumer welfare. Scale efficiencies in production lead to consumer welfare and lower prices even if they harm competitors. Profit maximization or exploitation of power based on merits should not be challenged by antitrust law. Horizontal practices and agreements that restrict freedom of choice of some parties can be efficient and procompetitive. Misguided antitrust application may frustrate innovative and welfare-enhancing ways of doing business. Aggressive but legitimate competitive actions against illegal anticompetitive behaviour have a potentially high welfare cost (Niels & ten Kate, 2004, pp 9, 10).

These principles are largely built on the work of Robert Bork, a US federal judge. He provided a highly influential interpretation of the Sherman Act in case law and regulation. The main intention of the Act, Bork argued, was to provide consumer welfare as the ultimate goal of antitrust (Bork, 1966). The argument goes that monopolistic industries with high entry barriers and few dominant companies do not necessarily imply harms to consumers. In fact, Bork argued that monopolistic companies operate under efficiencies of scale and vertical integration that outside competitors cannot reach. The conclusion was that they should not be penalized for their merits. Due to their efficiencies, they are able to provide commodities at the lowest prices, which ultimately improves consumer welfare. In one of his final published papers, Bork argued that imposing antitrust fines to Google 'would punish and therefore deter the same welfare-enhancing innovations that have made Google an effective competitor. Such use of antitrust law would weaken dynamic competition, as only successful firms would need to worry about being penalized for being winners' (Bork & Sidak, 2012, p 665).

There is widespread agreement among scholars critical of Bork that consumer welfare interpretations stifle regulation and lead to economic, political, and social harms. Timothy Wu, one of the most prominent antitrust scholars in the United States and one of the witnesses during the House Judiciary hearings, argues that Bork's interpretation misses the crucial point of the Sherman Act, which was to provide a democratic choice of economic structure and a check on the political and economic power of monopolies (Wu, 2018). Wu suggests a revised antitrust approach that would review past mergers, democratize the merger process through public debate, open cases against the biggest companies, break up existing monopolies, investigate existing markets and competition rules, and change antitrust goals towards competition protection (Wu, 2018). For Wu, the democratic ideal of the US economy is to have it decentralized and to foster competition. Scott-Morton and others (2019) follow a similar logic and argue that price should not be the only criterion for determining consumer welfare. Additional criteria should include privacy intrusion, surveillance, data protection, commercialization, and other factors that influence the quality of digital products. Consumer welfare comes from quality products that are readily available with sufficient innovation, competition, and market entry. These are all recognitions of the social character of economic processes surrounding platform business models.

Broader, historical arguments of the importance of antitrust are made by some authors (Abbate, 1999; Greenstein, 2015). Antitrust played an essential role for competitive innovation during privatization of the internet and commercialization of the World Wide Web in the late 1980s and early 1990s. The antitrust case against IBM was opened in 1969 and dismissed in 1982 without merit. The case against AT&T was filed in 1974. It settled and took effect in 1984. As Greenstein (2015, p 37) argues, these cases resulted in the fact that AT&T and IBM were unable to dominate telecommunications and computing markets, which opened the way for competition and innovation. AT&T was broken up into smaller companies, while IBM failed to expand into markets outside large-scale computing. Similarly, the browser war between Netscape and Microsoft in the 1990s led to an antitrust investigation. Microsoft was accused of bundling its Internet Explorer browser with the Windows OS as an aggressive business expansion strategy.[7] It earned Microsoft the nickname 'the evil company' among software engineers and smaller competitors (Arthur, 2012). The nickname was directly referenced by Google in its corporate motto 'Do not be evil' as a strategy of distancing from companies engaging in proprietary technology development and vertical organizational management.

Microsoft eventually ran Netscape out of business in 1998 as developers abandoned the platform. Simultaneously, Microsoft slowed down its internet initiatives and after 2001 Internet Explorer went years without another upgrade (Greenstein, 2015, p 332). The antitrust case led to the decision in 2000 that Microsoft should be split into two companies: one making operating systems and another making applications. The decision was never put into power and a settlement was reached in 2001. An outside panel would have full access to Microsoft's source code and systems. If one division opened up the APIs for a product to another Microsoft division, they had to be made publicly available. The goal was to prevent the use of secret and private APIs known only inside the company to enhance its own products at the expense of competitors (Arthur, 2012, pp 20, 21). The settlement opened the way for new web companies such as Google and Facebook and set the terrain for the expansion of data-driven business models and a new generation of tech monopolies.

Currently, a number of legal scholars argue that regulatory interventions and antitrust interpretations in relation to GAFAM are weak, inconsistent, and harmful in many ways. Khan (2016) argues that the consumer welfare doctrine cannot grasp the risk of predatory pricing and integration across distinct business lines by companies such as Amazon. Amazon pursued a long-term strategy of growth over profits, which was heavily rewarded by investors. Serving as an intermediary, Amazon also uses information collected on companies using its services to undermine them as competitors (Khan, 2016, p 710). Newman (2015) argues that the biggest issue for consumer welfare antitrust is grasping how markets operate in so-called zero-price conditions and multi-sided markets we discussed in more detail in Chapter 4. The main examples are Google and Facebook that offer their services free of charge to internet users. As he points out 'preeminent antitrust theorists have urged that without prices there can be no markets, and consequently no market power. This heavy methodological dependence on positive prices has led antitrust courts and enforcement agencies to overlook potentially massive welfare harms' (Newman, 2015, p 149). Even more problematically, antitrust allows vertical integration arguing that it improves corporate efficiency and results in lower prices for consumers. All horizontal coordination of economic activity is suspect and susceptible to antitrust scrutiny. Actors falling outside of the vertically integrated firm include workers' organizations and labour unions, small business cooperation, and even democratic regulation (Paul, 2019).

Economists of innovation and creative destruction, as well as antitrust legal scholars criticizing Robert Bork and demanding a decentralized and competitive economy, regularly miss how innovation results in an uneven distribution of risks and rewards, social and economic inequality (Lazonick & Mazzucato, 2013; Mazzucato, 2013, 2018b). Moreover, they miss the crucial point about capitalism: its tendencies to create monopolies and crises, along with monopolies and fierce competition co-existing on different levels of productive hierarchies (for example, application producers compete, while platform producers co-exist on the top dictating terms). Without such an understanding, antitrust is hailed as a panacea for limiting monopoly power, and labelled as the cause of monopoly power at the same time. The outcome of antitrust interpretation and implementation ultimately ends up being a political choice dependent on class, power, and stakes of involved actors. Looking at it from a long-term, historical perspective, market efficiency and competitive equilibrium are nothing more than views, personal stances based on a selective set of arguments on how the economy should operate. Those aligning with Bork and those criticizing Bork do not question this underlying assumption. Even if divestitures and monopoly breakups were introduced, new conditions would quickly open the route for a new generation of monopolies and a new gold rush to exploit data commodification.

Table 5.3: Centralization of capital by GAFAM (1987–2019)

Company	Google	Apple	Facebook	Amazon	Microsoft
Years active	2001–2019	1988–2019	2007–2019	1998–2019	1987–2019
# of acquisitions	234	108	77	83	221
Avg. annual #	13	3	7	4	7

Source: Moss (2019)

Relaxed implementation of antitrust legislation in the United States is certainly one of the reasons for the existence of large companies in the tech sector. As Table 5.3 shows, GAFAM made 723 acquisitions between 1987 and 2019. At the same time, only one transaction was challenged in the US federal court, which is far lower than the record for other industry sectors (Moss, 2019). The rate of FTC and DoJ challenges involving transactions in the area of data processing, hosting and related services was also far lower than the average for all transactions (Moss, 2019, p 6). Acquiring competing companies to gain access to data and new users was the reason behind some of the biggest acquisitions (see Table 5.4): Google's acquisition of YouTube; Apple's acquisition of Shazam; Facebook's acquisitions of WhatsApp, Instagram and Onavo; Amazon's purchase of Zappos, PillPack, Twitch Interactive; and Microsoft's acquisition of LinkedIn, Skype, and Github.

Capital accumulation on a world scale

GAFAM's scale of operations is truly global. Alphabet Inc. generated 54 per cent ($87 billion) of its 2019 revenue outside of United States. Apple Inc. generated 55 per cent ($143 billion) of their sales outside North and South America. Facebook generated 57 per cent ($40 billion) of its revenue outside of the United States. Amazon Inc. generated 31 per cent ($87 billion) of their net sales in international markets. Finally, Microsoft generated 63 per cent ($28 billion) of their income before tax from international markets in 2019. However, some national markets developed alternative digital services. For example, Google is not the main market player in China, Korea, Japan, or Russia. Google launched google.cn in 2006 while accepting to censor search results. It reached 27 per cent of the Chinese market share by 2010 challenging Baidu's 70 per cent share (Jin, 2015). In 2010, Google pulled out its operations from China due to reported cyberattacks and censorship of search results (Waddell, 2016). In 2014, Chinese authorities made Google's services largely inaccessible because of

Table 5.4: Top acquisitions by GAFAM ($ billion)

Company	Top five acquisitions
Google	Motorola Mobility ($12.5B, 2012) Nest Labs ($3.2B, 2014) DoubleClick ($3.1B, 2007) Looker ($2.6B, 2019) YouTube ($1.7B, 2006)
Apple	Beats Electronics ($3B, 2014) Dialog Semiconductor ($600M, 2018) Anobit Technologies ($500M, 2011) Shazam ($400M, 2017) NeXT Computer ($400M, 1996)
Facebook	WhatsApp ($22B, 2014) Oculus VR ($2B, 2014) Instagram ($1B, 2012) LiveRail ($500M, 2014) Onavo ($200M, 2013)
Amazon	Whole Foods ($13.7B, 2017) Ring ($1.2B, 2018) Zappos ($1.2B, 2009) PillPack ($1B, 2018) Twitch Interactive ($970M, 2014)
Microsoft	LinkedIn ($26.2B, 2016) Skype ($8.5B, 2011) Github ($7.5B, 2018) Nokia's Devices & Services Business ($7.2B, 2014) aQuantive ($6.3B, 2007)

Source: CB Insights (2019)

the anniversary of 1989 demonstrations on Tiananmen Square. The Chinese government played the role of gatekeeper by regulating Google, blocking Facebook and Twitter, and allowing growth of its domestic search engines and other digital services (Jin, 2015, p 81). Chinese companies Baidu, Alibaba, and Tencent now dominate the Chinese market. At the same time, only 1 per cent of Baidu's revenues come from international markets, 11 per cent of Alibaba's revenues stem come from outside China, and only 5 per cent of Tencent's revenues are from international markets (Fannin, 2018).

GAFAM's international dominance is the continuation of earlier forms of imperialism (Baran, 1956/1973; Magdoff, 1969; Lenin, 1999), especially the 'free flow of information' doctrine of cultural (Schiller, 1976, 1989, 1991) and media imperialism (Boyd–Barrett,

1977, 2006). It can be labelled as a form of platform imperialism (Jin, 2015). Communication and media industries are not just superstructure additions to the economic base but are, instead, reinforcing unequal economic development and promoting economic, political, and cultural ideas transmitted from the capitalist centre. Digital platforms amplify these processes. Accumulation of capital in the centre is governed by the self-centred production and circulation of capital. In the periphery, the reproduction of the system links exports with induced consumption and 'conveys a "dependence", in the sense that the periphery adjusts "unilaterally" to the dominant tendencies on the scale of the world system in which it is integrated, these tendencies being the very ones governed by the demands of accumulation at the centre' (Amin 2010, p 89).

Cultural imperialism developed in a world market in which production is determined in the core radiating outwards. Three major processes underpinned US cultural imperialism in the 1970s (Schiller, 1976). First, the ideology of the free flow of information synonymous with US. global hegemony. Second, technologies are shaped by production and capitalist social relations in which they are created and distributed. Third, communication policies become some of the main areas of class conflicts and interests. In the 1990s, new technologies were promoted as decentralized and democratic. It was argued that the internet brings an opportunity for multi-polar communication and distribution of power, which will put technology in the hands of citizens. Such a discourse was often no more than a new free flow of information strategy benefiting tech companies and serving ideological and profit-seeking motives of the system at large (Schiller, 1989, 1991) Earlier forms of analyses focused mostly on television programmes and content, while digital developments require a shift of focus towards computing and telecommunications (Boyd-Barrett, 2006). The platform business model introduced 'not only about forms of technological disparities but also forms of intellectual property, symbolic hegemony, and user commodity because these issues concentrate capital into the hands of a few U.S.-based platform owners' (Jin, 2015, p 12). Without physical, brick-and-mortar presence in many countries in which GAFAM realize profits, they leave nation-states and transnational entities such as the European Union without a possibility to demand democratic governance, fair and transparent data management and redistribution of their profits to public services through taxation. We will return to these issues in the following chapters.

6

Controlling, Processing, and Commercializing Data

In this chapter, we focus on the core dynamic between gathering and processing data with algorithms as means of production for generating and extracting surplus value, protected by patents, trade secrets, and copyrights. We do not know exactly what data companies collect, nor do we know exactly how algorithms process collected data. To study algorithms and data we are largely left with two main options: either to trace the flow of value in the form of money through technological forms, corporate production, and circulation, or to look at consequences of the deployment of (corporate) algorithms in various aspects of society (for example, credit scoring, recommendation systems, automobile navigation, personal assistants, news distribution, and so on). Taking the first option allowed us to focus on monopolization, advertising, regulation, and financialization in Chapters 3, 4, and 5. Now we turn to the social consequences of these techniques.

We do not argue that technological forms through algorithmic techniques establish full-blown, dystopian, and static control. Data-driven companies usually provide a range of behavioural options in line with their assessments of users and their data, thus providing a dynamic balance between flexibility and prediction. Yet, as instruments of perception, analytical techniques focus on human attentiveness of people and things of interest while, at the same time, discarding much of the context from which these persons and things emerged (Amoore & Piotukh, 2015). Control through technological forms is, therefore, a conditioning and structuring mechanism in which the range of options is constantly adapted and individualized in real time to allow profit making and commodity exchange to occur seamlessly in the background.

The rise of data-driven production needed a social and legal fabric on which to build. Corporate development needed openness for producing and sharing data among engineers and internet users. The first social foundation was secured through privatizing openness and knowledge in software production. This occurred through legal forms that allowed closure of software modifications, breaking up the chain of software sharing, enabling modifications to act as competitive advantages. We touched upon the difference between Free Software and Open Source in Chapter 2. The second foundation was secured by offering free-of-charge services. Free-of-charge services within the capitalist mode of production of advertising funded platforms are pre-commodities. They involve a form of non-monetary exchange of personal data for service use. Once scale and scope are secured by dominant companies, data exchange occurring through engagement with technological forms provides raw material for production of targeted adverts as intermediate commodities and simultaneously results in surveillance and market entry barriers. Capitalist production of data-driven targeted advertising ultimately undermines the news media industry and results in an impoverished public sphere and weak democracy.

Privatizing openness and knowledge

In the early decades of software, from the late 1950s to mid-1970s, large parts of production occurred collaboratively, with outputs such as source code and documentation, shared among engineers and often made publicly available without charge (Levy, 2010). Before the commercialization of the internet through the development of World Wide Web functionalities and web applications, communities of software and networking engineers developed a way of collaborating on production of software and networking protocols without a direct commercial incentive driving their activities. Early technologies that enabled these activities were driven by large public investments in combination with private research and originating in military investments during the Cold War (Abbate, 1999). Many participants in those collaborations were employed at universities and research centres, including students and specialists from other industries with active interest in this area. When software copyright started spreading through increasingly commercial software production, some of those early collaborative communities saw it as a threat to their existing practices and started rebelling (Chen, 2009, Part II), creating in the mid-1980s a peculiar set of licences they defined as Free Software. The goal was to enable protecting the software production under the conditions they were used to prior to the introduction of stricter and time-extended copyright laws.

The first version of General Public Licence (GPL) constructed Free Software as an umbrella term for software that can be shared with an anti-copyright, or Copyleft type of licensing, as the authors of the GPL licence named it (Stallman, 2001; S. Williams, 2002, Chapter 9). Copyleft defines a restrictive version of Free Software licences, mandating legally that when software released under such licences is modified and its modified copies distributed in any form, its source code must be released publicly under the same licence (Stallman, 2018). Since software is binary, forms of software installed and run by end users (for example, exe files on Windows) can be created from the source code and the replication of software with no-charge to end user is thus ensured. Furthermore, by mandating public availability of the source code, such licences also enabled the replication of the collaborative production process (in opposition to production within boundaries of a firm).[1]

GPL was a part of the wave of licences initiated by software engineering communities who wanted to release their work dictating the terms under which their work can be reused, under which terms a new code can be added to theirs. In effect, Free Software licences appeared in reaction to new laws and to commercial enterprises imposing onto the material form of software new social forms that were essential for the capitalist mode of production to operate. When software is used as means of production within the capitalist mode of production, in order for the producer to have an advantage based on investment and deployment of capital, means of production had to be privately owned. If software used as means of production was freely available, there would be no need to use money as capital to purchase it, and investors would not have an upper hand since anyone with available labour could utilize freely available means of production and start producing. More importantly, the capitalist mode of production relies on its outputs assuming commodity form in order to extract surpluses. It was not clear to the legal profession and courts in the US what form should the protection of software take, how to socially construct software as private property, and how to define its ownership.

Debating this issue and advocating contract law as opposed to copyright, Brown noted how it took years of debate to find the appropriate way to protect software as a form of private property, since given its novelty scholars and policy makers were unsure which route of protection to take (Brown, 1987, pp 1015–16). Brown also argued that lack of protection of user interface, graphical layout, and functionality of software, was 'a time bomb' (Brown, 1987). Ten years later, the social form of user interfaces was being constructed to fit the capitalist mode of production under the social form of copyright, albeit inconsistently and with a lot of problems in deciding on criteria (Castner, 1997). The change in the composition of those driving the software production, was vast – 'the academia-dominated, collegiate, programmer league of past years stands in stark contrast to the competitive, multinational, big business software industry of today' – leading to the conclusion that 'this seismic shift has led to ideological conflicts over the scope and propriety of software intellectual property protection' (Castner, 1997, pp 36–7).

The ideological clash is the clash of social forms of production, the dominant capitalist mode of production and the production practiced by early software producing communities whose social form, to a significant extent publicly financed, predates commercialization introduced by the penetration of capital and its logic in the field of software production. For commercial software companies, Free Software Copyleft licences were unacceptable as they faced the question of how can a company make profits if its products can be copied, shared, and modified with no payment by consumers and other producers. Put differently, if the product does not take the commodity form, how can surplus value be extracted and profits realized? Yet, large sections of software engineering communities reacted to the spreading of the capitalist mode of production in their field of work by using the legal system to construct Copyleft licences. It was a set of social forms different from those required by the capitalist production – a move that some researchers saw as a proof that 'the production of computer applications can be organised without intellectual property relations and, by extension, without mediation of capital' (Dafermos & Söderberg, 2009, p 59).

This move towards legal formalization and in part institutionalization of non-commodity production was not supported by all members of early engineering communities. A significant number of participants did not think their views were represented by the restrictive Free Software licences, considering Copyleft licences such as GPL obstacles for business involvement. Shunning people from the heart of Free Software movement, a group of those who believed that involvement of large businesses and venture capital was desirable organized a separate movement of software engineers, creating a new more permissive set of licences and a new brand, called Open Source. Under these licensees, sharing of modified source code was optional, enabling firms to close down their modifications, to stop the chain of replication of modifications publicly, allowing the addition of commodity form onto the existing freely shared software.[2]

To simplify talking about these types of licences, the term Open Source was coined as a permissive alternative to Free Software Copyleft licences, where the term 'free' in the name was judged to be undesirable to business leaders, whose funding and embrace of the software communities, Open Source founders believed, was essential. Hiding important differences, but helping to speak of an overlapping set of projects and participants, the common term FLOSS was coined to represent both Free Software and Open Source. By the time the World Wide Web and internet applications became mainstream, a vast majority of websites were delivered by such software (Apache web server dominated, as it still does, along with MySQL and PostgreSQL databases), while a significant portion of internet content was experienced through FLOSS browsers and other types of content reading software. Open Source did bring about huge investments from some of the major IT firms, such as IBM, Dell, and Oracle, which helped to both legitimize FLOSS production and to bring closer this type of more open and collaborative production process unfamiliar to profit making capitalist firms into their own productive chains.

Capital and Free Software as different social forms of production and regulation

Richard Stallman is the first engineer that rebelled against the closure of software source code by using legal means and forming accompanying projects, organizations, and concepts. He started the GNU project, initiated the creation of the GPL licence and its later derivatives, institutionalizing the fight against the commodification of software through the Free Software Foundation he founded. He became an icon for hacker and engineering communities, elevating his fight for the preservation of certain type of labour process and social form of output to a movement that captured the imagination of hackers and engineers worldwide (S. Williams, 2002). Eventually, encouraged by the Open Source approach, venture capitalist and large firms invested and integrated software in their chains of commodity production by utilizing permissive licencing. While the primary clash of those two approaches, Free Software Copyleft and Open Source permissive licences, comes down to whether the new modifications of the product can be closed down by legally defining the social form of a product, this was hardly ever discussed through the social and economic form determination approach.

Sabine Nuss was the first to discuss the contradictions in political positions held by Free Software and GPL proponents by utilizing the concept of social form (Nuss, 2006). She pointed out how many proponents of free sharing of digital products, not only in software but also in other occupations such as culture, objected to artificial creation of scarcity by legal means through copyright. The argument of such proponents, according to Nuss, is that knowledge and other digitally storable artefacts ought to be shared freely because of their digital character, due to being replicable at nearly zero cost. The discourse, Nuss points out, revolved around the concept of commons. The Creative Commons movement, inspired partly by the Free Software movement, is the largest institutionalized example of such extension of licencing to enable sharing, in the field of written word and arts in general. To affirm the production such as Free Software, not done for the sake of surplus value and without products that take the commodity-form, Nuss argues that it is necessary to grasp and challenge social forms that elements of capitalist production take. Additionally, we argue, it is essential to understand whatever production escapes capitalist mode of production, such as public sector outputs. The key advantage, Nuss argues, is the cooperation model, which enables fast and broad integration of producers in the production process, demonstrated by the fast development of internet technologies, which would have never occurred at such rate within the capitalist mode of production alone.

Stallman, however, responding by email to Nuss' earlier work on this topic, rejects the idea that the form of production process is the primary concern for the Free Software movement (Nuss & Stallman, 2005).[3] It is sharing of the product with other users in the form of source code that is the central concern of Free Software, while 'the word "commodity" is part of the Marxist mind-set that thinks in terms of economic value only', Stallman objects. He continues:

> To speak of 'realizing the value' assumes that the only value of a work consists of the money that could be made from it. There is more than one conceptual way to value a work. One value is _what you get in exchange for it_, and the other is _what it contributes to society_. For material commodities in a competitive market, the former tends to follow the latter (but watch out for externalities, such as pollution that neither the producer nor the consumer pays for). But that conclusion is not universally applicable. In cases where it is not applicable, the two kinds of 'value' have to be distinguished. (Nuss & Stallman, 2005)

Stallman acknowledges that if we imagine a different category of value applied to work as a way to measure positive contributions to society, economic value stemming from capitalist production of commodities follows closely such imaginary concepts when it comes to certain types of production. However, in other domains, such as software, he believes that we have to speak of two separate kinds of value, suggesting there is a valuable contribution made to society in the production of Free Software that could not have been created had the same software been produced in the form of commodity within the capitalist mode of production.

The argument on inadequacy of the economic concept of value is not new. From a different perspective, in Marxist feminist literature we can frequently find objections that the categories capturing capitalist production of surplus value are inadequate to encompass all spheres of work necessary for the social reproduction in totality, especially for the reproduction of labour power, such as unpaid household and care labour mostly performed by women. Nuss responds to Stallman by noting how capitalist production of value follows profits, creating massive unemployment, artificial scarcity, producing many useless objects while also not producing many other useful objects and services because producing them would not result in profits. Moving beyond the often-raised distinction between production of material and digital objects, such as software, Nuss argues that the passing of many restrictive copyright laws shows how the logic of capitalist production is valid for both material and digital objects. Put differently, the laws of appropriation are valid for all production that capital can make profitable. To do so, it has to impose certain social and economic form, such as commodity-form on the elements of production as it pulls them into its process of production, regardless of the type of materiality, digital or otherwise, that the product consists of.

Broadly speaking, Stallman is correct that these are two ways of producing, two social forms of production, or even two modes of production if we interpret Marx's concept of the mode of production in a manner that allows such understanding of Free Software. His mistake lies in not recognizing several key features of the capitalist mode of production, with the most important one being that surplus value production is the only direct goal. Such a goal makes it a predatory social form of production that will impose its social and economic determination of form on any activity that can integrate in its extraction of surplus value. More importantly, its influence goes beyond the elements directly under its control. To reach own goals, capitalist firms will rely on, or directly utilize, results and labour of any other form of production. In the case of software production, this predatory tendency can mean anything from additional selective imposition of commodity-form through strict software licencing, to supporting and promoting Free Software Copyleft production, depending on what fits any given capitalist business model in the context of its strategy and economic ecosystem. For Smith, this is a standard modus operandi of capitalist production, whose creation of wealth 'always crucially depended upon "free gits" that capital claimed as its own', with a long list of examples to support this claim:

> Gifts of nature, such as soil fertility developed over millions of years, or water and wind power, are examples. The cultural achievements of pre-capitalist societies, the development of cognitive and physical capacities outside the workplace, the unpaid care-labour of women, the scientific-technological knowledge developed in the early modern period, and the products of publicly funded research labs during the heyday of Fordism provide other illustrations. (Smith, 2013, p 243)

All mentioned elements and activities contribute to production of wealth. Yet, if their contribution to the production of capitalist commodities is not monetarily rewarded they are not considered to be value creating. Which brings us to the conceptual misunderstandings arising when various social forms of production of wealth and the capitalist production are intertwined. By confusing wealth and value, we often imprint our desires for overcoming the capitalist mode of production on other forms of production of wealth, such as Free Software. Although the imposition of value extraction, for Smith, will systematically hamper 'full development of immense potential of network technology', this has nothing to do with '"nature of technology" per se', but is 'due to the historically specific nature of technological change when it is subordinated under the social forms of capital' (Smith, 2010, p 221). The evidence offered by Smith is that a broad range of knowledge products can be made freely available, instead of money and armies of workers employed to figure out the best way to subsume these products under the capitalist social forms, supressing the potential of 'commons-based peer production', he concludes (Smith, 2010, p 209). In our understanding, Smith points out that technological forms we experience today are historically specific, shaped by legal forms, following the single goal to be profitable, to extract surplus value.

The egalitarian illusions resulting from the lack of adequate determinate abstractions

Neither Smith nor Nuss discuss specificities of different non-capitalist modes or social forms of production and the necessity to construct theoretical categories according to their own determinations of social form and laws of motion. However, wealth, like production, products, or labour, is a general abstraction. To appear, wealth has to take a social form. In most cases it becomes a commodity, present in various forms of production as a simple abstraction (pre-capitalist commodity production, artisan production), and having a determinate economic form only in societies where the capitalist mode of production dominates. As we have developed with Google and Facebook, when wealth is available at no monetary charge to end users, it can appear as a social form that transcends capitalist production. Yet, being an essential first step in the extraction of surplus value for this particular technological form of advertising-funded digital platforms, it is an element of the capitalist mode of production that leads consumers to final commodities, hence the term pre-commodity: not yet a commodity, but leading to one. Advertising provides the link between pre- and final commodities, hence the term intermediate commodity.

When wealth is provided through a social form that is free of charge to final consumers, the link between earning and consumption is severed for that particular social form and type of wealth. Such provision potentially reduces inequalities introduced through unequal distribution of income, the central mechanism by which an individual gains access to a portion of the overall social wealth. In many countries large sections of total wealth are produced in public sector, especially within health, education, and care domains. This type of production achieves an egalitarian effect by producing outputs that are not commodities, which are allocated according to a set of criteria and only weakly related to income of individuals. Yet, regardless of the shared feature of being available to end users free of direct monetary charge, the same egalitarian tendency cannot be assigned to pre-commodities, outputs available free of charge to consumers on digital platforms.

There are two key differences. First, unlike public sector outputs, pre-commodities are fully embedded in and functionally subordinated to the capitalist mode of production. Second, the funding of public sector outputs is achieved via taxation, citizens and private productive units collectively fund a vast array of products allocated in a variety of ways, planned in advance through budgeting, rarely taking the form of commodity and – despite the dependence of taxation on commodity production – not directly following the logic of surplus value extraction. The whole business model of producers such as Google and Facebook and their technological forms are constructed as an ecosystem geared to extract surplus value, thus contributing to all the negative tendencies typical for the capitalist mode of production, with new elements, such as surveillance and negative influence of the democratic processes, appearing only within digital platform monopolies. What initially may have seemed as an emancipatory potential is, in fact, a modified version of the capitalist mode of production, a technological form developed to operationalize a specific capitalist business model, revolving around pre-commodities, built out of digital materiality and broad international reach of networking technologies.

However, there are elements within the overall chain of production of these digital pre-commodities that are not fully functionally integrated in the capitalist mode production, with their own distinct social forms and perhaps even own casual mechanisms. As we discussed in earlier chapters, when Free Software released under Copyleft licences is produced by volunteers in a cooperative process of production without profit as the end goal, it cannot be considered produced under the capitalist mode of production. Let us recall that for Marx 'the means of production become capital only in so far as they have become separated from labourer and confront labour as an independent power' (Marx, 1861/1963, p 408). When 'the producer – the labourer – is the possessor, the owner, of his means of production ... they are therefore not capital' (Marx, 1861/1963), Marx continues his discussion of handicraftsman. The twist occurs when such a producer sells products as commodity on markets, thereby extracting surplus value for himself, without third party mediation, Marx notes. The tendency 'in the form of society in which the capitalist mode of production predominates' (Marx, 1861/1963), is that such production of commodities by owner-producer, whose 'production does not fall under the capitalist mode of production', is 'either gradually transformed into a small capitalist who also exploits the labour or other, or he will suffer the loss of his means of production' (Marx, 1861/1963, p 407).

Yet, engineers releasing software under Free Software Copyleft licences differ from artisan production discussed by Marx. Outputs of their work do not become commodities as licencing prevents it, ensuring availability of products to all consumers regardless of their individual income. This free-of-charge availability of outputs occurs without necessary embeddedness in the production of commodities in the manner of pre-commodities on advertising-funded digital platforms. In Free Software, the worker is not separate from the means of production, leading to a different social character, and different social form of the means of production. Free Software Copyleft products differ from Google and Facebook pre-commodities in several ways. Workers do not have to be paid wages to engage in production. Their cooperation is not formalized in a capitalist form or organization, such as a firm of some kind, nor is the process of production driven by the firm and its managers. Unlike the production of pre-commodities on advertising-financed digital platforms, the aim of Free Software Copyleft production is not to extract surplus value. The outputs are a social form of wealth with egalitarian tendencies, produced to an extent independently of the capitalist mode of production. Yet, given that Free Software Copyleft production often does not provide wages for producers, the reproduction of labour power of those engineers and hackers has to be financed elsewhere. When Free Software Copyleft producers are funded by capital, by wages within a capitalist productive unit, we have a combination of two social forms of production, with the Copyleft production to an extent functionally subordinated to the goals of surplus value extraction.

Privatizing knowledge and securing ownership

Regardless of the original goals and licensing arrangements of Free Software many FLOSS projects have been pulled into the capitalist mode of production (Barron, 2013; Birkinbine, 2015; Lund & Zukerfeld, 2020), as also evidenced by Microsoft's purchase of Github in 2018 for \$7.5 billion, one of the largest source code hosts for developers.[4] Beside Free Software, another domain outside of the capitalist mode of production that played an important part for the development of all digital platforms is publicly funded research. Initially, the goal of public research was not to make a profit and its outputs were publicly available without assuming the social form of commodity. In the United States, the Bayh-Dole Act of 1980 allowed publicly funded knowledge to be patented rather than remain in the public domain, which allowed the biotechnology industry to spin off from university research labs (Mazzucato, 2013). A state-supported and internationally implemented system of intellectual property rights (IPR) became an important element in commercialization of the internet and commodification of user data and software production. The system allows licensing agreements and privatization of different forms of knowledge, often profiting from public investments and FLOSS innovations. It legally codifies how knowledge can assume the social form required for the capitalist mode of production, the commodity form. It opens the trend of making smaller companies the target of larger corporations seeking to acquire IPR and skilled labour.

Computer software first started being patented after the 1981 Supreme Court decision in the Diamond v. Diehr case (Fuller, 1982). Once knowledge becomes property it is open for exchange in the market. Such an arrangement naturally requires the support of the state in managing ownership and exchange relations. The state sanctions a 'settlement, produced by the mobilisation of power, between the use of political authority to pattern the distribution of benefits and the use of the market mechanism'. The settlement decides on whether the authority or the market will become the leading distributional device (May, 2000, p 31).

The pharmaceutical industry was involved in long term lobbying in the United States for stronger IPRs (Lexchin, 2018), which led to the creation of the World Trade Organization (WTO) and the 1994 Agreement on Trade-Related Aspects of Intellectual Property Rights (TRIPS). The TRIPS agreement required uniform, minimum standards for all WTO countries in many areas, mostly notably in regulating industrial intellectual property (patents), and literary or artistic intellectual property (copyright).[5] According to the World Intellectual Property Organization (WIPO, 2020), copyright protection extends only to expressions and not to ideas, procedures, and methods of operation or mathematical concepts. Copyright protects the literal expressions of a computer program, while patents protect the ideas underlying computer programs with considerable commercial value.[6]

Ultimately, the IPR regime deepened existing economic inequalities between nation states, as most ownership rights are primarily concentrated in the most developed countries. International commercial laws that regulate global trade have become the backbone of maintaining monopoly privileges and one of the reasons for internationally consolidated market power of GAFAM in data–driven technology development.[7] As Harvey (2012, p 94) argues, '[t]he monopoly power of private property is therefore both the beginning and the end of all capitalist activity'. Pure market competition and free commodity exchange are rare and unstable devices for coordinating production and consumption. Political and economic relations are geared towards creating and sustaining individual monopoly privileges. Giving new monopoly rights on knowledge as property gives those rights prestige and legitimacy (Zukerfeld, 2017, p 248) and allows surplus profits to rise due to exclusive ownership over knowledge.[8]

Figure 6.1 shows the number of granted US patents to GAFAM. In 2019 alone, Microsoft was granted 3,144 patents, Alphabet

Figure 6.1: Granted US patents to GAFAM (2007–2019)

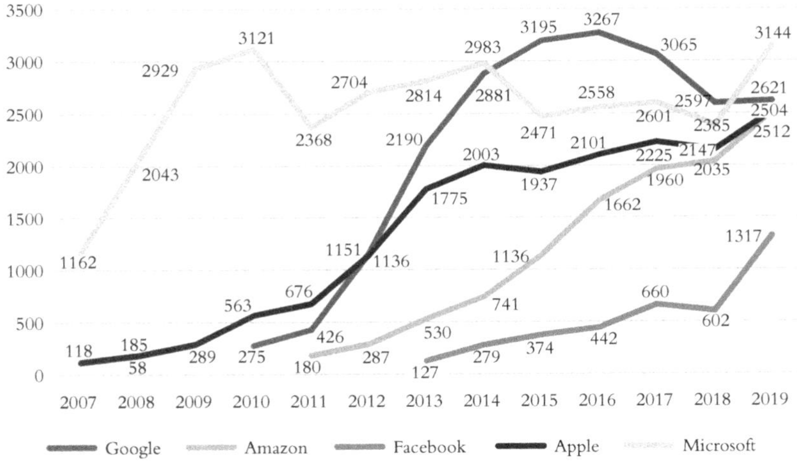

Source: Authors' analysis based on WIPO top 300 patent owners

(Google) 2,621, Apple 2,512, Amazon 2,504, and Facebook 1,317. Since 2013, GAFAM has consistently ranked among the top 300 patent owners in the US. In 2019, Microsoft was ranked number five on the list behind IBM (9,477), Samsung Electronics (8,735), Canon (4,102), and Intel (3,680). The majority of those patents are unlikely to achieve commodity status and profitability. However, the legal framework allows these companies to retain knowledge and technology dissemination rights as a way of protecting their research and developed investments.[9] Moreover, as patents expire after the legally defined period of 20 years, GAFAM are in the constant business of updating and further developing their digital services. For example, the PageRank algorithm expired in June 2019 and became public knowledge. However, already in October 2015, the company was granted an updated patent titled 'Producing a ranking for pages using distances in a web-link graph'. This 're-patenting' process is sometimes referred to as 'ever-greening' (Baker et al, 2017) and used as a strategy of extending proprietary rights beyond the legally defined period of 20 years for patent expiration.

It would be mistaken to view patents and their sheer number as a sign of innovation, investment, and technological advancement. The usual justificatory scheme for the existence and implementation of IPR is that it protects individual creators, allows a return on invested capital, and fosters innovation and economic growth (May, 2000). As Mazzucato (2013) argues, the rise in the number of patents does not indicate innovation but a change in patent laws and the rise in strategic reasons why patents are used. The number of patents that a company owns is an investment indicator for venture capitalists. Applying for multiple patents is a common strategy for emerging companies seeking capital investments. The international IPR framework allows transnational corporations to manage global value chains and capital accumulation on the basis of transnational patents and royalty incomes derived from them (Bryan et al, 2017). Once knowledge is privatized and commercialized, the vast majority of software production becomes far removed from the lofty ideals of free software promoters, with the expansion and growth of the capitalist mode of production being the biggest beneficiary. Despite this, FLOSS provided innovative outputs that are widely used by all organizations requiring technology in all sectors and social forms of production. Yet, IPR presents a major hurdle for all calls to secure public management and fair reward distribution from GAFAM. Their key technologies are deeply embedded in commercial logic of exploiting knowledge through markets, sanctioned by legal forms suited for privatization, commodification, and capital expansion.

Setting the rules of data engagement

Not all data is created equal and platform owners expend enormous computing, capital, and labour power (see Chapter 5) to continuously process and package data in useful formats for commodification and technical improvement. The first level is surface data, which consists of search entries, Facebook messages, Instagram posts, news articles, and other types of publicly visible and mostly accessible data that is the results of user engagement and activity on different digital platforms and the internet in general. This type of data is not of immediate commercial interest to platform owners but can be of interest to state surveillance mechanisms in areas such as anti-terrorism and hate speech. Surface data largely forms an area of contact between the private and the public sphere online. The second level is background data, which is a form of aggregate meta-data extracted from the user activities while generating surface data. Background data show platforms who, how, when, where, and how much is using certain services or is engaged around certain types of content. Analysing this type of data is extremely useful to advertisers since the resulting knowledge on users helps place and target advertisements to specific users, which increases their chances of selling advertised products. All platforms process surface data and analyse background data.

For advertising funded digital platforms, the process forms the backbone of their business model as it enables them to produce intermediate commodities sold to advertisers. Despite being the foundation of the entire business model, background data is largely hidden to platform users. It is also the point at which regulation imposes different privacy rules so that individual identities are not disclosed and processed by corporate and state surveillance mechanisms. The third level is technical data. It relates to platform usage, which is used directly to improve and optimize platform services. This type of data is also invisible to individual users. For example, if certain users at a specific location at a specific time receive a 'no search results' response from Google's search, this indicates two things. Either there is really no content for that specific search entry, or the algorithm does not 'understand' what the users are looking for. If the algorithm is unable to find what the users are searching, the consequences for the entire business model are obvious.

The story of advertising-funded platforms Google and Facebook, as well as GAFAM more broadly in terms of its diverse data commodification strategies, is not a story of controlled, state-sanctioned monopoly in which individual companies are chosen to become monopolies. It is a story of ruthless, cutthroat capitalist competition where rewards are reaped by those who withstand being swallowed up by bigger companies, by those who manage to attract venture capital and keep investors satisfied, and by those who take advantage of capital friendly regulation in the United States. At the same time, no capitalist monopoly wants insecurities and risks of competition on the one hand, or societal and democratic demands seeking accountability and public oversight on the other hand. As we will explore in this section further, data-driven, advertising business models within the capitalist mode of production ultimately create distorted technological forms that result in widespread surveillance, privacy breaches, technological, and economic enclosures.

Watching, sorting, and reselling data

Algorithmic solutions are not accepted automatically by internet users and advertisers. As we explained in Chapter 5, Google was competing with multiple search engines in the 1990s and early 2000s. Some of the competing engines included Infoseek, WebCrawler, Yahoo!, Lycos, AskJeeves, MSN Search, and many others. Apart from a unique technical solution for web search and information retrieval based on the free-of-charge use of the PageRank algorithm, Google's widespread adoption and commercial success was also the result of strategic contracts it signed with web businesses for providing search and advertising (Greenstein, 2015).

A similar story of initial competition before a dominant solution prevailed can be found in the history of social networking services (SNS) in the late 1990s. One of the first services was called Six Degrees.com, and it was founded in 1997. A wide number of SNS were launched in the following years including Live Journal, Black Planet, Lunar Storm, Cyworld, Couchsurfing, MySpace, Last FM, and many others (boyd & Ellison, 2007). Facebook was launched only in 2004 and many competing services soon disappeared and shut down completely. Facebook's dominance over the SNS market was strengthened by the purchase of Instagram for $1 billion in 2012, which allowed it to stifle competition and accumulate data across different services. Once algorithmic solutions are deployed by monopolistic companies, alternatives for their services are rare.

The archives of previous users' online activities become enclosed by companies that monitor every user action, store the resulting data, protect that data via intellectual property, and mine it for profit (Gehl, 2011). User engagement becomes locked within a constantly updated and individualized set of technical solutions. For example, Google reported 3,234 updates to its search algorithms in 2018, which was an average of almost nine updates per day (Moz, 2020). Some of these updates are the result of inputs from globally sourced and poorly paid search engine evaluators (Bilić, 2016). Each change affects the ranking of search results, which consequently affects not only the individual and/or collective user experience but also how the search engine optimization (SEO) and the advertising industry serves their customers.[10] The advertising and SEO industry as well as individual website owners all adapt to the rules Google sets and constantly updates: 'The power to include, exclude, and rank is the power to ensure which public impressions become permanent and which remain fleeting. That is why search services, social or not, are "must have" properties for advertisers as well as users' (Pasquale, 2015, p 61).

Its effectiveness in attracting advertising revenue depends on the precision and uniqueness of its data analytics, which depends on the quality and scale of surveillance over online activities of its users, which in turn depends on their search engine remaining the one that most users prefer. Surveillance was studied as a crucial aspect of many critical accounts of the media, advertising industry and the digital realm (for example, Gandy, 1993; Andrejevic, 2002; Lyon, 2005; Fuchs, 2008; Zwick & Denegri Knott, 2009; Allmer, 2012). However, surveillance is not only the direct outgrowth of contemporary digital technologies.

In fact, Foster and McChesney (2014) trace its current form back to the post World War II era development of the military-industrial complex in the United States. What they call surveillance capitalism is the result of corporate marketing revolutions based in Madison Avenue, and the creation of the warfare state dedicated to the imperial control of world markets and fighting the Cold War. In addition to the rise of financialization in the 1970s, these developments were accompanied by communications revolutions in the development of computers, digital technology, and the internet. The result, as they argue, was a universalization of surveillance associated with militarism, imperialism, and security; corporate-based marketing and the media system; and the world of finance. The critique was picked up by Zuboff (2015, 2019) who argued that surveillance has become one of the key mechanisms of capital accumulation in surveillance capitalism. While her approach is appealing when applied to GAFAM, it also leaves much to be desired. The term surveillance capitalism itself, although unattributed by Zuboff in her publications, was coined by Foster and McChesney (2014). As *Monthly Review* editors (Foster et al, 2018) argued, Zuboff divorced surveillance capitalism from class analysis and sidestepped the issue of the symbiotic relation between the military and private corporations – primarily in marketing, finance, high tech, and defence contracting.

According to Lyon (2005, p 20), the key aspect of surveillance is to allow social sorting, or classification of otherwise diverse populations into segments: 'the surveillance system obtains personal and group data in order to classify people and populations according to varying criteria, to determine who should be targeted for special treatment, suspicion, eligibility, inclusion, access, and so on'. As the advertising and marketing industry started realizing the potential of targeting consumers with scale and scope, the surveillance model expanded quickly. The expansion of the volume and precision of background data placed a premium on obtaining customer databases: 'it is now more efficient (faster, more flexible and cheaper) to manufacture customers as modular configurations of propensities, as calculations of possible future values and as purified groupings of selective homogeneity' (Zwick & Denegri Knott, 2009, pp 240, 241). While it is difficult to empirically study surveillance at the macro level of corporate and state monitoring, several major events in recent history have provided public evidence of the scale of these activities.

First, after the September 11 terrorist attacks in the United States there was widespread intensification of state surveillance as a form of pre-emptive security measure for reducing risks of future attacks (Lyon, 2003; Fuchs, 2008). The scope of surveillance activities received public attention more than a decade after the attacks when in 2013 Edward Snowden, an employee of Booz Allen Hamilton, a contractor of the National Security Agency (NSA), revealed the scope of surveillance activities undertaken by the US government in collaboration with telecommunications companies, internet companies, and European governments. His revelations of government documents were published in major newspapers in the US, the UK, and Germany. Microsoft, Google, Yahoo, and Facebook provided data on tens of thousands of individual profiles every six months (Ackerman & Rushe, 2014). As Lyon (2014) explains, Snowden's revelations displayed several trends in how surveillance is enacted with big data analytics. First, big data analytics and interconnected datasets increase capacity and intensify surveillance. Second, surveillance is driven by control motives, faith in technology, public–private partnerships, and user involvement. The quest for pattern discovery is used to justify unprecedented access to data. Third, big data surveillance revealed by Snowden opens the discussion of ethical principles involved in data-gathering and analysing practices. For the purpose of our book, corporate surveillance is a more intriguing development as it directly connects surveillance with the mode of production of GAFAM.

The second major event that displayed the use of big data analytics for surveillance purposes and massive privacy breaches occurred in 2018. In a nutshell, the scandal developed after it was revealed that Cambridge Analytica, a company partly owned by the hedge fund billionaire Robert Mercer, and headed by Trump's adviser Steve Bannon, used personal information taken from Facebook without authorization in early 2014 to build a system for profiling US voters (Cadwalladr & Graham-Harrison, 2018). It was later revealed that the company accessed more than 87 million individual profiles and used them to influence the 2016 US presidential campaign (Kang & Frenkel, 2018). The case is intriguing for at least three different reasons. First, it shows how big data surveillance can be leveraged for political purposes. Second, it shows how important it is for data-driven companies to have a wide pool of users from different population segments. Accumulated user background datasets allow specialized, niche targeting within a population of Facebook's 2.32 billion users worldwide in 2018 (Statista, 2020). Third, it shows weaknesses of digital economy regulation in the United States as data gathering and harvesting by third parties is becoming raw material for economic valorization and political mobilization.[11]

The United States' Federal Trade Commission (FTC) reached a settlement with Facebook in 2012 requiring the company to give consumers 'clear and prominent notice and obtaining their express consent before sharing their information beyond their privacy settings, by maintaining a comprehensive privacy program to protect consumers' information, and by obtaining biennial privacy audits from an independent third party' (FTC, 2012). In 2019, the FTC charged Facebook with a violation of the 2012 order and issued a US record $5 billion penalty (FTC, 2019a). In addition to the fine, a new 20-year settlement was imposed, which includes a privacy compliance system at the board of directors' level with the introduction of the independent privacy committee, individual privacy compliance officers, and third party assessors of the privacy program.[12] The FTC order and the increasing general public disillusionment with data services have some effect on behavioural adjustments by major companies even beyond these regulatory interventions. For example, Google, Safari, and Firefox have started blocking third-party cookies in their browsers to improve privacy settings on their properties (Bohn, 2020). Nonetheless, while the fine issued to Facebook is record-breaking and the privacy governance structure extensive, the underlying economic engine of surplus value extraction based on controlling, processing, and commercializing data through surveillance remains unchanged.

Erecting tollbooths and managing access points

Big data analyses are not possible without computer algorithms that extract patterns from otherwise large and unstructured datasets that are not possible to process manually. However, the technical implementation process also has direct economic benefits. For example, the financial sector, often credited with volatility and instability of its price mechanisms, has seen an increase in the usage of so-called high-frequency trading (HFT) algorithms for creating more predictable and profitable models of handling stock price changes and share price fluctuations. As MacKenzie (2017, p 191) explains, traditional exchanges such as the New York Stock Exchange (NYSE) had to fundamentally reorganize trading by creating technical systems within which algorithms had the data to predict prices and act on those predictions with minimum delay. Almost all US share-trading venues had to place their servers in the same building as an exchange's systems to avoid delays and minimize losses.

Pricing algorithms are widely used by Amazon, which consistently offers the lowest prices within its product offer in order to starve competition across different industries (Ezrachi & Stucke, 2016a; Khan, 2016). Wide acceptance of pricing algorithms displays three different trends that distort traditional rules of market competition as defined by mainstream economic theory (Ezrachi & Stucke, 2016b).

First, industries are shifting from a pricing environment where store clerks stamped prices on products to differential pricing where algorithms calculate and update prices. Second, firms harvest personal data to identify which emotion (or bias) will prompt users to buy products and what is the most users are willing to pay. Third, new types of relationships of competition and cooperation occur between super-platforms and independent apps. A most notable example of competition and cooperation managed by major platforms is Apple's iOS and Google's Android.[13]

During the January 2020 hearing before the Committee on the Judiciary in the United States[14] David Hanson, co-founder of a web application company, stated that software developers have to hand over 30 per cent of their revenue in the application store duopoly managed by Google and Apple (*Written Testimony of David Heinemeier Hansson, CTO & Cofounder, Basecamp*, 2020). Apple responded with a written reply stating that the payment by app developers 'reflects the value of the App Store as a channel for the distribution of developers' apps and the cost of many services – including app review, app development tools and marketing services'. In the same written response Apple states that developers are only charged 30 per cent for the first year of subscription, while the second and subsequent years include a 15 per cent charge (*Letter from Apple Inc. for the Record*, 2020). These charges reflect a broader trend of concentrated power in the digital industry, evident in the ability of only two players to control access points to the entire digital market for apps. The position of major players on the role of competition in the digital economy has shifted dramatically over the years. For example, in a 2008 Note to Google's users, Eric Schmidt, who was the CEO of Google at the time, wrote the following:

> The Internet as we know it is facing a serious threat. There's a debate heating up in Washington, DC on something called 'net neutrality' – and it's a debate that's so important Google is asking you to get involved. We're asking you to take action to protect Internet freedom. In the next few days, the House of Representatives is going to vote on a bill that would fundamentally alter the Internet. That bill, and one that may come up for a key vote in the Senate in the next few weeks, would give the big phone and cable companies the power to pick and choose what you will be able to see and do on the Internet. Today the Internet is an information highway where anybody – no matter how large or small, how traditional or unconventional – has equal

access. But the phone and cable monopolies, who control almost all Internet access, want the power to choose who gets access to high-speed lanes and whose content gets seen first and fastest. They want to build a two-tiered system and block the on-ramps for those who can't pay. Creativity, innovation and a free and open marketplace are all at stake in this fight. Please call your representative (202-224-3121) and let your voice be heard. (Schmidt, 2008)

Fast-forward 12 years to the 2020 Online Platforms and Market Power hearing and the following statement on the role of Google and Apple in the previously open and competitive digital economy stands out:

The central problem for a small software business like ours is that the once open internet has been colonized by the big tech giants, and they're erecting tollbooths everywhere. Tollbooths that restrict our access to customers, induce us to compromise our ethics, erode our self-determination, and ultimately threaten to suffocate us entirely. The power that these big tech companies wield over small tech companies is terrifying. If your presence ends up displeasing any of these conglomerates, they can make you essentially disappear from the marketplace with the press of a button – by relegating your position in their search engine to page 42, or by banning your application from their app stores altogether. The threat is very real, and all of us small tech operators instinctively internalize it, which often stifles dissent. This monopoly in search, which amounts to controlling the front door of the internet, allows Google to shake us down for protection money with ease. For years, we've been dealing with the problem that Google allows competitors to purchase ads on our trademark, blocking and misdirecting consumers from reaching our site. (Written Testimony of David Heinemeier Hansson, CTO & Cofounder, Basecamp, 2020)

The digital oligopoly deploys complex algorithmic mechanisms protected by IPRs to enforce its power and create profit-making opportunities for its shareholders, corporate owners, and managers. At the same time, their mechanisms erect access barriers for all outsiders. The oligopoly enforces power structures in which there are few winners, and many losers, which have to adapt to their rules of the game. It is a take-it-or-leave-it situation and a direct structural consequence of the way in which competition is enforced, promoted, and supported in the United States. Antitrust regulators simply favour the winner-take-all logic in zero-price markets of data-driven production. Monopoly power is not just an issue of accessing digital markets through Amazon, Apple, or Google. It is also a question of internet users' habits for accessing all digital data. The news industry is one of the biggest losers in this power game as it is affected by changing habits of internet users for accessing news on the hand, and competition for advertising revenue with global giants on the other hand.

Realization of value in advertising markets

The news media, and modern communication systems more broadly, occupy one of the central dynamics in the development of capitalism. At its core lies the continuing struggle over communications between public and private spheres. Within national media systems, this dynamic takes the form of institutional balancing between promoting privatized, commercial media production on the one hand, and public and non-profit media production on the other hand. Commercial outlets are predominantly funded by advertising investments making their communication structurally oriented towards consumers buying advertised products. Commercial media dedicate a large amount of print space, broadcasting time or digital space to advertising. At the same time, structural reliance on advertising moves their news production and editorial policies closer to the interests of advertisers as their primary funders.

This does not need to take the form of open promotion of interests of major advertisers. Nor does it mean that commercial media do not produce content of public interest. More often, their editorial policies take the form of supressing conflicting reports and not reporting on specific topics that might deter advertisers from buying their media space. The public media on the other hand, do not rely on advertising but usually on some form of licence fee or public tax, which funds news production. However, being reliant on public funding often involves being attentive to the interests of the government and political bodies, a point regularly stressed by neoliberals and other supporters of commercial media. All modern communications systems are constituted within this private-public dynamic. The US example is an extreme case of commercialization with a very weak public service element. The European Union, although with significant differences between Member States who have autonomy to organize their cultural sphere under the condition that it does not affect trade between Member States, promotes a more balanced approach between private and public media. The public service media still hold some significance in terms of audience shares, numbers of channels, and outlets. They still command trust among their audiences. However, this balance in the European system has also been eroding.

Digital advertising dominance, user habits, and disinformation

Prior to the rise of online communications, the media enjoyed a privileged position of being a focal point for accessing news, information, and some forms of entertainment for the whole population. This made the media natural allies for the advertisers' sales effort. The race for audience shares is a key competitive dynamic within the commercial media market. However, the close connection between news production and consumption around recognizable reporting styles, editorial policies, quality content and public issues has eroded in the digital sphere (McChesney, 2013). Digital platforms serve global audiences making the scale and precision of their operations unreachable by even the most widely consumed traditional media. As Turow (2011, p 69) convincingly outlined, the widespread usage of intermediary platforms such as Google and Facebook creates a 'new advertising food chain'. Algorithms allow advertising agencies to reach individuals in real time on whatever pages they land on the internet. This decoupling of audiences from context, Turow argues, marks a historic shift in deciding what content to support through advertising placement.

Reliance on big data and personalized marketing threatens connections that link citizens and groups via information, argumentation, empathy, and celebration as members of a shared social and civic space (Couldry & Turow, 2014, p 1710). Algorithmic recommendation systems steer audience habits and lock users within their personalized filter bubbles (Pariser, 2011). For example, search engines' autocomplete functions have a tendency to suggest slander and disinformation (Kayser-Brill, 2020). In a recent report, it was revealed that Facebook was aware of the role of recommendation systems in steering its users towards more divisive environments. However, the company did nothing to address the problem. According to an internal Facebook document from 2016, 64 per cent of all extremist group joins are due to companies' recommendation tools. Most of that activity comes from the platforms' 'Groups You Should Join' and 'Discover' algorithms (Seetharaman, 2020).

In 2018, the majority of internet users (65 per cent) in 37 countries worldwide preferred to access news through search, social media, email, mobile alerts, and news aggregators (Reuters Institute, 2019) instead of directly accessing news websites. Changing habits of news consumption is not the result of a coercive, ideological manipulation by corporations. It is based on convenience, free services, and smooth access to content offered by algorithms. As Marcuse (2007) argued, technology 'serves to institute new, more effective, and more pleasant forms of social control and social cohesion'. The convenient and pleasant form of controlling access points and data flows has direct economic consequences on the news industry, and consequently, on the public management of contemporary communications systems. Ideally, the news media engage in a complicated daily grind of news production that serves the purpose of informing populations, keeping governments and corporations in check. To create content, labour and other production costs are covered through public and/or commercial sources such as advertising. Once media sources become scarce and audiences are predominantly captured by platforms such as Google and Facebook, it becomes more difficult to produce news for the public interest, making it far more difficult for citizens to understanding and evaluate power structures governing their lives. Google and Facebook, however, are quick to point out that they are technology companies, not media companies producing content (Helft, 2008; BBC News, 2017).

Google and Facebook were major contributing parties in fake news and disinformation dissemination during the 2016 US presidential race, the UK Brexit campaign, and the European Parliament elections. Far-right groups used 'attention hacking' techniques to increase visibility, while the media's increasing dependence on social media, analytics and metrics, sensationalism, novelty over newsworthiness, and clickbait made them vulnerable to such media manipulations (Marwick & Lewis, 2017). During the 2018 Congressional hearing, Mark Zuckerberg, the CEO of Facebook, stated 'I consider us to be a technology company because the primary thing that we do is have engineers who write code and build product and services for other people' (Castillo, 2018).

This is a convenient position supported by immunity from liability for computer services that provide information from third parties granted by the 1996 Communications Decency Act. According to Section 230: 'No provider or user of an interactive computer service shall be treated as the publisher or speaker of any information provided by another information content provider'. Yet, as recent reports show, there was a conscious effort within the company to allow divisive content to thrive on the platform. As one internal presentation from

2018 stated: 'our algorithms exploit the human brain's attraction to divisiveness'. The document continues that, if left unchecked, Facebook would feed users 'more and more divisive content in an effort to gain user attention & increase time on the platform' (Seetharaman, 2020).

User attention brings digital advertising revenue, which Google and Facebook increasingly dominate worldwide. As Figure 6.2 shows, Google captured between a 40 and 62 per cent internet advertising share in European markets in 201.[15] The total size of the European internet advertising market as a whole in 2018 was €55.1 billion. It doubled in size since 2012 (IAB, 2019). In countries with higher internet penetration rates and higher internet advertising per capita, Google holds a higher market share. In Norway, Sweden, and Denmark it held more than 60 per cent of the internet advertising market share in 2018 according to our estimates. In Bulgaria, Greece, and Romania it holds a smaller market share, although still above 40 per cent. Facebook captured between 12 and 28 per cent of the internet advertising market

Figure 6.2: European online intermediate commodities circulation share in 2018 (Google)

Figure 6.3: European online intermediate commodities circulation share in 2018 (Facebook)

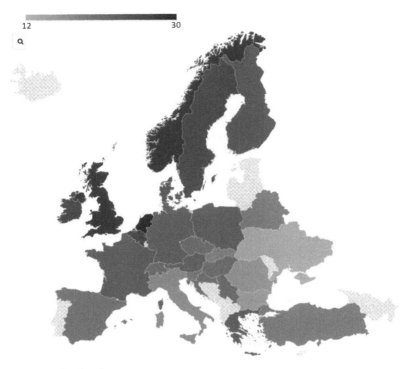

Source: Authors' analysis

(Figure 6.3), from the highest in the Netherlands, Norway, and the UK to the lowest in Russia, Ukraine, and Bulgaria.

Reluctant public interventionism

Public and non-profit alternatives to news production are not provided necessary support within the European union due to a legal system demanding deregulation of the media market and close monitoring of public spending (Donders & Pauwels, 2008). The position of journalism in the United States is even grimmer, given the highly commercialized media system. As McChesney (2013, pp 190, 191) argues, there are two key possibilities of doing journalism in the nexus between the internet and capitalism. First, if anyone can make money doing online journalism it will certainly be a very large, centralized operation, probably a monopoly or close to it. Second, wages paid to journalists can be slashed dramatically, while the workloads can be increased to levels previously unheard of. As David Chavern, president and CEO of the News Media Alliance, a non-profit trade association representing over 2,000 newspapers across the United States stated in the 2019 Hearing before the House Judiciary:

> News organizations face a collective action problem. It is in each of their interests to resist harmful or exploitative policies imposed by platform monopolists. It is in their interest to resist scraping, to demand attribution for their content, to demand better remuneration for their content, and to demand a greater focus on originality and reliability. But no news organization on its own can stand up to the platforms. The risk of demotion or exclusion from the platforms is simply too great. And the antitrust laws prevent news organizations from acting collectively, so the result is that publishers are forced to accept whatever terms or restrictions the dominant platforms choose to impose. (Testimony of David Chavern, President and CEO News Media Alliance, 2019)

Despite the need for state support schemes directed at public and non-profit media, financial aid for independent, professional journalism in the public interest remains a highly contested policy terrain (Murschetz, 2020). The existing policy and regulatory measures have been fragmented, despite the record-breaking fines in Europe and the United States in the fields of antitrust, privacy, and taxation. They deal with consequences of platform capitalism, not its root mechanisms of surplus vale extraction and income distribution.

There is a clear 'division of labour' among policy experts and regulators with limited understanding of the way in which platforms as specific capitalist technological forms lead to social and political consequences. Perhaps the most well thought through proposal was the digital taxation proposal at the EU level. The intent was to impose a 3 per cent tax at the point and in the countries where tech giants make profits, instead of where they report their revenues (European Commission, 2017c). While it proposed an EU-wide solution, it failed to get support from all EU Member States primarily because of opposition from Ireland, Sweden, and Denmark. However, where the EU-wide proposal failed conceptually was in connecting taxation with redistribution of new tax revenue to democracy strengthening purposes. There was no connection between the economic, social, and political. The redistribution of revenue to journalistic projects, investigative journalism, community media, and local journalism would challenge some of the weaknesses of the currently constructed public sphere and news production. However, such initiatives would only be a start since platforms have created new forms of exploitation, fragmentation, and casualization of labour (Graham & Woodcok, 2018; Huws, 2019, 2020) in other sectors of the economy.[16]

Conclusion: Contradictions and Alternatives to Data Commodification

The capitalist mode of production in which digital monopolies dominate as the most valuable companies is filled with contradictions. New material for commodification and capital accumulation is surface and background data, collected and processed from web search, social networking, cloud computing, apps, and other products and services. Much of the economic processes follow a familiar story in the history of capitalist development. Monopolies, seen by mainstream economics as nothing but aberrations from perfect competition, are, in fact, regularly occurring phenomena in the history of capitalism (Foster & McChesney, 2012; Harvey, 2014; Christophers, 2016). Yet, 'perfect monopolies' are equally hard to find as 'perfect competition' since there is almost never a single seller of a commodity in the market. Nonetheless, whether we talk about oil companies, banks, airlines, pharmaceutical companies, retailers, car manufacturers, or digital services, capital always has a tendency for concentration and centralization.

It is partially an economic process driven by the need to reduce uncertainties of competition, secure growth, maintain profit rates, control and exploit labour, and harness efficiencies of scale and scope. It is also a legal process since the state(s) organize market conditions for the exchange of commodities and boundaries for capital accumulation, expansion, and reproduction. Commodification of data requires multiple legal and regulatory interventions, primarily through privatization of scientific and technical discoveries, which is evident in the rise of intellectual property rights. Privatization of knowledge leads to private appropriation of wealth from technological innovation, usually funded in the early stages by massive public investments. The process results in growing income inequalities in economies of the capitalist centre where GAFAM are based. It also leads to extraction of value from peripheral countries where GAFAM secures a significant portion of their revenues. It leads to a skewed distribution of risks and rewards between public and private interests.

Yet societies are struggling to challenge digital monopolies. Idealizing capitalist production as the best and the most natural way to produce, constructed out of theoretical assumptions such as perfect competition and self-adjusting markets, this 'illusion of the economic' (Murray, 2002a) is built in the regulatory legal forms both in the US and in the EU, posing a significant obstacle to forming different policy perspectives. The marriage of convenience between mainstream economics and regulatory legal forms is often filled with own internal battles when diverging economic interests are represented by competing political sides, when lobbying forces of different industries and their branches collide in legislature making, or when legislators who interpret laws have diverging analyses on what is the best course of action.[1] The end result serves best the needs of the US to assert its dominance in digital platforms and data-processing business models through a regulatory and developmental fine-balancing act between the two needs: to foster competition and innovation, and to enable growth of monopolies.

Despite methodological shortcomings that result in theoretical accounts blind to social harms and consequences of contemporary technological forms, the illusion of the economic holds a firm grip on policy and expert debates in prominent places (influential academic journals, political institutions, mainstream media, and education), hindering the development of alternative theories and explanations. In this chapter, instead of repeating the conclusions we already draw in individual chapters, we extend those conclusions and our methodological approach to discuss possible roots of alternatives to the capitalist mode of production. First, we look at how and why free and open source production was captured by commercial interests. We try to answer if it can be re-invented to continue challenging commodification of knowledge. Second, we look at how taxation of digital monopolies can potentially tilt the balance of rewards towards public finances promoting democratic development. However, taxation does not directly challenge the economic engine of data commodification. Finally, we provide theoretical pathways for curbing digital monopoly power by democratizing underlying economic processes. We will argue that the rationale behind legal interventions should shift from protecting competition and extraction of surplus value towards protecting public interest, producing public wealth, and promoting social, technological, political, and economic alternatives to data commodification.

The capture and commercialization of FLOSS

It was argued in Chapters 2 and 6 that Free Software production is a peculiar, non-capitalist social form of production with egalitarian aspects. Given the lack of direct monetary reward for the work performed in such production, to be able to say more on its character we need to discuss how do households of those producers reproduce themselves. In the period before commercialization, from the late 1950s to mid-1990s, many Free Software producers were employed in non-profit or publicly funded organizations. Sharing the outputs, including the source code and documentation, recipes on how to put together and use software, was common part of the process of production. In the early days of Microsoft, in his infamous 1976 open letter to Homebrew Computer Club, Bill Gates posed the question of income of software producers, complaining that sharing BASIC, software he co-developed, instead of paying for it, prevents him from hiring more programmers (Gates, 1976). Gates spoke as a capitalist owner of the means of production, posing, from the perspective of his choice of the social form of production, an entirely valid question.

Gates' letter was published in hobbyist newsletters, and as Levy documented, 'all hell broke loose in the hacker community', with Gates receiving 'between three and four hundred letters, only five or six containing the voluntary payment he suggested that owners of pirated BASIC send him', concluding 'many of the letters were intensely negative' (Levy, 2010, pp 232–3). The reaction demonstrates the extent to which the capitalist mode of production, whose rules Gates was trying to impose, was foreign to the community of software producers at the time. The conflict, as Chopra and Dexter correctly observe, was 'indicative of an emerging tension in the hacker community', and 'this divergence would also underwrite the schism, in the 1990s, between the free software and open source movements' (2008, p 12). In this period, a separate Open Source movement was created within cooperative communities of hackers and software engineers in order to promote permissive legal licensing of Free Software. It gave private investors security over the social form of output and production, removing the obstacle in the form of Free Software Copyleft licences as a form of public wealth unsuitable to surplus value extraction.

Essentially, in both cases of Bill Gates clashing with early software producers and Open Source with Free Software Copyleft proponents, the conflict erupted between two social forms of production. Reproduction, Lebowitz noted and developed in his work on socialist countries and their attempts to develop alternatives to capitalist production, is always contested (2010, pp 98, 121). The dominant capitalist mode struggling to impose a particular 'mode of regulation through which accumulation occurs', regulation being defined as 'institutional forms, procedures and habits which either coerce or persuade private agents to conform' (Lipietz, 1987, p 33). With software, we can see how two different social forms of production struggle to impose their own logic and determine the social and economic form of elements and processes of production. In the case of digital matter where the character of the content enables near-zero cost copying and easy improvement on existing output (provided the source material is distributed), it is the legal text of a copyright licence that defines key aspects of the social form of output. In the domain of digitally storable entities, the mode of regulation of the capitalist mode of production rests on legal forms shaped by legal definitions and on their enforceability. Contrary to the physical matter, where private ownership of products and their distribution in the form of commodities guarantees that the physical exchange has to occur for the accompanying potential extraction of surplus value. The material character of digital entities necessitates a larger and more complex system of legal form.

Free Software producers tried to hack copyright laws,[2] creating Copyleft, a specific type of copyright licences that define a legally enforceable social form of software that we call public wealth, constructing their own mode of regulation for protecting their social form of production. However, typical for the liberal narratives of digital commons, and to a large extent for many progressive understandings of commons applied to the digital sphere, there is very little, if anything said by the advocates of different social forms of production such as Free Software about the conditions necessary for its reproduction. Relying on self-organization and high levels of motivation, doing what they love and what they are passionate about, generations of software engineers and hackers have demonstrated that, as Nuss correctly observed, collaborative and productive work does not have to be driven by monetary rewards. We add, however, that while monetary rewards do not have to be direct, nor the driving force, all of those software producers have had their costs of living met somewhat while producing Free Software.

Therefore, the liquid wealth they were able to draw upon had to exist, either in the form of income that does not directly enforce the production of Free Software, or in the form of savings. Given that many Free Software engineers are paid to produce public wealth in various organizations during their paid working time, the difficult questions of the social form of money paying their wages, and of a mode or a social form of production they are part of ought to be raised. Academic institutions and research centres as large employers of Free Software engineers were part of this different social form of production. Gradually, this field of production became dominated by capitalist firms. The model Gates advocated imposed itself and the vast majority of top hackers and software engineers that used to do their work to an extent voluntarily or at least not under the direct supervision of organizations that paid their wages now do so on corporate salaries. The capitalist mode of production has largely imposed itself. However, some elements of the previously dominant social form of software production still remain, both in the form of collaborative practices and in the form of the old model. The overall goals and to a large extent the social forms of product of software have been subordinated to capital, confirming Marx's insight on the predatory character of the capitalist mode of production.

Nowhere is this more visible than in the development of Android, Google's mobile operating system. Google selectively took Free Software it required (Linux kernel) utilizing those parts that were under an Open Source licence. It also ignored the legal requirements of Open Source software (Java API) for over a decade, building the best and most popular mobile operating system in the meantime by combining public wealth and what may be seen as piracy. The move was executed with such a fine-grained understanding of the legal grey areas that the litigation between Oracle, the owner of Java, and Google has been ongoing for years.[3]

Transnational capital and taxation

Corporate taxation allows societies to ensure provision of essential services ranging from health care and education to non-profit and public service media. Thus far, most digital companies have escaped taxation almost completely and have left societies and their respective fiscal policies impoverished.[4] The overall goal of the European Commission is to promote a unified market by implementing the Digital Single Market Strategy (European Commission, 2015) in a geopolitical struggle to position Europe between the United States and

China in terms of digital development (European Political Strategy Centre, 2019). This implies direct confrontation with some of the largest companies.

In 2016, the European Commission (2016) concluded that Ireland granted tax benefits of up to €13 billion to Apple by allowing it to pay substantially less tax than other businesses, which is illegal under EU state aid rules. Apple paid an effective corporate tax rate that declined from 1 per cent in 2003 to 0.005 per cent in 2014 on the profits of its corporate segment Apple Sales International (ASI). It avoided taxation on almost all profits generated by sales in the entire EU because it recorded all sales in Ireland rather than in the countries where products were sold. Ireland and Apple, which employs around 6,000 people in Cork, appealed the Commission's ruling. The General Court of the European Union (GCEU) delivered its final judgement in July 2020 and concluded that the Commission 'was wrong to declare that ASI and AOE[5] had been granted a selective economic advantage and, by extension, State Aid' (General Court of the European Union, 2020). The Court annulled the earlier decision leaving the European Commission with the possibility to appeal to the European Court of Justice. While Apple paid extremely low taxes, the situation is far more complicated with trading and sales of data, as for example in the advertising market. Apple sells its physical products (iPhones, iPads, and so on) in physical stores, while online advertising is handled exclusively in the digital realm. Therefore, the key issue is where to tax these companies due to the lack of physical, and legal, presence in countries where they generate revenue (see Figures 6.2 and 6.3).

The EU proposed two directives to harmonize taxation policies in the Single Market: the Corporate taxation of a significant digital presence[6] (European Commission, 2018b) and the Digital services tax[7] (European Commission, 2018c). The concept of 'significant digital presence' is a novelty in tax legislation and the proposed Directive based it on revenues generated in a Member State from supplying digital services, number of users of digital services, and the number of business contracts for a digital service.[8] The second proposal was created as an interim solution to fix the immediate problems of untaxed economic activity. The Digital Services Tax (DST) intended to apply taxation measures to revenues created from certain digital services such as selling online advertising space, intermediary activities allowing users to interact and facilitate the sale of goods and services, and sale of data generated from user-provided information (European Commission, 2018c).[9] However, the Council of the European Union failed to reach an agreement on those proposals with some delegations rejecting it 'as a matter of principle irrespective of technical revisions' (Ivanovski & McIntosh, 2019). Nordic countries and Ireland vetoed the EU plans in March 2019, which led to the introduction of unilateral digital taxes in many countries.

Figure 7.1 shows the status of DSTs in European countries as of May 2020. Austria, France, Hungary, Italy, Turkey, and the UK introduced unilateral digital taxes. Czechia, Poland, Slovakia, and Spain proposed DSTs in their countries. Latvia, Norway, and Slovenia have announced or shown intentions of introducing a DST. After the 2018 Directives were stalled at the Council level, the resulting consensus was that the process should be moved to the global level of OECD and G20 discussions on digital taxation. The EU competition officer Margrethe Verstager stated: 'The best thing at present is a global solution, but if we want solutions in a reasonable time, then Europe must step forward' (Ivanovski & McIntosh, 2019).

Figure 7.1: Digital Service Taxes in Europe (May 2020)

Source: Adapted from Bunn et al (2020, p 19)

However, OECD talks resulted in tensions and trade disputes, in particular between France and the US. After France introduced a DST in 2019, the United States responded by publishing a list of items, including cheese and wine, with new 100 per cent tariffs in December 2019. The two sides agreed to pause the collection of taxes and tariffs until multilateral discussions at the level of OECD conclude. However, the United States nearly pulled out of the talks in June 2020 over a plan for a new global tax framework, and the Trump administration announced investigations into a number of countries that introduced DSTs including the UK, Italy, Brazil, and Indonesia (Williams, 2020). In July 2020, the United States announced it would impose tariffs of 25 per cent on \$1.3 billion worth of French goods, further escalating the trade dispute (Williams, 2020). The European Union urged the United States to return to negotiations but said it stood ready to make a new proposal to harmonize the fragmented Digital Single Market in the EU if those talks failed (Lomas, 2020; Shalal, 2020).

A broader conceptual problem with the proposed EU directives was that they stop at levelling the competitive field within the Single Market by holding perfect competition as the normative ideal. In itself, that proves to be an enormous task due to multiple political hurdles ranging from strong sovereigntist parties in Member States and the EU Parliament, and long-standing tax haven policies in some Member States, to retaliatory policies and trade threats from the Trump administration. A common EU taxation policy needs to be created, in order to ensure that transnational companies contribute to public finances. However, taxation policy should be considered a starting point, in the second stage more broadly aligned with a broader set of policies aiming to democratize societies in the digital age for the long run. The surplus value extraction model on digital platforms has become one of the centrepieces of the contemporary capitalism, generating unprecedented levels of wealth extraction for individual owners and some shareholders.

Future taxation policies should aim at alleviating those public interests most harmed by such digital business models – for example, labour issues surrounding the gig economy and precarious, flexible platform labour or the mediated public sphere and the public information environment. This should not imply salvaging the struggling news industry. It should, instead, promote and fund independent journalism, fact checking, media pluralism, social inclusiveness, human rights, labour rights, and even provide support for a renewed welfare state, fit for the 21st century (Social Prosperity Network & Institute for Global Prosperity, 2017; Huws, 2020). Based on the current unilateral taxation in Austria, France, Hungary, and the UK, the contribution to their overall annual tax revenue would range between 0.04 per cent and 0.07 per cent (Geringer, 2020). The DST(s) will not have dramatic fiscal effects, but their societal and public effects could be significant if properly distributed with the purpose of strengthening democratic processes.[10]

Beyond capital, data commodification, and surplus value extraction

The problem with taxation and other forms of legal interventions and regulatory measures is that they do not alter the existing mode of production. So how do we tackle contradictions of capitalism as pertaining to digital monopolies if FLOSS is pulled into the capitalist mode of production and if regulation only minimizes social harms leaving the business model marked by capital, data commodification, and surplus value extraction intact? How can regulatory interventions through taxation or antitrust, as the necessary first steps towards alleviating the power of monopolies, be further advanced for the betterment of social, political, economic, and technological development beyond what we have with the capitalist mode of production in all its forms?

We contribute to such debates by forging a specific theoretical and empirical analysis revolving around social and economic determination of forms and casual mechanisms. The *Monthly Review* perspective opens up the question of an alternative redistributive logic necessary to eradicate seemingly irrational surplus allocation under capitalist mode of production. The Frankfurt School offered a historically famous critique of consumer society and commodity fetishism, yet it often remained trapped in its own negative dialectics. In other words, it provided unique answers as to what is wrong in capitalist society, but seldom did it venture into conjuring alternatives. With theoretical mediation across different generations of interpreters, some of their insights can still be applied to contemporary technological forms and technological fetishisms. Finally, the social form analysis allows us to understand how social and economic determination of forms operates within the capitalist mode of production, how it shapes specific social forms and their ordering, all connected with real causal mechanisms resulting from the operationalization of the capital–driven production of surplus value. This methodological approach and overall understanding of the production, allocation, and consumption is the starting point for theorizing alternative social forms and social forms of production beyond surplus value extraction and data commodification.

Reigning monopolies in

For theorists of monopoly capitalism (for example, Baran, 1956/1973; Baran & Sweezy, 1968; Foster, 2014a), the main argument is that under monopoly conditions the economy produces more than it consumes, which leads to overaccumulation and the problem of surplus absorption. The economy becomes closely tied to investments, primarily by the state, as the military becomes one of the central mechanisms for surplus absorption, the other mechanisms being consumption and waste. On the surface, it resembles left-Keynesian perspectives with regard to the potential to reform capitalism. However, as Foster argues, economic theory after Keynes was interested in the broader concept of growth, while neo-Marxian analyses suggested that growth under capitalism is synonymous with capital's self-expansion associated with class-based accumulation (2014a, p 148). As Sweezy himself stated, the Keynesians 'tear the economic system out of its social context and treat it as though it were a machine to be sent to a repair shop there to be overhauled by an engineer state' (cited in Foster, 2014a, pp 148, 149). However, the theory of monopoly capitalism requires a 'dynamic conception of political change and its relation to the accumulation process' (Foster, 2014a, p 155) that would move beyond reasoning of surplus absorption.

Let us, for the sake of considering alternatives to the capitalist mode of production, remain within the reasoning of surplus absorption by treating it as a political problem, while keeping the concept of surplus value intact. As we showed in Chapter 2, surplus value for those platforms funded by advertising is extracted from the circulation of commodities, which means that platforms perform a vital function for commodity producers seeking faster capital realization and reproduction. At the same time, platforms seek to increase their profit and accumulate capital by taking a larger share of the global circulation of commodities and by controlling technological innovation through different mechanisms (legal protection of IPR, mergers and acquisitions, and so on). The strategy depends on private appropriation of rewards from technological innovation, which results in socioeconomic inequality and socialization of risks (that is, privacy abuse, surveillance, disinformation, tax avoidance, regulation, labour issues, and so on).

It creates different accumulation problems from the ones described by the school of monopoly capitalism in the 1960s and 1970s. GAFAM depends largely on legal forms, which allow it to take a cut from growing economies through surplus value extraction and exclusive ownership of technology. Moreover, capital accumulation cannot occur without legal mediation because intangible technology can be easily copied and reproduced. Specific forms of intellectual property such as copyright and patents are the condition for the intangibles such as code, software, data to be defined and treated as elements within the capitalist mode of production, as capital and commodity. This means that production, consumption, and usage (within chains of production) of technological forms cannot be solely theorized from an economic perspective. In other words, socio-political factors are essential for construction of capital and commodities as prerequisites for private accumulation of wealth.

Uncontrolled capital accumulation opens up the question of social distribution of rewards from technological innovation on digital platforms. Their business models were built on top of publicly funded and developed telecommunications infrastructure, public education in computing and engineering, household investments in digital equipment, and internet user activities such as online socialization and political engagement. This is the point of departure for political action in digital monopoly platform conditions. Societies and the public should have a stake in managing how technological forms serve their needs instead of being subordinated to what is often ideologically engineered as a technical necessity in the form of latest commodities aiding profit-seeking goals. The public has the right to demand redistribution of rewards from innovation to develop underfunded public services, democratize technology and the economy, and promote new sets of digital rights. Justifications for such political actions are not moral. They are social and economic, based on understanding how digital monopolies extract surplus value, weaken technological diffusion, hamper innovation, and pauperize populations while depriving them of potential gains from the utilization of technological forms within different social and economic forms of production.

Re-imagining technological forms

Our experiential horizon of technological forms is circumscribed by their design characteristics and profit-seeking motives embedded in them. These forms implement solutions that allow people to socialize, network, search for information, read news, and participate in politics, store information, do business, and purchase commodities. At the same time, experiential dimensions of technological forms in our everyday lives allow companies to commodify our digital traces, monitor our everyday activities, invade our privacy, trade our personal data, distribute disinformation, and exploit platform labour all in order to streamline and improve the efficiency of connecting advertisers with potential consumers. From a purely economic standpoint, improving algorithms to perform these activities as quickly, efficiently, and precisely as possible is perfectly rational. At the same time, distributing disinformation and hate to enhance emotional engagement on digital platforms and increase profit rates is downright dystopian.

Technological forms are contradictory since they are experiential, embedded in everyday lives on the one hand, and systemic and capitalist, key to capital accumulation, on the other hand. They are rational (technical, scientific, mathematical) and instrumental within the capitalist mode of production, but that does not entail progressive social values nor does it enhance democratic processes (performing surveillance, distributing fake news, helping spread prejudice, feeding fear and conspiracies). How is it possible that such technological forms exist? Why are they to such a degree outside of social responsibility and oversight? How can we theoretically describe their contradictory existence by reconciling these seemingly polar opposites? Can we change technological forms to reflect human needs better?

One of the main contributions of the Frankfurt School to Marxian theory is their sweeping critique of instrumental rationality in markets, administration, and technology as explained in Chapter 2. Rationality is not inherently progressive as it also unleashes destructive forces of dominance. Hence, rationality is not neutral as it implies a system of mostly unspoken interests. This is particularly relevant with digital platforms because corporations controlling platforms often resort to technical arguments to justify their business models and distance themselves from social harms they help create. The critique of instrumental rationality is necessary to deal with technological fetishism as it allows us to understand technologies as socially constructed and, more importantly, as embedded in a broader chain of commodities exchanged for surplus value extraction.

There is nothing inherently bad about technologies and technics, as Marcuse called the technical apparatus of technology. The social and economic determination of forms defines the final shape that technical solutions (for social networking, web search, and so on) acquire as technological forms within the capitalist mode of production, making them into tools for control and dominance along the way. As Feenberg (2014, p 120) argues, the Frankfurt School developed rudiments for a concept of social bias appropriate for the analysis of rational systems. He extends and summarizes this position clearly:

> As technologies develop, their social background is forgotten, covered by a kind of unconsciousness that makes it seem as though the chosen path of progress was inevitable and necessary all along. This is what gives rise to the illusion of pure rationality. That illusion obscures the imagination of future alternatives by granting existing technology and rationalized social arrangements an appearance of necessity they cannot legitimately claim. Critical theory demystifies this appearance to open up the future. It is neither utopian nor dystopian but situates rationality within the political where its consequences are a challenge to human responsibility. (2014, p 120)

Data commodification and capital accumulation are the final outcomes of cumulative public investments, innovations from engineering communities, commercialization efforts and financial market crashes, permissive regulatory environments, capital expansion through mergers and acquisitions, and other developments described in Chapters 5, and 6. All of these conditions influenced how means of production and labour were utilized to produce technological forms, commodify captured usage data, and accumulate capital.

By evoking social conditions that gave birth to the rise of contemporary technological forms, and challenging their profit-seeking mechanisms of surplus value extraction, different types of technological forms can be envisioned. Marcuse argued for the development of new science (1971) but did not provide a pathway for such a utopian goal. As Feenberg (2014) argues, he failed to distinguish between science and technology, which opened his argument for widespread criticism. As one of the intellectual figures of the New Left in the 1960s, Marcuse also called for the Great Refusal, which implied resistance to various systems of dominance. Refusal to participate in surplus value extraction mechanisms that cause social harms came recently from a coalition of different civil rights and other groups under the name Stop Hate for Profit.

In June 2020, the group called major advertisers to boycott Facebook and stop advertising on the platform due to the company's reluctant approach to deal with hate speech during parliamentary elections and social protests in the United States. A few days after the boycott started, more than 800 companies worldwide stopped advertising on

Facebook, including some big brand names such as Coca-Cola and Unilever (Scola, 2020). The coalition issued a list of ten demands to Facebook such as establishing a civil rights expert among Facebook's executives to evaluate products and policies for discrimination, bias, and hate (Stop Hate for Profit, 2020). This is certainly a common way of protesting, much in line with historical types of boycotts. However, it is also unique in targeting the economic foundations of a technological form.

Although the boycott had an immediate effect on Facebook's market value, the ultimate success of such refusals will depend on how much they will threaten Facebook's long-term revenue streams and if they will expand the boycott to include users. Facebook relies on major advertisers, but it also relies on a long tail of small advertisers targeting niche audiences. Responding to the boycott, Mark Zuckerberg said that the company will not change its policies because of a threat to a small percentage of their revenue, guessing that the advertisers will be back on the platform because the boycott is 'just a reputational issue' (Sonnemaker, 2020). In order to be successful, the boycott should also include a big section of Facebook's 2.32 billion users worldwide (Statista, 2020).

The corporate business model is held together by capital, advertising, and legal forms as much as it is by social habit and daily routines of its users. So far, Facebook's users do not consider platform usage to be a political matter and it is likely that the majority of them never will. While not physically or legally coerced, they rely on their daily habits in conditions of hardly existing alternative platforms. Regardless of immediate or long-term success, the boycott opens the way for envisioning and imagining different technological forms that would serve human needs and democratic goals better. If algorithms can be constructed to deliver consumers to advertisers, they could also be streamlined to perform socially responsible, democratic functions. The history of social protests teaches us that the tipping point for change is often the result of long-term struggles and pressures for realizing a different type of society.

Public wealth and value: recognition, advocacy, and public policy

Behind the visible outputs of digital monopoly platforms, there is a vast, yet poorly visible, history of public wealth production on which the development of contemporary commodity-based platforms depended on. One of the common attributes of this background wealth production – such as publicly funded not-for-profit production of science and technology, Free Software, and similar productions – is that it is available free of direct (at the point of use) monetary charge to end users. While this feature is shared by the central products of advertising-funded digital platforms, the social and economic forms of these productions differ significantly. Advertising-funded digital platforms are firmly embedded in the global production and valorization of commodities. Social forms of production not driven by nor under the direct control of capital are not autonomous from it either. They are also to various extents functionally integrated and subordinated to the needs of reproduction of the capitalist mode of production. However, they nevertheless constitute different social forms of production, whose characters can be theoretically grasped and captured by considering their specificities. To refer to outputs of such productions, to denote non-commodity social forms of wealth with a single term, we use the concept public wealth. We say that production of public wealth occurs in the background due to the lack of conceptual and theoretical apparatus to grasp its peculiar features.

Despite our methodological commitment to value-form theories that tie us to the internal link between value and money for production within the capitalist mode of production, we keep an open mind for different approaches. For instance, an integrated understanding of value and wealth production, hopefully encompassing other social forms of production, beyond the capitalist one, may be equally, if not more, productive in the long run.[11] For now, given this link between wealth and value, it follows that all monetized producers of public wealth, including those we find in public sector, non-governmental institutions, do produce value within the capitalist mode of production; national accounts recognize this by equating their output with inputs in monetary terms. However, from the perspective of policymaking and advocacy in favour of recognition, improvement, and expansion of the production of public wealth and value, this equation of output and input and the focus on monetary aggregates alone remain major obstacles. Put differently, as long as national accounts show it is only the commodity producing units that are capable of delivering surpluses, it will remain difficult for policy arguments and public sector advocates to argue in favour of the expansion of the production of public wealth.[12]

A methodological approach by which the existence of various social forms of production and their specificities can be accounted for and to an extent integrated in the dominant mainstream narratives and statistical accounts of wealth and value production would enable us to escape the current situation. It would move us beyond positions in which the production of public wealth and value is seen at best, even by the governments themselves, as the supporting framework for commodity production (Mazzucato, 2018a, Chapter 8). While economic theories, especially in the mainstream of the discipline, tend to claim neutrality from social affairs and objectivity in their approach, the social construction of statistical sets, the underlying data that economic theories have to use to validate their propositions, is especially visible in national accounts. There, the state and science combine their authority, using it predominantly to facilitate markets and competition (Desrosières, 2010, pp 334–5) through historical construction and international consolidation of standards, driven by a blend of economic and political motivations and goals (Schmelzer, 2016; Coyle, 2017b).

The free of monetary charge products, such as those we focus on in the book, and research and development of intangible products rank among the biggest problems in 'adequately observing and measuring many aspects of "real life"' (Vanoli, 2017, pp 247–8). With intangibles, products that can be stored digitally and replicated at near zero-cost, there are two distinct types of valuations that can be applied: private, when consumption or use of a product is limited by designating it as private property (an entity that can be privately owned), and social, when products can be copied and used freely by anyone (Nakamura, 2010, p S143). Since the great social value of works has to be restricted in order for private value to be achievable, Nakamura asks, how do we reconcile those two valuations?

In our understanding, the first valuation is achieved through legal forms that enable construction of the commodity form for the purposes of surplus value extraction. It is a political regulation by which a specific social form of output is brought into existence so that economic determination of form suitable to the capitalist mode of production can take place. The second one is a form of public wealth, whose better understanding remains to be developed. Yet, utilizing the existing system for the construction of legal forms to construct non-commodity alternatives in order to fend off the intrusion of the capitalist mode of production into non-commodified sphere has a limited reach. The alternative use of licensing by FLOSS, Creative Commons, and Open Publishing, seems to 'frequently fail to secure broader transformative effects as the competitive forces of the market appropriate, marginalize, or make obsolete the alternatives they advocate' (Medak & Mars, 2019, p 55). Recognizing the specificities of social and economic determination of forms of such productive efforts and bringing them under an umbrella concept of public wealth production, one that captures the production beyond the capitalist mode of production in a way that can be fitted into existing statistical and accounting frameworks, would make public wealth advocacy and policy making easier. Such an approach should be able to connect public investments with the proliferation of intangible wealth, and with other forms of productions whose provision can be socially constructed as public wealth.

Data, democracy, and development

Data has been hailed as the new oil. The largest datasets are currently locked inside technological forms and business models within commodity chains. While there is a justified fear of governments' uses of citizens' data, it is currently poorly regulated and deployed solely as the means to private wealth through surplus value extraction. Yet, covering the consumption side, raw, anonymized data on our on-line behaviour and more generally on our recordable interactions and transactions can be reconceptualized and deployed as a raw material that informs the production of all sorts of public wealth. On the production side, value is being extracted by the most developed countries from the rest of the world in a variety of ways (Smith, 2015). While the political force to do so seems currently beyond any plausibly imaginable scenario, there are proposals,[13] even within the national accounting literature, to come up with international standards for data collection on firms and their activities (Nakamura & Nakamura, 2015). Such an approach would improve the analysis of global flows of funds, materials and produced outputs, opening up the space for alternative narratives and accounts of value and wealth production.

In a narrower and more strictly economic sense, such raw data feeds would provide us with unprecedented insights on both production and consumption. Extending the notion of democracy into the economic sphere, Nakamura and Nakamura argue, is the sign of a true democracy, so that populations can express their views on how their needs are met within the current socio-economic arrangements. The public could be asked to participate in the construction of alternatives indexes and dashboards showing the variety of measurements, moving beyond the current strong focus on single measure approach while having public debates on what moving beyond GDP may be (Coyle, 2017a). In a broader socio-economic sense, the extent, the productive contribution, and the location of the burden of household activities could be understood far better through household data analysis. The contribution of household activities to the overall production of wealth may be accounted for and its production imagined alternatively accordingly, taking into account social reproduction as a whole (Bhattacharya, 2017).

Finally, there is the broadest sense of reproduction, one that includes natural resources along with social and economic aspects. In this literature, where public wealth gets frequently referred to indirectly, with occasionally explicit mention of the term as a positive entity but without any definition, data of all kinds may be used to envisage the totality of human interactions with nature, accounting better for the human interaction with the finite biophysical infrastructure of the planet (Domazet et al, 2020).[14]

In all those scopes, from the strictly economic to the broadest eco-social one, standardization and access to a broad range of diverse data on production, consumption and all of their constitutive elements would enable the construction of arguments for more production of public wealth in a variety of forms. While private commodity production gets its validation and socialization through the act of exchange, the production of public wealth by the public sector, NGOs, or within networks of self-organized producers, requires planning and budgeting. That is where its socialization resides. The political processes and supporting institutional architecture are unavoidable elements of the systemic approach to such productive arrangements.

Extending the coverage of populations with new types of public wealth productions, especially those that strive to be universally available to all according to agreed criteria, in the mould of public health and education, would benefit immensely from access to data and from implementation of technological forms constructed for such purposes. In publicly funded productions, given their more direct and open socialization, lacking the need to be closed down as private activities, as capital-driven productions do, 'externalities' can finally be accounted for. Both in the sense of finite biophysical resources, and in the sense of the potential for full emancipation of all that keeps getting simultaneously propelled forward and shackled by the self-expansion of capital as the goal of human development in itself.

If the production of public wealth overpowers capitalist commodities, so that wealth starts appearing as a collection of public social forms, the development of human beings and their material and social well-being may change qualitatively. Through a democratic takeover and control of use of data as raw material by which decisions on the production of public wealth may be made, human development may cease to be a side effect of the capital-driven economic sphere. The seemingly endless growth of private forms of wealth and accompanying inequalities that privilege the tiny minority may cease to be attractive as a promise of equality of opportunity through individual ownership and control over wealth and labour of other humans. Democratizing data and re-imagining technological forms beyond the currently existing surplus value extracting digital platforms could be an important step toward post-capitalist sustainable development based on public wealth.

Notes

Chapter 1

[1] During 2019 an impressive number of policy papers and studies were written to inform regulators in different countries. Some of them include the Joint Memorandum of the Belgian, Dutch and Luxembourg Competition Authorities; the report by the German 'Kommission Wettbewerbsrecht 4.0'; the report prepared by the BRICS countries entitled 'Digital Era Competition: A BRICS View'; the 'Stigler Report' prepared in the US by the 'Stigler Committee on Digital Platforms'; the 'Digital platforms inquiry' by the Australian Competition Authority; the Report of the European Commission on 'Competition policy for the digital era'; and the 'Furman Report' on 'Unlocking digital competition' prepared for the British government.

[2] Microsoft was founded in 1975, Apple in 1976.

[3] For tables with date of drafts, publications, and topics, see Reuten (2003), p 150; Heinrich (2009), pp 86–7; Roth (2010), p 1227. For the overall context of this issue, see Roth (2009); Linden and Hubmann (2018), pp 18–20.

[4] Michael Heinrich summarizes this position with clarity: 'The Marxian opus is a gigantic body of fragmentary theoretical work. Not only does it consist of unpublished and unfinished works; Marx's own research programme remained largely uncompleted. Above all, Marx's theoretical development does not consist solely of continuities, but also of a series of breaks. One cannot therefore regard Marx as a quarry from which to extract quotations, nor can one, without regard for context, pass off certain texts as "the" position of Marx. But that is exactly the common method among both many Marxists and many critics of Marx (2007).

[5] 'Marx's economic texts, as a whole, show on the one hand that there is no such thing as a completed major work by the name of Capital, and that on the other hand Marx's other economic writings cannot simply be classified as "preparatory works" which lead – as was thought when work on the MEGA2 began – towards Capital in a teleological fashion. The completion of the MEGA2's section on Capital shows that the section precisely does not reconstruct a "work" or a final theory formation, but documents Marx's unfinished research process' (Linden & Hubmann, 2018, p 25).

[6] For the advice to public sector institutions on grasping how algorithms operate, see AI Now Institute (2018); Whittaker et al (2018). For an overview of the use of algorithms on digital platforms in relation to labour and regulation, see Prug and Bilić (2021).

Chapter 2

[1] For the differences in this broad grouping of interpretations see Bidet (2007); Heinrich (2009); Elbe (2013).

[2] See Reuten and Williams (1989), p 62; Murray (1997); Smith (1997), pp 182–6; Murray and Badeen (2016).

[3] A more detailed understanding of the method by which Marx approached his construction of different social forms, the logic and procedure by which he identified the inadequacy of the categories utilized by the economists would help us to move beyond what we inherit from Marx's work, carrying our interpretation of his approach to contemporary issues of monopolistic digital platforms. This goes against the trend among the value-form and New Readings of Marx type of literature, where there is 'less consideration of empirical factors' than in many other strands of Marxism, and where focus instead falls largely on 'general laws of how capitalism proceeds through a series of social forms' (Pitts, 2017, p 3). However, we believe that extending Marx's approach of social and economic determination of forms carries a lot of promise for two research directions. First, for grasping the variations within the capitalist mode of production. Second, for grasping social and economic forms and causal mechanisms within other social forms of production, along with their position within the overall capitalist social formation and its systemic logic of expansion through realization of surplus value.

[4] Clarke also used the term 'determinate abstractions' to differentiate Marx's method from political economists, stating that such abstractions correspond to 'determinate social processes' (1991, p 141).

[5] There are different approaches to how Marx constructs his categories. Reuten partially sides with Murray's approach on social forms, but does not take up notions such as general and determinate abstractions (2000, pp 140–1). From his early works, Marx committed to an understanding of production, consumption and exchange as economic forms and categories that are historical and transitory (1846, pp 97, 102). His goal was 'to show that in the social domain naturalistic entities do not exist', with human needs, utility, wealth always defined and subsumed 'within a socio-historical constellation' (Reuten, 2003, p 153). Murray argues that Marx 'paid close attention to the logic and content of scientific categories' (1988, p xiv), examining their construction, criticizing idealist thinking that approaches the objects under study with 'some external, preconceived logic' (Murray, 1988, p 41). For example, such an approach stands in a stark contrast with neoclassical foundations, whose categories are fixed and given in advance, irrespective of the possibly changing object under study. For the neoclassical school, the point Marx raises has no relevance. Social type of production, social conditions in which individuals produce and consume, and the social form of the consumed outputs (predominantly commodities in capitalism) do not matter for the self-interested, utility-maximizing individual whose behaviour propels all systems of production in all ages forward, regardless of the social arrangements and the socio-economic form determination that necessarily takes place in human societies.

[6] One of the best examples of the mainstream approach is found in international standards for national accounting, debated and developed since 1947, used by the national statistical offices worldwide. The current standard for national accounting defines products as outputs with two kinds, goods, and services, without any reference to their specific social character (OECD, 2009, para. 6.10). Defining goods and services, transferable ownership and market transactions are

understood to be aspects that define production: 'Goods are physical, produced objects for which a demand exists, over which ownership rights can be established and whose ownership can be transferred from one institutional unit to another by engaging in transactions on markets' (OECD, 2009, para. 6.16). This is how the specific character of the public sector production is not considered by the conceptual framework.

7   Marx often wrote about social forms through critical evaluations of other political economists, pointing out their inability to 'grasp the difference between labour as a producer of something useful, a use value, and labour as a producer of exchange value, a specific social form of wealth' (Marx, 1859, p 277). From the first known draft to the final published versions of *Capital*, he introduces the duality of useful objects in the first paragraphs, emphasizing how usefulness of an object to humans is indifferent to the 'determined economic form', and thus, 'use value as such lies outside of the sphere of investigation of political economy' (Marx, 1859, p 270). Again, this is the approach opposite to that of neoclassical economics, where utility of an object, its use value we may say, is precisely the starting point and the centre of the theoretical approach around which the rest of the framework revolves and on top of which nearly everything else, including the theory of value, is built. Marx elaborated this methodological insights for ordering the two types of abstractions for the first time in Grundrisse (Marx, 1857/1987, p 195). Yet, he did not consistently stick to this method in *Capital*, presenting and developing both types of abstractions simultaneously instead (Murray, 1988, p 126, 2002b, p 162). This, however, does not stop from us re-reading the work through the lens of this methodological commitment to social and economic determination of form, applying the approach to contemporary phenomena.

8   In such cases when production is not driven by the extraction of surplus value, labour is not directly supervised nor directed by capitalist firms, and outputs do not take the commodity form, a series of questions – that we tackle at the end of this chapter and in subsequent chapters – arise. Primarily, what social form do means of production, labour, and other elements of production take in non-capitalist social forms of production? Moreover, which laws of motion, or what causal mechanisms, if any, drive such productions? If we pose a question whether Marx thought that human productive activity can take social forms other than what we find in the dominant capitalist form, his answer seems positive and logically necessary so given the methodology of social forms: 'wage labour is not an absolute, but rather a historical form of labour. It is not necessary for production that the worker's means of subsistence should confront him in an alienated form as capital. But the same is true of the other elements of capital' (1861, p 139). None of this means that productions with different social forms occurring in societies where the capitalist mode of production dominates escape being shaped to a certain extent by the dominant capitalist production and its needs. The key questions are rather concerning the functional integration of different social forms of production in the dominant mode of production and recognizing the specificities by which they differ despite of their minority position.

9   The legitimate questions are which of the two options is conceptually and analytically more meaningful and which can be drawn out more consistently from Marx's work as an interpretation that captures both what we think Marx had in mind along with our contemporary object of research. With the first option, social forms of production, we quickly run into problems with Marx's writing. For instance, in *Theories of Surplus Value*, Marx's economic manuscripts written

in preparation for *Capital*, discussing 'the labour of handicraftsmen and peasants in capitalist society', Marx writes how 'their production does not fall under the capitalist mode of production'. He unambiguously affirms the co-existence of different ways of producing as modes of production, with the dominant capitalist mode both imposing its surplus value producing logic on other modes and having a tendency to turn every activity into capitalist production (Marx, 1861/1963, pp 407–9). Equally so, Marx's assertion on the importance of the domination of single mode of production from the opening sentence of the first volume of *Capital* – in societies in 'which the capitalist mode of production prevails', 'the wealth ... appears as an "immense collection of commodities"' (1872/1976, p 125) – is a notion recurring throughout his work.

[10] A mistaken reading, such as Dobb's, Banaji argues, takes the existence of wage labour to be sufficient for the capitalist mode of production to be present. However, in the capitalist mode of production, Banaji contends, generalization of commodity labour power and the mobility of labour power 'became as essential to the laws of motion of capital as the ability of capital itself to operate on the world-scale' (Banaji, 2010).

[11] Marx spoke of 'form', 'determination of form', Rubin notes, pointing out how the meaning was expressed by Marx variety of terms: 'economic form', 'social form', 'historical-social form', 'social determination of form', 'economic determination of form', 'historical-social determination of form' (Rubin, 1928/1973, p 39).

[12] For an admission of this problem and subsequent attempts to overcome it within the neoclassical economics through various refinements through closely related research projects, such as marginal rate of substitution, indifference curves and revealed preferences, see Hamilton and Banco Mundial (2006), pp 15–18; Lenfant (2012); Hands (2014). For critiques, see Lewin (1996); Mirowski and Hands (1998); Syll (2016).

[13] The path towards social change from the perspective of the working class was to overthrow reified consciousness and to free itself from servitude. Commodity is the universal category of society as a whole (Lukács, 1972, p 86). 'Commodity relations' have decisive importance for the objective evolution of society and the stance adopted by humans towards it. Commodity becomes crucial to the subjugation of consciousness to the forms in which reification finds expression. However, there are key differences in the way he and Marx understood key dynamics and social forms within capitalism. For Lukács, capitalism is essentially a static, abstract quantitative form that is superimposed on the true nature of the concrete, qualitative, social content (Postone, 2003, p 92). Marx, on the other hand, did not analyse capitalism as structures that hide the 'real' historical Subject such as the proletariat. He saw those structures as fundamental relations of capitalist society which were historically dynamic (2003, p 96). The reification concept provided an approach that attempted to bridge economic and subjective categories.

[14] Perhaps the most theoretically elaborate relation between commodity form and thought form can be found in the work of Sohn-Rethel (1978), a distant affiliate of the Frankfurt School. His key concept was 'real abstraction', not the exclusive privilege of thought, but also an essential characteristic of human action. The commodity abstraction is therefore not thought-induced since it originates in human actions (Sohn-Rethel, 1978, p 20). Commodity exchange always occurs in specific historical conditions within specific spatial-temporal activities. The salient feature of the act of exchange is the separation, or abstraction, of the use of commodities from their exchange: 'this is an abstraction not in mind, but in fact.

It is a state of affairs prevailing at a definite place and lasting a definite time. It is the state of affairs which reigns on the market' (Sohn-Rethel, 1978, p 25). What Sohn-Rethel aims to do is to link social forms of commodity production with forms of cognition and action.

[15] Weber uses the term value to denote cultural value such as ethical positions and worldviews, not as an economic term denoting value-form theory and similar approaches.

[16] Such a conceptualization of potential transformation of capitalism through the establishment of new science and technology was a source of criticism pointed towards Marcuse by Jurgen Habermas. For an overview of the debate see Agger (1976) and Habermas (1987).

[17] Unlike many of the Frankfurt School theorists, often chastised for their cultural pessimism, Marcuse was active in writing about alternatives (for example, Marcuse, 1971). As Agger (1976, p 166) argues, Marcuse's concern with technological domination does not split him off from the critique of political economy. It adds another dimension to the critique of domination.

[18] In a different context, a similar argument about the social role of technology is visible. Under the Nazi regime, radio and mass media were the main tools for propaganda and indoctrination: 'In technology, there is no truth and falsehood, right and wrong, good and evil – there is only adequacy and inadequacy to a pragmatic end. Accordingly, under National Socialism, all standards and values, all patterns of thought and behaviour are dictated by the need for the incessant functioning of the machinery of production, destruction and domination' (Marcuse, 1998, p 161).

[19] For an account of the early history of the commercial software production from the1960s and 1970s, see Johnson (2002).

[20] In 1975, at the founding meeting of one of the historically important hobbyist engineers' club, Homebrew Computer Club, discussing what they wanted in the club 'the words people used most were "cooperation" and sharing' (Levy, 2010, p 202). The club inspired Steve Wozniak to start working on the computer that became the first Apple computer model (Levy, 2010, Chapter 12).

[21] This was sometimes called the viral effect of the Copyleft licences and it defined the fundamental difference between the two models, the proprietary and the free one: 'what distinguishes the models are the concepts of progress and the accompanying means of advancement ... In the classic schema of intellectual property, the granting of private rights fosters incentive for creation and invention. ... The very goal of copyleft is the promotion of knowledge based on the broadest possible distribution of work, on the 'creation of a common foundation to which each person can add his/her contribution, but from which no one can remove a contribution' (Dusollier, 2002, pp 286–8).

[22] Another concept that was frequently deployed by researchers to conceptualize FLOSS production was commons (Berry, 2008, Chapter 3), 'global common goods', or even 'global software commons' (Barron, 2013, p 616). The literature that develops and uses terms such as commons and peer-to-peer production to conceptualize specificities, differences of software and other production of similar kind is vast. The focus of the literature on modes of governance (more dominant in peer-to-peer focused accounts), digital non-commodified outputs and localized, mostly self-organized groups (coops, micro production), along with aversion to inclusion of monetized production (dominant commodity production and public sector outputs), puts it at odds with our approach. Nevertheless, we still see

significant overlap, and while it would be productive to engage with the commons and peer-to-peer literature, we lack space to do so in this book. For an overview of commons literature, see Hess (2008) and for peer-to-peer see *The Journal of Peer Production* and P2P Foundation publications.

23   There is a long-standing history of mainstream theorist deploying the term public to signify specific categories and theories aimed at advocating the capitalist mode of production, such as public goods, or public choice theory.

24   Throughout her work, and especially with the concepts such as entrepreneurial state and public value, Mariana Mazzucato has been demonstrating and explicitly referring to the importance of new rhetoric and a new vocabulary to think about the production beyond commodities and markets (Mazzucato, 2015, p 15, 2018a, sec. Preface).

25   For the story of how some leading members of Free Software movement where excluded from the Open Source founding meetings and the logic and rhetoric behind it, see Prug (2014), pp 54–6.

26   There is large body of work on this, for a useful introduction from the Open Source advocates who built successful businesses through this approach, see Goldman et al (2005), Introduction.

27   Some studies suggest that the behaviour of firms and their involvement in FLOSS communities should be observed from the perspective of firms' goals (Jullien & Zimmermann, 2011).

28   A study of 684 software developers in 287 FLOSS projects found out while it was often theorized that 'better jobs, career advancement' drove participation, 'enjoyment-based intrinsic motivation, namely how creative a person feels when working on the project, is the strongest pervasive driver' of individual motivations for participating (Lakhani & Wolf, 2003).

29   For Google Maps revenue estimates and analysis, see Franek (2019).

30   See Chapter 6. In *Capital* Vol II with the section on transportation (Marx, 1864/1978, pp 225–9) and Olsen (2017, pp 125–7).

31   Activities leading to the sales of final commodities, such as 'marketing, accounting, data processing, transportation, storage, maintenance, security' (OECD, 2009, para. 6.215), are called intermediate consumption in national accounting, reflecting their character as an expense consuming the potential value present in commodities. For a proposal that the cost of advertising on media with free content should be treated as final, instead of intermediate, consumption, and thus be included in GDP, see Nakamura (2015). For the complex relationship between calculations of logistics costs and the way GDP is calculated, see Candemir and Çelebi (2017).

32   See Chapters 5 and 6.

Chapter 3

1   See Hilferding (1910/2005); Lenin (1999).

2   For a discussion of the concept of economic surplus see Barclay et al (1975); Dawson and Foster (1991); Davis (1992); Foster (2014a).

3   The contemporary scholarship, such as Christoph Menke's (2020) extensive genealogy of modern rights, exposes many occasions of incompleteness and one-sidedness in Pashukanis' work, which prevented him to capture important aspects and contradictions arising out of the form of rights, that is, the legal form and the liberal discourse that supports it. Nonetheless, reading authors like Menke also affirms the soundness of the direction Pashukanis had taken the inquiry of modern

legal form, in particular, the centrality of the relationship between commodity and legal form for understanding the basic logic of capitalist system.

4   For an overview of the recent debates on the character of monopolies in contemporary platform capitalism and for an emerging new legal doctrine on monopoly see Khan (2016); Glick (2019).

Chapter 4

1   The problem with neoclassical economics is not only their focus on price, as Newman puts it, but also their focus on the consumption side, through their concept of utility, and their associated neglect of production side, which includes the neglect of profit making as the logic that drives producers and their actions. This leads to further neglect of circulation as the necessary phase of production in which outputs have to be sold, turned into revenue stream in order for value of the product, in the monetary sense, to be realized and divided among the involved actors. In our approach, platform businesses such as Google web search or Facebook social network develop by attracting users on one side of the platform, and producers of final commodities who pay for advertising in order to attract users to buy their products, on the other side of the platform. Some businesses generate revenue from consumers though subscriptions or through other types of payment, but the general model relies on dominating two separate sets of exchanges simultaneously: monetary one with advertisers, and non-monetary one with users who give consent to provide flows of data in return.

2   For an overview see Turow (2011); Hardy (2014), pp 135–56; McStay (2016).

3   Paul Baran was also a close friend of Herbert Marcuse. For their correspondence see Foster (2014b).

4   He explicitly criticizes Baran and Sweezy for falling back to media manipulation: 'But Baran and Sweezy fail to pursue in an historical materialist way the obvious issues which are raised by demand-management-via-advertising under monopoly capitalism. What happens when a monopoly capitalist system advertises? Baran and Sweezy answer ... *psychological* manipulation' (Smythe, 1977, p 4).

5   With regard to the printed press, Baker (1992) detailed four different ways in which the media adapt their messages when overly dependent on advertising revenue. First, they tend to treat advertisers' interests charitably in their reports. Second, the media create a buying mood favourable to advertisers. Third, the media try to make their content less partisan and less controversial to avoid offending advertisers' potential customers. Fourth, the media tend to favour audiences with greater purchasing power. Similarly, Hardy (2014, pp 152–4) outlines multiple factors that enhance advertising influence on media, which includes issues such as market conditions, marketing effectiveness, advertiser-media placement, corporate ownership and relationships, producer/produser cultures, user activities – practices and cultures, marketers' influence as media content providers, as well as governance and regulation.

6   Kevin Kelly's work is representative of this wave of writers (Kelly, 1998).

7   Fuchs, for example, points out his work on establishing alternative communication systems to defend the audience labour argument (2014a, pp 282–3).

8   Fuchs clarifies his position further: 'if the users become productive, then in terms of Marxian class theory this means that they become productive labourers who produce surplus value and are exploited by capital, because for Marx productive labour generates surplus. Therefore, the victims of exploitation of surplus value in

cases like Google, YouTube, MySpace, or Facebook are not merely those employed by these corporations for programming, updating, and maintaining the soft and hardware, performing marketing activities, and so on, but also the users and the produsers engaged in the production of user-generated content. New media corporations do not (or hardly) pay the users for the production of content. One accumulation strategy is to give them free access to services and platforms, let them produce content. ... While no product is sold to the users, the users themselves are sold as a commodity to advertisers. ... Capitalist Internet produsage is an extreme form of exploitation, in which the produsers work completely for free and are therefore infinitely exploited' (Fuchs, 2010, p 191).

Chapter 5

1 Patenting of publicly funded research in the US was introduced by the Bayh-Dole Act of 1980.

2 Some of the reasons behind the decision to register in Delaware include: (1) incremental royalty expense deductions in non-combined reporting states; (2) potential exclusion of foreign royalty income from the tax base in combined reporting states; (3) creation of a constitutional challenge to the taxation of foreign royalty income of Alphabet; and (4) domestic IP licence benchmark for foreign affiliates to allow for repatriation of offshore cash by higher royalty payments (Bogenschneider & Heilmeier, 2016).

3 In 2017, biggest advertisers in the US across all media were Comcast Corp. ($5.745 billion), Procter & Gamble Co. (4.387 billion), AT&T (3.520 billion), Amazon (3.379 billion) and General Motors Co. (3.244 billion). Worldwide, the biggest media advertising spenders were Samsung Electronics. Co. ($11.2 billion), Procter & Gamble Co. (10.5 billion), L'Oréal (8.6 billion), Unilever (8.5 billion), Nestlé (7.2 billion) (Neustar, 2018).

4 As of August 2020, Alphabet Inc. is 68.36 per cent owned by institutional investors, the biggest ones being Vanguard Group Inc., Blackrock Inc., Price T Rowe Associates Inc., and State Streets corp.

5 Digital Millennium Copyright Act in the US, E-Commerce Directive in Europe, The General Data Protection Regulation in the EU, court decisions on the right to be forgotten from the Court of Justice of the European Union, court decisions that require Google to suppress content not just in the jurisdiction of the issuing court, but also for all users worldwide, the US and international laws that restrict distribution of materials considered harmful to children, laws with regard to content removals and disclosure obligations such as the Network Enforcement Act in Germany, data protection laws, data localization laws, privacy laws, and so on (Alphabet Inc., 2018).

6 The Department of Justice (2020) argues that Google: (a) entered into exclusivity agreements that forbid preinstallation of any competing search service; (b) entered into tying and other agreements that force preinstallation of its search applications in prime locations on mobile devices and make them undeletable, regardless of consumer preferences; (c) entered into long-term agreements that require Google to be the default – and *de facto* exclusive – general search engine on Apple's popular Safari browser and other Apple search tools; (d) used monopoly profits to buy preferential treatment for its search engine on devices, web browsers,

and other search access points, creating a continuous and self-reinforcing cycle of monopolization.

[7] In 1997 an internal memo from Microsoft surfaced and contained four strategies: (1) identify the market leader; (2) emulate the market leader; (3) steal the vision, provide an integration path; (4) integrate, leverage, and erode (Greenstein, 2015, p 312).

Chapter 6

[1] Critics have argued that copyright is not an appropriate mechanism for social productions of volunteer and jointly authored collaborative work, since it 'fails to provide a proper toolkit for structuring the relationships among collaborators regarding their joint output', and 'it may also erect barriers to creating new content through collaboration', so that, in summary, 'the individualistic focus on the sovereignty of the owner regarding the use of the work and the legal power to exclude others, which is the essence of the proprietary approach to copyright, may conflict with the fundamentals of social production' (Elken-Koren, 2011, pp 337–8).

[2] See how a software engineer turned journalist describes the differences between Copyleft and Open Source licences and benefit of the later to profit making companies (Barr, 2001).

[3] See also the critique of idealizations of Free Software as a germ of a post-capitalist society (Nuss & Heinrich, 2001) and contextualization provided by Medak (2013).

[4] As Birkbine demonstrated with his analysis of Oracle acquisition of MySQL AB and subsequent development of MySQL community fork MariaDB, there are significant differences of FLOSS production within the capitalist mode of production, with hybrid social forms of production, erecting legal boundaries to the imposition of commodity form. In the author's words: 'MariaDB represents another example of how communities of FLOSS projects maintain the ability to protect their commons-based resource against unwanted corporate influence' (Birkinbine, 2015, p 11).

[5] For patents, registered knowledge that becomes property must be new, not obvious, useful, or applicable in industry. Copyright covers literary works, artistic works, musical works, maps, technical drawings, photography, and audio-visual works.

[6] To be more precise: 'A patent provides its owner the exclusive right over the commercial exploitation of the invention for a limited period of time in return for disclosing the invention to the public. The theory behind the system is that the financial reward flowing from the exploitation of the patent and the public disclosure of the resulting inventions would encourage further innovation, thereby raising the technical level of a nation's industry with the obvious resultant trade advantages' (WIPO, 2003).

[7] A case in point are long-running legal battles and patent wars between Samsung, Apple, and HTC, some of the largest smartphone manufacturers (see Jin, 2015).

[8] Yet it is important to stress that monopoly profits can be secured by any monopolistic firm, irrespective of whether its products are immaterial or, instead, fully corporeal and tangible (Parkhurst, 2019, p 84).

[9] An intriguing side story is Google's famous 20 per cent rule, which allowed their workers to devote 20 per cent of their time to different side projects of their choosing in order to be more creative and innovative, hoping. This internal attempt to mimic how workers select their own projects and tasks in FLOSS production

resulted in some side projects growing into widely used products such as Google News, Gmail, and AdSense. Naturally, ownership over these products remains with the company, with social form of output determined by the needs of Google's business model. This suggests that the self-selection of projects and tasks by workers is not intrinsic to Free Software social form of production.

10   Unlike traditional advertising, the SEO industry provides consultation on how to improve 'organic' search results, which are not paid as advertisements. The SEO industry follows each update and then provides consultation to website owners on how to organize and manage content and improve placement on Google's organic search results. The total worth of the SEO industry in the United States is estimated to reach $80 billion in 2020 (McCue, 2018).

11   The European Union's General Data Protection Regulation (GDPR) (European Parliament, 2016) is often hailed as a benchmark for data protection worldwide. However, while offering unique solutions to data protection, there are also major problems with this directive, as it does not sufficiently connect data privacy with antitrust legislation (Cremer et al, 2019).

12   A detailed list of requirements is available in FTC (2019b).

13   All of these technical solutions result in different technological forms that can economically be determined as either commodities or pre-commodities, depending on whether they imply a monetary exchange or not. All of them imply some sort of data exchange, which is necessary for their proper functioning on the user side, and on the owner side.

14   Subcommittee on Antitrust, Commercial and Administrative Law of the US House of Representatives.

15   These calculations are estimates and not exact figures. Estimates are based on the calculation methodology developed by Dwayne Winseck from Carleton University, Canada, and used for market share calculations in the Canadian Media Concentration Research project, available at www.cmcrp.org/ (accessed 5 June 2020). The methodology was applied in Bilić and Primorac (2018). The main data sources for the estimate include SEC Form 10-Ks for Google and Facebook, Internet Advertising Bureau's (IAB) European AdEx reports, and Statista for national Internet users and Facebook users. The figures include calculations for all European countries present in the IAB AdEx reports. The countries that are not included in those reports are Cyprus, Estonia, Latvia, Liechtenstein, Lithuania, Luxembourg, Malta, and Portugal.

16   Remaining taxation proposals are unilateral (Geringer, 2020) and led by France, which looks to tax digital giants directly and improve the status of the news industry. France is the first state in which antitrust authorities ordered Google to negotiate with publishers to pay for the news content shown in search results (Chavern, 2020).

Chapter 7

1   For example, in the case of legislators' practices, Castner notes how 'although Congress formally extended copyright protection to computer programs nearly twenty years ago, key court decisions and many commentators have doggedly argued such protection is either inappropriate or very narrow' (Castner, 1997, p 39). Another example are the differences in decisions of juries, judges, and appeal courts in litigations involving the question of whether copyright protection should cover application public interfaces (Frankel & Forrest, 2018; von Lohmann, 2017).

[2] For many useful insights through the prism of hacking the existing socio-economic order, see Söderberg (2007).

[3] Google has been in court for years of JAVA API with Sun, now owned by Oracle. For the roots of Google/Oracle conflict, see Gratz and Lemley (2017); Menell (2016), sec. B, and for why Android team selected Java and their own Java Virtual Machine (it allowed them to use an Open Source licence, instead of less permissive GPL), see Menell (2016), sec. The Android Platform.

[4] According to the European Commission (2017b), digital international companies operating in the business to consumer (B2C) model paid 10.1 per cent, while the digital international companies in the business to business (B2B) model paid 8.9 per cent effective tax rate in the European Union Members States. At the same time, companies operating within a traditional international business model producing and selling physical goods paid an average 23.2 per cent effective tax rate.

[5] Apple Operations Europe (AOE).

[6] The full name is Council Directive laying down rules for corporate taxation of a significant digital presence.

[7] The full name is Council Directive on a common system of a digital service tax on revenues resulting from provision of certain digital services.

[8] Significant digital presence is reached if one of the following criteria are met. Revenues from providing digital services to users in a jurisdiction exceeds €7,000,000 in a tax period. The number of users of a digital service in a Member State exceeds 100,000 in a tax period. The number of business contracts for digital services exceeds 3,000 (European Commission, 2018b). This measure was intended to tax corporate profits in countries where they are made and to integrate this new taxation policy within the scope of the Common Consolidated Corporate Tax Base.

[9] Tax revenues were to be collected by Member States where users are located and applied only to companies with total annual worldwide revenue of €750 million and EU revenues of €50 million to avoid burdening smaller start-ups and scale-up businesses. A 3 per cent tax rate was expected to generate €5 billion in revenues a year for Member States (2018c).

[10] For example, it could easily be envisioned that a DST tax revenue is used for funding independent regulatory bodies that would allocate funds to democracy strengthening projects and initiatives, in addition to monitoring and regulating digital markets. The Digital Competition Expert Panel proposed to the UK government an establishment of a digital regulator for monitoring competition in the digital market. See Furman et al (2019).

[11] For an approach that defends physiological concept of abstract labour through a critique of Rubin's approach to value-form theory, see Kicillof and Starosta (2007), and for a critical evaluation that situates it in a broader context of related Marxist debates, see Bonefeld (2014), Chapter 6.

[12] The paradox that medical equipment produces no net return when used in a public hospital but does so when used in a private clinic is recognized in national accounting literature, with the conclusion that 'the present method of valuing non-market output significantly understates the contribution of general government to GPD' (OECD, 2014, p 115). Intuitively, both provide new added value, with output being more valuable than its inputs. However, the surplus shows only in private, commodified, surplus value oriented activity. One way to re-think contributions of public wealth may be to reconceptualize the notion of surplus beyond added

value in monetary terms. De-growth literature seems the logical field to engage with for such questions, but we lack the space to do so here.

[13] For the most concrete practical set of proposals focused on the importance of data and it uses beyond current technological forms, see DiEM25 (2019).

[14] For a de-growth based perspective on uses of technology for post-capitalist development, see Medak (2017), and for number of promising approaches towards a political economy of de-growth, see Chertkovskaya et al (2019).

References

Abbate, J. (1999). *Inventing the Internet*. MIT Press.

Ackerman, S.A., & Rushe, D. (2014). Microsoft, Facebook, Google and Yahoo release US surveillance requests. *The Guardian*. www.theguardian.com/world/2014/feb/03/microsoft-facebook-google-yahoo-fisa-surveillance-requests

Agger, B. (1976). Marcuse & Habermas on new science. *Polity*, *9*(2), 158–81. https://doi.org/10.2307/3234393

AI Now Institute. (2018). *Algorithmic Accountability Policy Toolkit*. AI Now Institute. https://ainowinstitute.org/aap-toolkit.pdf

Albritton, R. (2003). Superseding Lukács: A contribution to the theory of subjectivity. In R. Albritton & J. Simoulidis (Eds), *New Dialectics and Political Economy* (pp 60–77). Palgrave Macmillan.

Allmer, T. (2012). *Towards a Critical Theory of Surveillance in Informational Capitalism*. Peter Land.

Alphabet Inc. (2017). 2016 10-K form. www.sec.gov/Archives/edgar/data/1652044/000165204417000008/goog10-kq42016.htm

Alphabet Inc. (2018). 2017 10-K form. www.sec.gov/Archives/edgar/data/1652044/000165204418000007/goog10-kq42017.htm

Alphabet Inc. (2020). 2019 10-K form. www.sec.gov/Archives/edgar/data/1652044/000165204420000008/goog10-k2019.htm

Al-Rayes, H.T. (2012). Studying main differences between Android and Linux operating systems. *International Journal of Electrical and Computer Sciences*, *12*(5), 46–9.

Althusser, L. (2014). *On the Reproduction of Capitalism: Ideology and Ideological State Apparatuses*. Verso.

Amazon Workers and Supporters. (2018, 20 June). *'Stop Treating Us Like Dogs!': Worker Resistance at Amazon in Poland*. Pluto Press. www.plutobooks.com/blog/worker-resistance-amazon-poland/

Amin, S. (2010). *The Law of Worldwide Value*. Monthly Review Press.

Amoore, L., & Piotukh, V. (2015). Life beyond big data: Governing with little analytics. *Economy and Society*, *44*(3), 341–66. https://doi.org/10.1080/03085147.2015.1043793

Ananny, M. (2016). Toward an ethics of algorithms: Convening, observation, probability, and timeliness. *Science, Technology, & Human Values, 41*(1), 93–117. https://doi.org/10.1177/0162243915606523

Ananny, M., & Crawford, K. (2018). Seeing without knowing: Limitations of the transparency ideal and its application to algorithmic accountability. *New Media & Society, 20*(3), 973–89. https://doi.org/10.1177/1461444816676645

Andrejevic, M. (2002). The work of being watched: Interactive media and the exploitation of self-disclosure. *Critical Studies in Media Communication, 19*(2), 230–48. https://doi.org/10.1080/07393180216561

Arthur, C. (2012). *Digital Wars: Apple, Google, Microsoft and the Battle for the Internet.* Kogan Page.

Asay, M. (2005). Open Source and the commodity urge: Disruptive models for a disruptive development process. In C. DiBona, M. Stone, & D. Cooper (Eds), *Open Sources 2.0: The Continuing Evolution* (pp 103–19). O'Reilly Media.

Backhaus, H.G. (1980). On the dialectics of the value-form. *Thesis Eleven, 1*(1), 99–120. https://doi.org/10.1177/072551368000100108

Baker, C.E. (1992). Advertising and a democratic press. *University of Pennsylvania Law, 140*(6), 2097–43.

Baker, D., Jayadev, A., & Stiglitz, J. (2017). *Innovation, Intellectual Property, and Development: A Better Set of Approaches for the 21st Century.* AccessIBSA.

Banaji, J. (2010). *Theory as History: Essays on Modes of Production and Exploitation.* Brill Academic Publishers.

Baran, P. (1973). *The Political Economy of Growth.* Penguin Books.

Baran, P., & Sweezy, P. (1968). *Monopoly Capital: An Essay on the American Economic and Social Order.* Modern Reader Paperbacks.

Baran, P., & Sweezy, P. (2013a). The quality of monopoly capitalist society: Culture and communications. *Monthly Review, 65*(3), 43–64.

Baran, P., & Sweezy, P. (2013b). Theses on advertising. *Monthly Review, 65*(3), 34–42.

Barbrook, R., & Cameron, A. (1996). The Californian ideology. *Science as Culture, 6*(1), 44–72. https://doi.org/10.1080/09505439609526455

Barclay, W.J., & Stengel, M. (1975). Surplus and surplus value. *Review of Radical Political Economics, 7*(4), 48–64. https://doi.org/10.1177/048661347500700404

Barr, J. (2001, 23 May). Live and let license. *ITWorld.* https://web.archive.org/web/20030207093359/http://www.itworld.com/AppDev/350/LWD010523vcontrol4/

Barron, A. (2013). Free software production as critical social practice. *Economy and Society, 42*(4), 597–625. https://doi.org/10.1080/03085147.2013.791510

BBC News. (2017). *Google News Boss: "We Don't Produce Media."* BBC News. www.bbc.com/news/av/technology-41251246/google-news-boss-we-re-not-a-media-company

Bellofiore, R., & Riva, T.R. (2015). The Neue Marx-Lektüre. Putting the critique of political economy back into the critique of society. *Radical Philosophy*, *189*, 24–36.

Berry, D.M. (2008). *Copy, Rip, Burn: The Politics of Copyleft and Open Source: The Politics of Open Source.* Pluto Press.

Bhattacharya, T. (Ed.). (2017). *Social Reproduction Theory: Remapping Class, Recentring Oppression.* Pluto Press.

Bidet, J. (2007). New interpretations of capital. In S. Kouvelakis & J. Bidet (Eds), & G. Elliott (Trans.), *Critical Companion to Contemporary Marxism* (pp 369–83). Brill.

Bilić, P. (2016). Search algorithms, hidden labour and information control. *Big Data & Society*, *3*(1), 205395171665215. https://doi.org/10.1177/2053951716652159

Bilić, P. & Primorac, J. (2018). The digital advertising gap and the online news industry in Croatia. *Media Studies*, *9*(18), 62–80.

Bilić, P. & Prug, T. (2020). Google's post-IPO development: Risks, rewards, and shareholder value. *Internet Histories*. https://doi.org/10.1080/24701475.2020.1864959

Birkinbine, B.J. (2015). Conflict in the commons: Towards a political economy of corporate involvement in free and Open Source Software. *The Political Economy of Communication*, *2*(2), 3–19.

Bogenschneider, B., & Heilmeier, R. (2016). Google's "Alphabet soup" in Delaware. *Houston Business and Tax Law Journal*, *16*(1), 31.

Bohn, D. (2020, 14 January). Google to 'Phase Out' Third-party Cookies in Chrome, but Not for Two Years. The Verge. www.theverge.com/2020/1/14/21064698/google-third-party-cookies-chrome-two-years-privacy-safari-firefox

Bonefeld, W. (2014). *Critical Theory and the Critique of Political Economy: On Subversion and Negative Reason.* Bloomsbury 3PL.

Bork, R.H. (1966). Legislative intent and the policy of the Sherman Act. *Journal of Law and Economics*, *9*, 7–48.

Bork, R.H. (1993). *The Antitrust Paradox* (2nd edn). Free Press.

Bork, R.H., & Sidak, J.G. (2012). What does the Chicago School teach about internet search and the antitrust treatment of Google? *Journal of Competition Law & Economics*, *8*(4), 663–700. https://doi.org/10.1093/joclec/nhs031

Borodovsky, L. (2020, 22 June). Stock market continues to ignore looming US political risks. *The Wall Street Journal.*

boyd, danah m., & Crawford, K. (2012). Critical questions for big data: Provocations for a cultural, technological, and scholarly phenomenon. *Information, Communication & Society*, *15*(5), 662–79. https://doi.org/10.1080/1369118X.2012.678878

boyd, danah m., & Ellison, N.B. (2007). Social network sites: Definition, history, and scholarship. *Journal of Computer-Mediated Communication*, *13*(1), 210–30. https://doi.org/10.1111/j.1083-6101.2007.00393.x

Boyd-Barrett, O. (1977). Media imperialism: Towards an international framework for the analysis of media systems. In J. Curran & M. Gurevitch (Eds), *Mass Communication and Society* (pp 116–35). Edward Arnold.

Boyd-Barrett, O. (2006). Cyberspace, globalization and empire. *Global Media and Communication*, *2*(1), 21–41. https://doi.org/10.1177/1742766506061815

Boyle, J. (2003). The second enclosure movement and the construction of the public domain. *Law and Contemporary Problems*, *66*(1/2), 33–74. JSTOR.

Braverman, H. (1998). *Labor and Monopoly Capital: The Degradation of Work in the Twentieth Century* (25th anniversary ed). Monthly Review Press.

Brin, S., & Page, L. (1998, 14 April). *The Anatomy of a Large-Scale Hypertextual Web Search Engine*. Seventh International World-Wide Web Conference (WWW 1998), Brisbane, Australia.

Brown, V.F. (1987). The incompatibility of copyright and computer software: An economic evaluation and a proposal for a marketplace solution comment. *North Carolina Law Review*, *66*(5), 977–1022.

Bryan, D., Rafferty, M., & Wigan, D. (2017). Capital unchained: Finance, intangible assets and the double life of capital in the offshore world. *Review of International Political Economy*, *24*(1), 56–86. https://doi.org/10.1080/09692290.2016.1262446

Bunn, D., Asen, E., & Enache, C. (2020). *Digital Taxation around the World*. Tax Foundation.

Burnette, E. (2008, 4 June). Patrick Brady dissects Android. *ZDNet*. www.zdnet.com/article/patrick-brady-dissects-android/

Burrell, J. (2016). How the machine 'thinks': Understanding opacity in machine learning algorithms. *Big Data & Society*, *3*(1), 205395171562251. https://doi.org/10.1177/2053951715622512

Cadwalladr, C., & Graham-Harrison, E. (2018, 17 March). Revealed: 50 million Facebook profiles harvested for Cambridge Analytica in major data breach. *The Guardian*. www.theguardian.com/news/2018/mar/17/cambridge-analytica-facebook-influence-us-election

Candemir, Y., & Çelebi, D. (2017). An inquiry into the analysis of the transport and logistics sectors' role in economic development. *Transportation Research Procedia*, *25*, 4692–707. https://doi.org/10.1016/j.trpro.2017.05.317

Caraway, B. (2011). Audience labor in the new media environment: A Marxian revisiting of the audience commodity. *Media, Culture & Society*, *33*(5), 693–708. https://doi.org/10.1177/0163443711404463

Carchedi, G. (2009). The fallacies of 'new dialectics' and value form theory. *Historical Materialism*, *17*(1), 145–69.

Castillo, M. (2018, 11 April). *Zuckerberg Tells Congress Facebook Is Not a Media Company: 'I Consider Us to Be a Technology Company'*. CNBC. www.cnbc.com/2018/04/11/mark-zuckerberg-facebook-is-a-technology-company-not-media-company.html

Castner, M. (1997). Copyright law: The software user interface student comment. *Adelphia Law Journal*, *12*, 33–92.

Cavallone, E. (2020). *Tech Giants Are Serious about Lobbying in Brussels*. Euronews. www.euronews.com/2020/01/14/tech-giants-are-serious-about-lobbying-in-brussels

CB Insights. (2019). *Visualizing Tech Giants' Billion-Dollar Acquisitions*. CB Insights Research. www.cbinsights.com/research/tech-giants-billion-dollar-acquisitions-infographic/

Chattopadhyay, P. (2012). Competition. In B. Fine & A. Saad-Filho (Eds), *The Elgar Companion to Marxist Economics*. Edward Elgar.

Chavern, D. (2020, 19 April). Opinion: Google and Facebook must pay for local journalism. *The New York Times*. www.nytimes.com/2020/04/19/opinion/coronavirus-newspapers-journalism.html

Chen, S. (2009). To surpass or to conform: What are public licenses for. *University of Illinois Journal of Law, Technology & Policy*, *2009*(1), 107–40.

Chertkovskaya, E., Paulsson, A., & Barca, S. (Eds). (2019). *Towards a Political Economy of Degrowth*. Rowman & Littlefield Publishers.

Chopra, S., & Dexter, S.D. (2008). *Decoding Liberation: The Promise of Free and Open Source Software*. Routledge.

Christophers, B. (2016). *The Great Leveler: Capitalism and Competition in the Court of Law*. Harvard University Press.

Clarke, S. (1991). *Marx, Marginalism and Modern Sociology: From Adam Smith to Max Weber* (2nd edn). Palgrave Macmillan.

Cockshott, P. (2013). Heinrich's idea of abstract labour. *Critique*, *41*(2), 287–97.

Cohen, J.E. (2017). Law for the platform economy. *U.C. Davis Law Review*, *51*, 133.

Couldry, N., & Turow, J. (2014). Advertising, big data, and the clearance of the public realm: Marketers' new approaches to the content subsidy. *International Journal of Communication*, *8*, 1710–26.

Court of Justice of the European Union. (2010). *Press Release No 32/10: Judgement in Joined Cases C-236/08 to C-238/08, Google France and Google Inc. Et al V Louis Vuitton Malletier et al* https://ec.europa.eu/commission/presscorner/detail/en/CJE_10_32

Coyle, D. (2017a). The future of the national accounts: Statistics and the democratic conversation. *Review of Income and Wealth*, *63*(s2), S223–37. https://doi.org/10.1111/roiw.12333

Coyle, D. (2017b). The political economy of national statistics. In K. Hamilton & C. Hepburn (Eds), *National Wealth: What Is Missing, Why It Matters*. Oxford University Press. https://doi.org/10.1093/oso/9780198803720.003.0002

Cremer, J., de Monjoye, Y.A., & Schweitzer, H. (2019). *Competition Policy for the Digital Era*. European Commission.

Dafermos, G., & Söderberg, J. (2009). The hacker movement as a continuation of labour struggle. *Capital & Class*, *33*(1), 53–73. https://doi.org/10.1177/030981680909700104

Davis, J.B. (1992). *The Economic Surplus in Advanced Economies*. Edward Elgar.

Davis, L., & Orhangazi, Ö. (2019). Competition and monopoly in the US economy: What do industrial concentration data tell? *Political Economy Research Institute*, 68.

Dawson, M., & Foster, J.B. (1991). The tendency of the surplus to rise, 1963–1988. *Monthly Review*, *43*(4), 37–50. https://doi.org/10.14452/MR-043-04-1991-08_4

Dellinger, A.J. (2019). *How the Biggest Tech Companies Spent Half a Billion Dollars Lobbying Congress*. Forbes. www.forbes.com/sites/ajdellinger/2019/04/30/how-the-biggest-tech-companies-spent-half-a-billion-dollars-lobbying-congress/

Department of Justice. (2020). *Justice Department Sues Monopolist Google for Violating Antitrust Laws*. www.justice.gov/opa/pr/justice-department-sues-monopolist-google-violating-antitrust-laws

Desrosières, A. (2010). *The Politics of Large Numbers: A History of Statistical Reasoning* (C. Naish, Trans.; New edn). Harvard University Press.

Detter, D., & Fölster, S. (2018). Unlocking public wealth. *Finance and Development*, *55*(1). www.imf.org/external/pubs/ft/fandd/2018/03/detter.htm

Devine, K.L. (2008). Preserving competition in multi-sided innovative markets: How do you solve a problem like Google. *North Carolina Journal of Law & Technology*, *10*(1), 61.

Diakopoulos, N. (2015). Algorithmic accountability: Journalistic investigation of computational power structures. *Digital Journalism, 3*(3), 398–415. https://doi.org/10.1080/21670811.2014.976411

DiEM25. (2019). *Technological Sovereignty: Democratising Technology and Innovation* (No. 2; Green Paper). DiEM25.

Domazet, M., Rilović, A., Ančić, B., Andersen, B., Richardson, L., Brajdić Vuković, M., Pungas, L., & Medak, T. (2020). Mental models of sustainability: The degrowth doughnut model. In *Encyclopedia of the World's Biomes* (pp 276–86). Elsevier. https://doi.org/10.1016/B978-0-12-409548-9.12143-8

Donders, K., & Pauwels, C. (2008). Does EU policy challenge the digital future of public service broadcasting? *Convergence: The International Journal of Research into New Media Technologies, 14*(3), 295–311.

Dourish, P. (2016). Algorithms and their others: Algorithmic culture in context. *Big Data & Society, 3*(2), 205395171666512. https://doi.org/10.1177/2053951716665128

Doyle, G. (2002). *Understanding Media Economics*. SAGE.

Drahos, P. (2016). *A Philosophy of Intellectual Property* (1st edn). Routledge.

Durand, C., & Gueuder, M. (2018). The profit–investment nexus in an era of financialisation, globalisation and monopolisation: A profit-centred perspective. *Review of Political Economy, 30*(2), 126–53. https://doi.org/10.1080/09538259.2018.1457211

Dusollier, S. (2002). Open source of copyleft: Authorship reconsidered. *Columbia Journal of Law & the Arts, 26*(Issues 3 + 4), 281–96.

Dyer-Witheford, N. (2015). *Cyber-proletariat: Global Labour in the Digital Vortex*. Between the Lines; Pluto Press.

Elbe, I. (2013, October). Between Marx, Marxism, and Marxisms: Ways of reading Marx's theory. *Viewpoint Magazine*. https://viewpointmag.com/2013/10/21/between-marx-marxism-and-marxisms-ways-of-reading-marxs-theory/

Elbe, I. (2018). Helmut Reichelt and the new reading of Marx. In B. Best, W. Bonefeld, & C. O'Kane (Eds), *The SAGE Handbook of Frankfurt School Critical Theory* (Vol. 1, pp 367–85). SAGE.

Elken-Koren, N. (2011). Tailoring copyright to social production copyright culture, copyright history. *Theoretical Inquiries in Law, 12*(1), 309–48.

European Commission. (2015). *COM(2015) 192 final: A Digital Single Market Strategy for Europe*. https://eur-lex.europa.eu/legal-content/EN/TXT/HTML/?uri=CELEX:52015DC0192

European Commission. (2016). *Press Release – State Aid: Ireland Gave Illegal Tax Benefits to Apple Worth up to €13 Billion*. https://ec.europa.eu/commission/presscorner/detail/en/IP_16_2923

European Commission. (2017a). *Antitrust: Commission Fines Google €2.42 Billion* [Text]. https://ec.europa.eu/commission/presscorner/detail/en/IP_17_1784

European Commission. (2017b). *Communication from the Commission to the European Parliament and the Council: A Fair and Efficient Tax System in the European Union for the Digital Single Market.* https://eur-lex.europa.eu/legal-content/EN/TXT/?uri=CELEX%3A52017DC0547

European Commission. (2017c, 20 September). *Fair Taxation of the Digital Economy* [Text]. Taxation and Customs Union – European Commission. https://ec.europa.eu/taxation_customs/business/company-tax/fair-taxation-digital-economy_en

European Commission. (2018a). *Press Release – Antitrust: Commission Fines Google €4.34 Billion for Illegal Practices Regarding Android Mobile Devices to Strengthen Dominance of Google's Search Engine.* http://europa.eu/rapid/press-release_IP-18-4581_en.htm

European Commission. (2018b). *Proposal for a Council Directive Laying Down Rules Relating to the Corporate Taxation of a Significant Digital Presence.* https://eur-lex.europa.eu/legal-content/EN/TXT/?uri=CELEX%3A52018PC0147

European Commission. (2018c). *Proposal for a Council Directive on the Common System of a Digital Services Tax on Revenues Resulting from the Provision of Certain Digital Services.* https://eur-lex.europa.eu/legal-content/EN/TXT/?uri=COM%3A2018%3A148%3AFIN

European Commission. (2019). *Antitrust: Google Fined €1.49 Billion for Online Advertising Abuse* [Text]. https://ec.europa.eu/commission/presscorner/detail/en/IP_19_1770

European Parliament. (2016). Regulation (EU) 2016/679 of the European Parliament and of the Council of 27 April 2016 on the protection of natural persons with regard to the processing of personal data and on the free movement of such data, and repealing Directive 95/46/EC (General Data Protection Regulation). *Official Journal of the European Union, 119*, 1–88.

European Political Strategy Centre. (2019). *Rethinking Strategic Autonomy in the Digital Age.* European Commission.

Ezrachi, A., & Stucke, M.E. (2016a). *Virtual Competition: The Promise and Perils of the Algorithm-driven Economy.* Harvard University Press.

Ezrachi, A., & Stucke, M.E. (2016b). Virtual competition. *Journal of European Competition Law & Practice, 7*(9), 585–6. https://doi.org/10.1093/jeclap/lpw083

Fannin, R. (2018). China's bat won't battle the fangs in the US anytime soon. *Forbes.* www.forbes.com/sites/rebeccafannin/2018/05/21/dont-count-on-chinas-baidu-alibaba-tencent-to-go-mainstream-in-the-u-s/

Feenberg, A. (1996). Marcuse or Habermas: Two critiques of technology. *Inquiry*, *39*(1), 45–70. https://doi.org/10.1080/00201749608602407

Feenberg, A. (2010). *Between Reason and Experience: Essays in Technology and Modernity*. MIT Press.

Feenberg, A. (2014). *The Philosophy of Praxis: Marx, Lukacs, and the Frankfurt School*. Verso.

Feenberg, A. (2017). *Technosystem: The Social Life of Reason*. Harvard University Press.

Fisher, E. (2010). *Media and New Capitalism in the Digital Age: The Spirit of Networks*. Palgrave Macmillan.

Fisher, E. (2012). How less alienation creates more exploitation: Audience labour on social network sites. *TripleC: Communication, Capitalism & Critique. Open Access Journal for a Global Sustainable Information Society*, *10*(2), 171–83. https://doi.org/10.31269/triplec.v10i2.392

Forbes. (2019). *The World's Most Valuable Brands*. Forbes. www.forbes.com/powerful-brands/list/

Foster, J.B. (2014a). *The Theory of Monopoly Capitalism: An Elaboration of Marxian Political Economy*. Monthly Review Press.

Foster, J.B. (Ed.). (2014b). The Baran Marcuse correspondence. *Monthly Review*, *65*(10). https://monthlyreview.org/commentary/baran-marcuse-correspondence/

Foster, J.B. (2016). Monopoly capital at the half-century mark. *Monthly Review*, *68*(3), 1–25. https://doi.org/10.14452/MR-068-03-2016-07_1

Foster, J.B., & McChesney, R.W. (2012). *The Endless Crisis: How Monopoly-Finance Capital Produces Stagnation and Upheaval from the USA to China*. Monthly Review Press.

Foster, J.B., & McChesney, R.W. (2014). Surveillance capitalism: Monopoly-finance capital, the military–industrial complex, and the digital age. *Monthly Review*, *66*(3). https://monthlyreview.org/2014/07/01/surveillance-capitalism/

Foster, J.B., McChesney, R., & Jonna, J. (2011). Monopoly and competition in twenty-first century capitalism. *Monthly Review*, *62*(11), 1–39.

Foster, J.B., Clark, B., & Michael, Y. (2018). Notes from the editors. *Monthly Review*, *70*(2). https://monthlyreview.org/2018/06/01/mr-070-02-2018-06_0/

Franek, K. (2019). *How Google Maps Makes Money: With Visuals and Revenue Estimate*. www.kamilfranek.com/how-google-maps-makes-money/

Frankel, S.J., & Forrest, E. (2018). Essay: What remains of fair use for software after Oracle v. Google. *New York University Journal of Intellectual Property & Entertainment Law*, *8*(2), 310–23.

Friedman, M. (1982). *Capitalism and Freedom*. University of Chicago Press.

FTC. (2012, 10 August). *FTC Approves Final Settlement with Facebook*. Federal Trade Commission. www.ftc.gov/news-events/press-releases/2012/08/ftc-approves-final-settlement-facebook

FTC. (2019a). *FTC's $5 Billion Facebook Settlement: Record-breaking and History-making*. Federal Trade Commission. www.ftc.gov/news-events/blogs/business-blog/2019/07/ftcs-5-billion-facebook-settlement-record-breaking-history

FTC. (2019b, 24 July). *FTC Imposes $5 Billion Penalty and Sweeping New Privacy Restrictions on Facebook*. Federal Trade Commission. www.ftc.gov/news-events/press-releases/2019/07/ftc-imposes-5-billion-penalty-sweeping-new-privacy-restrictions

Fuchs, C. (2008). *Internet and Society: Social Theory in the Information Age*. Routledge.

Fuchs, C. (2010). Labor in informational capitalism and on the internet. *The Information Society*, 26(3), 179–96. https://doi.org/10.1080/01972241003712215

Fuchs, C. (2014a). Dallas Smythe reloaded: Critical media and communication studies today. In L. McGuigan & V. Manzerolle (Eds), *The Audience Commodity in a Digital Age: Revisiting Critical Theory of Commercial Media* (pp 267–88). Peter Lang. https://westminsterresearch.westminster.ac.uk/item/8yq8x/dallas-smythe-reloaded-critical-media-and-communication-studies-today

Fuchs, C. (2014b). *Digital Labour and Karl Marx*. Routledge, Taylor & Francis Group.

Fuchs, C. (2015). Dallas Smythe today – The audience commodity, the digital labour debate, Marxist political economy and critical theory. Prolegomena to a digital labour theory of value. In C. Fuchs & V. Mosco (Eds), *Marx and the Political Economy of the Media* (pp 522–99). Brill. https://doi.org/10.1163/9789004291416_019

Fuchs, C. (2017). Towards Marxian internet studies. In C. Fuchs & V. Mosco (Eds), *Marx in the Age of Digital Capitalism* (pp 22–67). Haymarket Books.

Fuchs, C., & Fisher, E. (Eds). (2015). *Reconsidering Value and Labour in the Digital Age*. Palgrave Macmillan.

Fuller, R.A. (1982). Algorithm patentability after Diamond v. Diehr. *Indiana Law Review*, 15, 713–32.

Furman, J., Coyle, D., Fletcher, A., McAuley, D., & Mardsen, P. (2019). *Unlocking Digital Competition: Report of the Digital Competition Expert Panel*. UK Government.

Gandesha, S. (2018). Totality and technological form. In B. Best, W. Bonefeld, & C. O'Kane (Eds), *The SAGE Handbook of Frankfurt School Critical Theory* (Vol. 2, pp 642–60). SAGE.

Gandy, Jr., O.H. (1993). *The Panoptic Sort: A Political Economy of Personal Information*. Westview Press.

Gates, B. (1976, 3 February). *An Open Letter to Hobbyists*. https://archive.nytimes.com/www.nytimes.com/library/cyber/surf/072397mind-letter.html

Gehl, R.W. (2011). The archive and the processor: The internal logic of Web 2.0. *New Media & Society*, *13*(8), 1228–44. https://doi.org/10.1177/1461444811401735

General Court of the European Union. (2020). *Press Release No. 90/20: The General Court of the European Union Annuls the Decision Taken by the Commission Regarding Irish Tax Rulings in Favour of Apple*. https://curia.europa.eu/jcms/jcms/Jo2_7052/en/?annee=2020

Geringer, S. (2020). National digital taxes: Lessons from Europe. *South African Journal of Accounting Research*, 1–19.

Gillespie, T. (2010). The politics of 'platforms'. *New Media & Society*, *12*(3), 347–64. https://doi.org/10.1177/1461444809342738

Gillespie, T. (2014). The relevance of algorithms. In T. Gillespie, P.J. Boczkowski, & K.A. Foot (Eds), *Media Technologies* (pp 167–94). MIT Press. https://doi.org/10.7551/mitpress/9780262525374.003.0009

Glick, M. (2019). Antitrust and economic history: The historic failure of the Chicago School of antitrust. *The Antitrust Bulletin*, *64*(3), 295–340. https://doi.org/10.1177/0003603X19863586

Goldman, R., Gabriel, R.P., & Meyer, C. (2005). *Innovation Happens Elsewhere: Open Source as Business Strategy* (1st edn). Morgan Kaufmann.

Google Inc. (2003). *Google Acquires Applied Semantics*. http://googlepress.blogspot.com/2004/04/google-acquires-applied-semantics.html

Google Inc. (2006). 2005 10-K form. www.sec.gov/Archives/edgar/data/1288776/000119312506056598/d10k.htm

Google Inc. (2008). 2007 10-K form. www.sec.gov/Archives/edgar/data/1288776/000119312508032690/d10k.htm

Google Inc. (2009). 2008 10-K form. www.sec.gov/Archives/edgar/data/1288776/000119312509029448/d10k.htm

Graham, M., & Woodcok, J. (2018). Towards a fairer platform economy: Introducing the Fairwork Foundation. *Alternate Routes*, *29*, 242–53.

Gratz, J., & Lemley, M.A. (2017). Platforms and interoperability in Oracle v. Google special issue: Software interface copyright. *Harvard Journal of Law & Technology (Harvard JOLT)*, *31*(Special Issue), 603–14.

Greenstein, S.M. (2015). *How the Internet Became Commercial: Innovation, Privatization, and the Birth of a New Network*. Princeton University Press.

Habermas, J. (1987). *Toward a Rational Society: Student Protest, Science, and Politics*. Polity Press.

Hamilton, K., & Banco Mundial. (2006). *Where Is the Wealth of Nations? Measuring Capital for the 21st Century*. World Bank.

Hands, D.W. (2014). Paul Samuelson and revealed preference theory. *History of Political Economy*, *46*(1), 85–116. https://doi.org/10.1215/00182702-2398939

Hardt, M., & Negri, A. (2000). *Empire*. Harvard University Press.

Hardt, M., & Negri, A. (2004). *Multitude*. Hamish Hamilton.

Hardy, J. (2014). *Critical Political Economy of the Media*. Routledge.

Harvey, D. (2012). *Rebel Cities: From the Right to the City to the Urban Revolution*. Verso.

Harvey, D. (2014). *Seventeen Contradictions and the End of Capitalism*. Oxford University Press.

Haskel, J., & Westlake, S. (2018). *Capitalism without Capital: The Rise of the Intangible Economy*.

Hein, E. (2014). *Distribution and Growth after Keynes: A Post-Keynesian Guide*. Edward Elgar.

Heinrich, M. (2007). Invaders from Marx: On the uses of Marxian theory, and the difficulties of a contemporary reading. *Left Curve*, *31*, 83–8.

Heinrich, M. (2009). Reconstruction or deconstruction? Methodological controversies about value and capital, and new insights from the critical edition. In Riccardo Bellofiore & R. Fineschi (Eds), *Re-reading Marx: New Perspectives after the Critical Edition* (pp 72–98). Palgrave Macmillan.

Heinrich, M. (2012). *An Introduction to the Three Volumes of Karl Marx's Capital* (A. Locascio, Trans.). Monthly Review Press.

Helft, M. (2008, 10 August). Is Google a media company? *The New York Times*. www.nytimes.com/2008/08/11/technology/11google.html

Hesmondhalgh, D. (2010). User-generated content, free labour and the cultural industries. *Ephemera*, *10*(3/4), 267–84.

Hess, C. (2008). *Mapping the New Commons* (SSRN Scholarly Paper ID 1356835). Social Science Research Network. https://doi.org/10.2139/ssrn.1356835

Hilferding, R. (2005). *Finance Capital: A Study in the Latest Phase of Capitalist Development* (1st edn). Routledge.

Hillis, K., Petit, M., & Jarrett, K. (2013). *Google and the Culture of Search*. Routledge Taylor & Francis Group.

Himmelweit, S. (1998). Mode of production. In T. Bottomore, L. Harris, V.G. Kiernan, & R. Miliband (Eds), *A Dictionary of Marxist Thought* (2nd edn, pp 379–81). Blackwell Publishing Limited.

Horkheimer, M., & Adorno, T.W. (2002). *Dialectic of Enlightenment: Philosophical Fragments*. Stanford University Press.

Hornborg, A. (2014). Technology as fetish: Marx, Latour, and the cultural foundations of capitalism. *Theory, Culture & Society*, *31*(4), 119–40. https://doi.org/10.1177/0263276413488960

Hubbard, J. (2004). Open Source to the core. *Queue*, *2*(3), 24–31. https://doi.org/10.1145/1005062.1005064

Hudis, P. (2013). *Marx's Concept of Alternatives to Capitalism*. Haymarket Books.

Huws, U. (2013). Working online, living offline: Labour in the internet age. *Work, Organisation, Labour & Globalisation*, 7(1), 1–11.

Huws, U. (2019). *Labour in Contemporary Capitalism: What Next?* Palgrave Macmillan UK. https://doi.org/10.1057/978-1-137-52042-5

Huws, U. (2020). *Reinventing the Welfare State*. Pluto Press. www.plutobooks.com/9780745341842/reinventing-the-welfare-state

IAB. (2019). *AdEx Benchmark 2018*. Internet Advertising Bureau (IAB) Europe.

Internet Live Stats. (2020). *1 Second – Internet Live Stats*. www.internetlivestats.com/one-second/

Introna, L.D., & Nissenbaum, H. (2000). Shaping the web: Why the politics of search engines matters. *The Information Society*, *16*, 169–85.

Irani, L. (2015). The cultural work of microwork. *New Media & Society*, *17*(5), 720–39. https://doi.org/10.1177/1461444813511926

Ivanovski, A., & McIntosh, B. (2019). *EU Tax Policy Report, January – June 2019*. CFE Tax Advisers Europe.

Jessop, B. (1990). *State Theory: Putting Capitalist States in their Place*. Penn State University Press.

Jessop, R. (1990). Mode of production. In J. Eatwell, M. Milgate, & P. Newman (Eds), *The New Palgrave: Marxian Economics* (pp 289–96). Macmillan.

Jhally, S., & Livant, B. (1986). Watching as working: The valorization of audience consciousness. *Journal of Communication*, *36*(3), 124–43. https://doi.org/10.1111/j.1460-2466.1986.tb01442.x

Jin, D.Y. (2015). *Digital Platforms, Imperialism, and Political Culture*. Routledge.

Johnson, L. (2002). Creating the software industry-recollections of software company founders of the 1960s. *IEEE Annals of the History of Computing*, *24*(1), 14–42. https://doi.org/10.1109/85.988576

Jullien, N., & Zimmermann, J.B. (2011). Floss firms, users and communities: A viable match? *Journal of Innovation Economics Management*, 7(1), 31–53.

Kang, C., & Frenkel, S. (2018, 4 April). Facebook says Cambridge Analytica harvested data of up to 87 million users. *The New York Times*. www.nytimes.com/2018/04/04/technology/mark-zuckerberg-testify-congress.html

Kayser-Brill, N. (2020). *Ten Years on, Search Auto-complete Still Suggests Slander and Disinformation*. AlgorithmWatch. https://algorithmwatch. org/en/story/auto-completion-disinformation/

Keen, S. (2011). *Debunking Economics – Revised and Expanded Edition: The Naked Emperor Dethroned?* (Revised, expanded edn). Zed Books.

Kelly, K. (1998). *New Rules for the New Economy* (1st edn). Viking.

Khan, L.M. (2016). Amazon's antitrust paradox. *Yale Law Journal, 126*, 710–805.

Kicillof, A., & Starosta, G. (2007). On materiality and social form: A political critique of Rubin's value-form theory. *Historical Materialism, 15*(3), 9–43. https://doi.org/10.1163/156920607X225852

Kincaid, J. (2007). Production vs. realisation: A critique of fine and Saad-Filho on value theory. *Historical Materialism, 15*(4), 137–65.

King, J.E. (2012). *The Microfoundations Delusion: Metaphor and Dogma in the History of Macroeconomics*. Edward Elgar.

Kitchin, R. (2014). Big data, new epistemologies and paradigm shifts. *Big Data & Society, 1*(1), 205395171452848. https://doi.org/10.1177/2053951714528481

Kolasky, W.J. (2004). What is competition? A comparison of US and European perspectives. *The Antitrust Bulletin, 49*(1–2), 39.

Krishnamurthy, S. (2005). An analysis of Open Source business models. In J. Feller, B. Fitzgerald, S.A. Hissam, & K.R. Lakhani (Eds), *Perspectives on Free and Open Source Software* (pp 279–96). MIT Press.

Lakhani, K.R., & Wolf, R.G. (2003). *Why Hackers Do What They Do: Understanding Motivation and Effort in Free/Open Source Software Projects* (http://ssrn.com/paper=443040) [MIT Sloan Working Paper].

Lazonick, W. (2014). *Profits without Prosperity: How Stock Buybacks Manipulate the Market, and Leave Most Americans Worse Off*. www. ineteconomics.org/research/research-papers/profits-without-prosperity-how-stock-buybacks-manipulate-the-market-and-leave-most-americans-worse-off

Lazonick, W., & Mazzucato, M. (2013). The risk-reward nexus in the innovation–inequality relationship: Who takes the risks? Who gets the rewards? *Industrial and Corporate Change*, *22*(4), 1093–128. https://doi.org/10.1093/icc/dtt019

Lazonick, W., Mazzucato, M., & Tulum, Ö. (2013). Apple's changing business model: What should the world's richest company do with all those profits? *Accounting Forum*, *37*(4), 249–67. https://doi.org/10.1016/j.accfor.2013.07.002

Lazzarato, M. (1996). Immaterial labour. In P. Virno & M. Hardt (Eds), *Radical Thought in Italy: A Potential Politics* (pp 132–47). University of Minnesota Press.

Lebowitz, M. (2010). *The Socialist Alternative: Real Human Development*. Monthly Review Press.

Lee, F., & Björklund Larsen, L. (2019). How should we theorize algorithms? Five ideal types in analyzing algorithmic normativities. *Big Data & Society*, *6*(2), 205395171986734. https://doi.org/10.1177/2053951719867349

Lee, M. (2011). Google ads and the blindspot debate. *Media, Culture & Society*, *33*(3), 433–47. https://doi.org/10.1177/0163443710394902

Lee, M. (2019). *Alphabet: The Becoming of Google*. Routledge.

Lenfant, J.-S. (2012). Indifference curves and the ordinalist revolution. *History of Political Economy*, *44*(1), 113–55. https://doi.org/10.1215/00182702-1504077

Lenin, V.I. (1999). *Imperialism: The Highest Stage of Capitalism*. Resistance Books.

Leslie, S.W. (2000). The biggest 'angel' of them all: The military and the making of Silicon Valley. In M. Kenney (Ed.), *Understanding Silicon Valley: The Anatomy of an Entrepreneurial Region* (pp 48–67). Stanford University Press.

Levy, S. (2010). *Hackers: Heroes of the Computer Revolution – 25th Anniversary Edition* (1st edn). O'Reilly Media.

Letter from Apple Inc. For the Record (2020). Testimony of Apple Inc. https://judiciary.house.gov/calendar/eventsingle.aspx?EventID=2386

Lewin, S.B. (1996). Economics and psychology: Lessons for our own day from the early twentieth century. *Journal of Economic Literature*, *34*(3), 1293–323.

Lexchin, J. (2018). The pharmaceutical industry in contemporary capitalism. *Monthly Review*, *69*(10). https://monthlyreview.org/2018/03/01/the-pharmaceutical-industry-in-contemporary-capitalism/

Linden, M. van der, & Hubmann, G. (2018). Introduction. In *Marx's Capital: An Unfinishable Project?* (Vol. 159, pp 1–30). Brill. https://brill.com/abstract/book/edcoll/9789004367159/BP000001.xml

Lipietz, A. (1987). *Mirages and Miracles: The Crisis in Global Fordism*. Verso.

Livant, B. (1979). The audience commodity: On the 'blindspot' debate. *Canadian Journal of Political and Social Theory*, *3*(1), 91–117.

Lomas, N. (2020). EU digs in on digital tax plan, after US quits talks. *TechCrunch*. https://social.techcrunch.com/2020/06/18/eu-digs-in-on-digital-tax-plan-after-us-quits-talks/

Lotz, C. (2018). The culture industry. In B. Best, W. Bonefeld, & C. O'Kane (Eds), *The SAGE Handbook of Frankfurt School Critical Theory* (Vol. 2, pp 973–87). SAGE.

Luchetta, G. (2014). Is the Google platform a two-sided market? *Journal of Competition Law & Economics*, *10*(1), 185–207. https://doi.org/10.1093/joclec/nht026

Lukács, G. (1972). *History and Class Consciousness: Studies in Marxist Dialectics*. MIT Press.

Lund, A., & Zukerfeld, M. (2020). *Corporate Capitalism's Use of Openness: Profit for Free?* Springer International Publishing. https://doi.org/10.1007/978-3-030-28219-6

Lunden, I. (2018). Amazon's share of the US e-commerce market is now 49%, or 5% of all retail spend. *TechCrunch*. http://social.techcrunch.com/2018/07/13/amazons-share-of-the-us-e-commerce-market-is-now-49-or-5-of-all-retail-spend/

Lyon, D. (2003). *Surveillance after September 11*. Polity Press.

Lyon, D. (2005). *Surveillance as Social Sorting: Privacy, Risk and Automated Discrimination*. Taylor and Francis.

Lyon, D. (2014). Surveillance, Snowden, and big data: Capacities, consequences, critique. *Big Data & Society*, *1*(2), 205395171454186. https://doi.org/10.1177/2053951714541861

MacKenzie, D. (2017). A material political economy: Automated trading desk and price prediction in high-frequency trading. *Social Studies of Science*, *47*(2), 172–94. https://doi.org/10.1177/0306312716676900

Magdoff, H. (1969). *The Age of Imperialism*. Monthly Review Press.

Magdoff, H., & Sweezy, P. (1987). *Stagnation and the Financial Explosion*. Monthly Review Press.

Mager, A. (2012). Algorithmic ideology: How capitalist society shapes search engines. *Information, Communication & Society*, *15*(5), 769–87. https://doi.org/10.1080/1369118X.2012.676056

Mandel, E. (1976). *Late Capitalism*. NLB.

Marcuse, H. (1971). *An Essay on Liberation*. Beacon Press.

Marcuse, H. (1998). *Collected Papers of Herbert Marcuse. Technology, War, and Fascism Volume 1 Volume 1* (D. Kellner, Ed.). Routledge.

Marcuse, H. (2007). *One-dimensional Man: Studies in the Ideology of Advanced Industrial Society*. Routledge.

Marcuse, H. (2009). *Negations*. MayFlyBooks.

Marr, B. (2018). How much data do we create every day? The mind-blowing stats everyone should read. *Forbes*. www.forbes.com/sites/bernardmarr/2018/05/21/how-much-data-do-we-create-every-day-the-mind-blowing-stats-everyone-should-read/

Marwick, A., & Lewis, R. (2017). *Media Manipulation and Disinformation Online*. Data & Society Research Institute.

Marx, K. (1846). Letter from Marx to Pavel Vasilyevich Annenko. In *Collected Works: Letters, 1844–51* (Vol. 38, pp 95–106). International Publishers. www.marxists.org/archive/marx/works/1846/letters/46_12_28.htm

Marx, K. (1859). A contribution to the critique of political economy. Part One. In *Collected Works: 1857–1861* (Vol. 29, pp 257–421). Lawrence & Wishart.

Marx, K. (1861). Economic manuscript of 1861–63, Notebooks 1–7. In *Collected Works: Marx 1861–3* (Vol. 30). Lawrence & Wishart.

Marx, K. (1963). *Theories of Surplus Value* (S. Ryazaskaya, Ed.; E. Burns, Trans.; Vol. 1). Progress Publishers.

Marx, K. (1967). *Capital* (Vol. 1). Progress Publishers.

Marx, K. (1976). *Capital* (Vol. 1). Penguin.

Marx, K. (1978). *Capital* (D. Fernbach, Trans.; 2nd edn, Vol. 2). Penguin.

Marx, K. (1981). *Capital* (Vol. 3). Penguin.

Marx, K. (1987). *Collected Works: Marx 1857–61* (Vol. 28). Lawrence & Wishart.

Marx, K. (1996). *Capital: Vol. 1*. Lawrence & Wishart.

Marx, K. (1998). *Capital: Vol. 3*. Lawrence & Wishart.

Marx, K. (2010). *Collected Works: Capital Volume I* (Vol. 35). Lawrence & Wishart.

Marx, K. (2015). *Marx's Economic Manuscript of 1864–1865* (F. Moseley, Ed.). Brill.

Marx, K., & Engels, F. (1974). *The German Ideology, Part One*. Lawrence & Wishart.

Mattick, Jr., P. (1998). Economic form and social reproduction: On the place of 'Book II' in Marx's critique of political economy. In C.J. Arthur & G. Reuten (Eds), *The Circulation of Capital: Essays on Volume Two of Marx's Capital* (pp 17–32). Macmillan.

May, C. (2000). *A Global Political Economy of Intellectual Property Rights: The New Enclosures?* Routledge.

Mayer-Schönberger, V., & Cukier, K. (2014). *Big Data: A Revolution That Will Transform How We Live, Work, and Think Cover.* Eamon Dolan/Mariner Books.

Mazzucato, M. (2013). *The Entrepreneurial State: Debunking Public vs. Private Myths in Risk and Innovation.* Anthem Press.

Mazzucato, M. (2015). *The Entrepreneurial State: Debunking Public vs. Private Sector Myths* (Revised). Public Affairs.

Mazzucato, M. (2018a). *The Value of Everything: Making and Taking in the Global Economy.* Allen Lane.

Mazzucato, M. (2018b). The entrepreneurial state: Socializing both risks and rewards. *Real-World Economics Review, 84,* 17.

McChesney, R.W. (2013). *Digital Disconnect.* The New Press.

McCue, T.J. (2018). *SEO Industry Approaching $80 Billion But All You Want Is More Web Traffic.* Forbes. www.forbes.com/sites/tjmccue/ 2018/07/30/seo-industry-approaching-80-billion-but-all-you-want-is-more-web-traffic/

McStay, A. (2016). *Digital Advertising.* Palgrave Macmillan.

Medak, T. (2013, 28 April). *Reconsidering Economics, Struggles and Autonomy in the Digital Commons.* DPU May Day School, Ljubljana, Slovenia. http://tom.medak.click/posts/commons/

Medak, T. (2017). *Technologies for an Ecological Transition: A Faustian Bargain?* [Working Paper]. Institute For Political Ecology, Zagreb.

Medak, T., & Mars, M. (2019). System of a takedown: Control and de-commodification in the circuits of academic publishing. In A. Lison (Ed.), *Archives* (pp 47–68). University of Minnesota Press and Meson Press.

Meehan, E.R. (1984). Ratings and the institutional approach: A third answer to the commodity question. *Critical Studies in Mass Communication, 1*(2), 216–25. https://doi.org/10.1080/15295038409360032

Menell, P.S. (2016). API copyrightability Bleak House: Unraveling and repairing the Oracle v. Google jurisdictional mess. *Berkeley Technology Law Journal, 31*(3), 1515–96.

Menke, C. (2020). *Critique of Rights* (C. Turner, Trans.; 1st edn). Polity.

Milios, J., Dimoulis, D., & Economakis, G. (2002). *Karl Marx and the Classics: An Essay on Value Crises and the Capitalist Mode of Production* (illustrated edn). Ashgate Publishing Limited.

Miller, T., & Maxwell, R. (2017). Apple Inc. In B. Birkinbine, R. Gomez, & J. Wasko (Eds), *Global Media Giants* (pp 369–82). Routledge.

Mirowski, P., & Hands, W. (1998). A paradox of budgets: The postwar stabilization of American neoclassical demand theory. In *From Interwar Pluralism to Postwar Neoclassicism* (pp 260–89). Duke University.

Mischel, L., & Wolfe, J. (2019). *CEO Compensation Has Grown 940% since 1978: Typical Worker Compensation Has Risen only 12% during That Time.* Economic Policy Institute. www.epi.org/publication/ceo-compensation-2018/

Mittelstadt, B.D., Allo, P., Taddeo, M., Wachter, S., & Floridi, L. (2016). The ethics of algorithms: Mapping the debate. *Big Data & Society*, 1–21.

Montalban, M., Frigant, V., & Jullien, B. (2019). Platform economy as a new form of capitalism: A Régulationist research programme. *Cambridge Journal of Economics*, *43*(4), 805–24. https://doi.org/10.1093/cje/bez017

Mosco, V. (2004). *The Digital Sublime: Myth, Power, and Cyberspace.* MIT Press.

Mosco, V. (2014). *To the Cloud: Big Data in a Turbulent World.* Paradigm Publishers.

Moss, D.L. (2019). *The Record of Weak US: Merger Enforcement in Big Tech.* American Antitrust Institute.

Moulier-Boutang, Y. (2011). *Cognitive Capitalism.* Polity Press.

Moz. (2020). *Google Algorithm Update History.* Moz. https://moz.com/google-algorithm-change

Murdock, G. (1997). Blindspots about Western Marxism: A reply to Dallas Smythe. In P. Golding & G. Murdock (Eds), *The Political Economy of Media. Volume 1* (pp 465–75). Edward Elgar.

Murdock, G., & Golding, P. (2016). Political economy and media production: A reply to Dwyer. *Media, Culture & Society*, *38*(5), 763–69. https://doi.org/10.1177/0163443716655094

Murdock, I. (2005). Open Source and the commoditization of software. In C. DiBona, M. Stone, & D. Cooper (Eds), *Open Sources 2.0: The Continuing Evolution* (pp 91–102). O'Reilly Media.

Murray, P. (1988). *Marx's Theory of Scientific Knowledge.* Humanities Press International.

Murray, P. (1997). Redoubled empiricism: The place of social form and formal causality in Marxian theory. In *New Investigations of Marx's Method* (pp 38–65). Humanities Press.

Murray, P. (1998). Beyond the 'commerce and industry' picture of capital. In C.J. Arthur & G. Reuten (Eds), *The Circulation of Capital: Essays on Volume Two of Marx's Capital* (pp 33–66). Macmillan.

Murray, P. (2000). Marx's 'Truly social' labour theory of value: Part I, abstract labour in Marxian value theory. *Historical Materialism*, *6*(1), 27–66. https://doi.org/10.1163/156920600100414551

Murray, P. (2002a). The illusion of the economic. The Trinity formula and the 'religion of everyday life'. In M. Campbell & G. Reuten (Eds), *The Culmination of Capital: Essays on Volume Three of Marx's Capital* (pp 246–72). Palgrave.

Murray, P. (2002b). Reply to Geert Reuten. *Historical Materialism*, *10*(1), 155–76. https://doi.org/10.1163/156920602760231695

Murray, P. (2005). The new giant's staircase. *Historical Materialism*, *13*(2), 61–84. https://doi.org/10.1163/1569206054127228

Murray, P. (2016). *The Mismeasure of Wealth* (Lam edn). BRILL.

Murray, P. (2018). Critical theory and the critique of political economy: From critical political economy to the critique of political economy. In B. Best, W. Bonefeld, & C. O'Kane (Eds), *The SAGE Handbook of Frankfurt School Critical Theory* (Vol. 2, pp 764–82). SAGE.

Murray, P., & Badeen, D. (2016). A Marxian critique of neoclassical economics' reliance on shadows of capital's constitutive social forms. *Crisis and Critique*, *3*(3), 8–28.

Murschetz, P.C. (2020). State aid for independent news journalism in the public interest? A critical debate of government funding models and principles, the market failure paradigm, and policy efficacy. *Digital Journalism*, 1–20.

Myers, B.A. (1998). A brief history of human–computer interaction technology. *Interactions*, *5*(2), 44–54. https://doi.org/10.1145/274430.274436

Nakamura, A.O., & Nakamura, L.I. (2015, 17 April). *The System of National Accounts and Alternative Economic Perspectives*. IARIW–OECD Special Conference: 'W(h)ither the SNA?,' Paris. http://iariw.org/papers/2015/nakamura.pdf

Nakamura, L. (2010). Intangible assets and national income accounting. *Review of Income and Wealth*, *56*(1). http://papers.ssrn.com/abstract=1630588

Nakamura, L. (2015). Advertising, intangible assets, and unpriced entertainment. In A. Bounfour & T. Miyagawa (Eds), *Intangibles, Market Failure and Innovation Performance* (pp 11–26). Springer International Publishing.

Nakamura, L., Samuels, J., & Soloveichik, R. (2017). Measuring the 'free' digital economy within the GDP and productivity accounts. In *Economic Statistics Centre of Excellence (ESCoE) Discussion Papers* (DP-2017-03; Economic Statistics Centre of Excellence Discussion Papers). Economic Statistics Centre of Excellence. https://ideas.repec.org/p/nsr/escoed/escoe-dp-2017-03.html

Net Market Share. (2020). *Operating System Market Share*. https://netmarketshare.com/operating-system-market-share

Neustar. (2018). *AdAge: Marketing Fact Pack 2019*.

Newman, J.M. (2015). Anti-trust in zero-price markets: Foundations. *University of Pennsylvania Law Review, 164*(1), 149–206.

Newman, J.M. (2018). The myth of free. *George Washington Law Review, 86*(2), 513–86.

Newman, J.M. (2019). Antitrust in digital markets. *Vanderbilt Law Review, 72*(5), 1497–562.

Niels, G., & ten Kate, A. (2004). Introduction: Antitrust in the US and the EU – Converging or diverging paths? *The Antitrust Bulletin, 49*(1–2), 1–27. https://doi.org/10.1177/0003603X0404900101

Nuss, S. (2006, 30 September). *Property and Public Goods in View of Copyright and Copyleft*. Value, Property, Public Goods, and Labour in Digitalized Capitalism, Thessaloniki, Greece. http://wbk.in-berlin.de/wp_nuss/wp-content/uploads/2006/10/thessal_input.pdf

Nuss, S., & Heinrich, M. (2001, April). *Warum Freie Software dem Kapitalismus nicht viel anhaben kann*. First Oekonux Conference, Dortmund, Germany. http://erste.oekonux-konferenz.de/dokumentation/texte/nuss.html

Nuss, S., & Stallman, R. (2005, 7 September). *Paper 'Digital Property' by Sabine Nuss – Response to Stallman* (Letter to oekonux). www.oekonux.org/list-en/archive/msg02796.html

OECD. (2009). *System of National Accounts 2008*. OECD.

OECD. (2014). *Understanding National Accounts: Second Edition: 2014* (2nd revised edn). OECD.

Olsen, E.K. (2009). Social ontology and the origins of mode of production theory. *Rethinking Marxism, 21*(2), 177–95. https://doi.org/10.1080/08935690902743096

Olsen, E.K. (2017). Productive and unproductive labor. In D. Brennan, D. Kristjanson-Gural, C.P. Mulder, & E.K. Olsen (Eds), *Routledge Handbook of Marxian Economics* (1st edn, pp 122–34). Routledge. https://doi.org/10.4324/9781315774206-12

O'Reilly, T. (2005). *What Is Web 2.0: Design Patterns and Business Models for the Next Generation of Software*. www.oreilly.com/pub/a/web2/archive/what-is-web-20.html

Orhangazi, Ö. (2008). Financialisation and capital accumulation in the non-financial corporate sector: A theoretical and empirical investigation on the US economy: 1973–2003. *Cambridge Journal of Economics, 32*(6), 863–86. https://doi.org/10.1093/cje/ben009

Orhangazi, Ö. (2018). The role of intangible assets in explaining the investment–profit puzzle. *Cambridge Journal of Economics*. https://doi.org/10.1093/cje/bey046

Pagano, U. (2014). The crisis of intellectual monopoly capitalism. *Cambridge Journal of Economics*, *38*(6), 1409–29. https://doi.org/10.1093/cje/beu025

Pagano, U., & Rossi, M.A. (2009). The crash of the knowledge economy. *Cambridge Journal of Economics*, *33*(4), 665–83. https://doi.org/10.1093/cje/bep033

Papadimitriou, S., & Moussiades, L. (2018). Mac OS versus FreeBSD: A comparative evaluation. *Computer*, *51*(2), 44–53. https://doi.org/10.1109/MC.2018.1451648

Pariser, E. (2011). *The Filter Bubble: What the Internet Is Hiding from You*. Penguin Books.

Parkhurst, B. (2019). Digital information and value: A response to Jakob Rigi. *TripleC: Communication, Capitalism & Critique. Open Access Journal for a Global Sustainable Information Society*, *17*(1), 72–85. https://doi.org/10.31269/triplec.v17i1.1078

Parry, G., Newnes, L., & Huang, X. (2011). Goods, products and services. In M. Macintyre, G. Parry, & J. Angelis (Eds), *Service Design and Delivery* (pp 19–29). Springer US. https://doi.org/10.1007/978-1-4419-8321-3_2

Pashukanis, E., & Milovanovic, D. (2001). *The General Theory of Law and Marxism* (1st edn). Transaction Publishers.

Pasquale, F. (2015). *The Black Box Society: The Secret Algorithms That Control Money and Information*. Harvard University Press.

Paul, S. (2019). Antitrust as allocator of coordination rights. *UCLA Law Review*, *67*(2), 4–64.

Pistor, K. (2019). *The Code of Capital: How the Law Creates Wealth and Inequality*. Princeton University Press.

Pitts, F.H. (2017). *Critiquing Capitalism Today: New Ways to Read Marx*. Springer International Publishing.

Postone, M. (1996). *Time, Labor, and Social Domination: A Reinterpretation of Marx's Critical Theory*. Cambridge University Press.

Postone, M. (2003). Lukács and the dialectical critique of capitalism. In R. Albritton & J. Simoulidis (Eds), *New Dialectics and Political Economy* (pp 78–100). Palgrave Macmillan.

Prado, J. (2018). Prospects for organizing the tech industry. *Notes from Below*. https://notesfrombelow.org/article/prospects-for-organizing-the-tech-industry

PricewaterhouseCoopers. (2018). *IAB Internet Advertising Revenue Report: 2017 Full Year Results*. www.iab.com/topics/ad-revenue/

Prug, T. (2014). *Hacking the Economy and the State: Towards an Egalitarian and Participatory Conception of Production and Allocation* [PhD Thesis, Queen Mary, University of London]. https://qmro.qmul.ac.uk/xmlui/handle/123456789/11751

Prug, T., & Bilić, P. (2021). Work now, profit later: AI between capital, labour, and regulation. In P. Moore & J. Woodcock (Eds), *Augmented Exploitation: Artificial Intelligence, Automation and Work*. Pluto Press.

Qiu, J.L. (2016). *Goodby iSLave: A Manifesto for Digital Abolition*. University of Illinois Press.

Reuten, G. (1988). Value as social form. In M. Williams (Ed.), *Value, Social Form and the State* (pp 42–61). Palgrave Macmillan.

Reuten, G. (2000). The interconnection of systematic dialectics and historical materialism. *Historical Materialism*, 7(1), 137–65. https://doi.org/10.1163/156920600100414669

Reuten, G. (2003). Karl Marx: His work and the major changes in its interpretation. In *A Companion to the History of Economic Thought* (p 148166). Blackwell.

Reuten, G., & Williams, M. (1989). *Value Form and the State: The Tendencies of Accumulation and the Determination of Economic Policy in Capitalist Society*. Routledge.

Reuters Institute. (2019). *Digital News Report 2018*. University of Oxford, Reuters Institute for the Study of Journalism. www.digitalnewsreport.org/survey/2018/

Richter, F. (2020). *Amazon Leads $100 Billion Cloud Market*. Statista Infographics. www.statista.com/chart/18819/worldwide-market-share-of-leading-cloud-infrastructure-service-providers/

Rieder, B., & Sire, G. (2014). Conflicts of interest and incentives to bias: A microeconomic critique of Google's tangled position on the Web. *New Media & Society*, 16(2), 195–211. https://doi.org/10.1177/1461444813481195

Rigi, J., & Prey, R. (2015). Value, rent, and the political economy of social media. *The Information Society*, 31(5), 392–406. https://doi.org/10.1080/01972243.2015.1069769

Roberts, S.T. (2016). Commercial content moderation: Digital labourers' dirty work. *Media Studies Publications*, 12. https://ir.lib.uwo.ca/commpub/12

Roberts, S.T. (2018). Digital detritus: 'Error" and the logic of opacity in social media content moderation. *First Monday*, 23(3). https://doi.org/10.5210/fm.v23i3.8283

Robinson, B. (2015). With a different Marx: Value and the contradictions of Web 2.0 capitalism. *The Information Society*, 31(1), 44–51. https://doi.org/10.1080/01972243.2015.977634

Rochet, J.C., & Tirole, J. (2003). Platform competition in two-sided markets. *Journal of the European Economic Association*, *1*(4), 990–1029. https://doi.org/10.1162/154247603322493212

Roth, R. (2009). Karl Marx's original manuscripts in the Marx-Engels-Gesamtausgabe (MEGA): Another view on capital. In *Re-reading Marx: New Perspectives after the Critical Edition* (pp 27–49). Palgrave Macmillan.

Roth, R. (2010). Marx on technical change in the critical edition. *European Journal of the History of Economic Thought*, *17*(5), 1223–51. https://doi.org/10.1080/09672567.2010.522239

Rotta, T., & Teixeira, R. (2019). The commodification of knowledge and information. In M. Vidal, T. Smith, T. Rotta, & P. Prew (Eds), *The Oxford Handbook of Karl Marx* (pp 378–400). Oxford University Press. https://doi.org/10.1093/oxfordhb/9780190695545.013.23

Rubin, I.I. (1973). *Essays on Marx's Theory of Value* (M. Samardžija & F. Perlman, Trans.; 3rd edn). Black Rose Books.

Saad-Filho, A. (2002). *The Value of Marx: Political Economy for Contemporary Capitalism*. Pluto Press.

Schiller, H.I. (1976). Communication and cultural domination. *International Journal of Politics*, *5*(4), 1–127.

Schiller, H.I. (1989). *Culture Inc.: The Corporate Takeover of Public Expression*. Oxford University Press.

Schiller, H.I. (1991). Not yet the post-imperialist era. *Critical Studies in Mass Communication*, *8*(1), 13–28. https://doi.org/10.1080/15295039109366777

Schmelzer, M. (2016). *The Hegemony of Growth: The OECD and the Making of the Economic Growth Paradigm*. Cambridge University Press.

Schmidt, E. (2008, 14 September). *A Note to Google Users on Net Neutrality*. https://web.archive.org/web/20080914170535/http://www.google.com/help/netneutrality_letter.html

Scholz, T. (Ed.). (2013). *Digital Labour: The Internet as Playground and Factory*. Routledge.

Scola, N. (2020). Inside the Ad Boycott That Has Facebook on the Defensive. *POLITICO*. www.politico.com/news/magazine/2020/07/03/activists-advertising-boycott-facebook-348528

Scott Morton, F., Bouvier, P., Ezrachi, A., Julien, B., Katz, R., Kimmelman, G., Melamed, A.D., & Morgenstern, J. (2019). *Stigler Committee on Digital Platforms: Market Structure and Antitrust Subcommittee*. Stigler Center for the Study of Economy and the State. https://research.chicagobooth.edu/stigler/media/news/committee-on-digital-platforms-final-report

Seetharaman, J.H. and D. (2020, 26 May). Facebook executives shut down efforts to make the site less divisive. *Wall Street Journal*. www.wsj.com/articles/facebook-knows-it-encourages-division-top-executives-nixed-solutions-11590507499

Sell, S.K. (2003). *Private Power, Public Law: The Globalization of Intellectual Property Rights* (Illustrated edn). Cambridge University Press.

Shalal, A. (2020, 10 July). EU urges US to return to negotiations at OECD on digital taxes. *Reuters*. www.reuters.com/article/us-usa-trade-france-eu-idUSKBN24B2EV

Smith, F., & Woods, L. (2005). A distinction without a difference: Exploring the boundary between goods and services in the World Trade Organization and the European Union. *Columbia Journal of European Law*, *12*(1), 1–52.

Smith, J. (2015). Imperialism in the twenty-first century. *Monthly Review*, *67*(3), 82–97.

Smith, T. (1997). Marx's theory of social forms and Lakatos's methodology of scientific research programs. In F. Moseley & M. Campbell (Eds), *New Investigations of Marx's Method* (pp 176–98). Humanities Press.

Smith, T. (1998). The capital/consumer relation in lean production: The continued relevance of Volume Two of *Capital*. In C.J. Arthur & G. Reuten (Eds), *The Circulation of Capital: Essays on Volume Two of Marx's Capital* (pp 67–94). Macmillan.

Smith, T. (2010). Technological change in capitalism: Some Marxian themes. *Cambridge Journal of Economics*, *34*(1), 203–12. https://doi.org/10.1093/cje/bep048

Smith, T. (2013). The 'general intellect' in the Grundrisse and beyond. *Historical Materialism*, *21*(4), 235–55. https://doi.org/10.1163/1569206X-12341321

Smyrnaios, N. (2018). *Internet Oligopoly: The Corporate Takeover of Our Digital World*. Emerald Publishing Limited. https://doi.org/10.1108/9781787691971

Smythe, D.W. (1977). Communications: Blindspot of Western Marxism. *CTheory*, *1*(3), 1–27.

Smythe, D.W. (2005). On the audience commodity and its work. In M.G. Durham & D.M. Kellner (Eds), *Media and Cultural Studies: Keyworks* (1st edn, pp 230–56). Wiley-Blackwell.

Social Prosperity Network, & Institute for Global Prosperity. (2017). *Social Prosperity for the Future: A Proposal for Universal Basic Services*. Institute for Global Prosperity, University College London.

Söderberg, J. (2007). *Hacking Capitalism: The Free and Open Source Software (FOSS) Movement*. Routledge.

Sohn-Rethel, A. (1978). *Intellectual and Manual Labour: A Critique of Epistemology*. Macmillan.

Sonnemaker, T. (2020). *Mark Zuckerberg Reportedly Said Facebook is 'Not Gonna Change' in Response to a Boycott by More Than 500 Advertisers over the Company's Hate-speech Policies*. Business Insider. www.businessinsider.com/zuckerberg-facebook-not-gonna-change-due-to-advertising-boycott-report-2020-7

Srnicek, N. (2017). *Platform Capitalism*. Polity Press.

Srnicek, N. (2018). Platform monopolies and the political economy of AI. In J. McDonnell (Ed.), *Economics for the Many* (pp 152–63). Verso.

Stallman, R. (2001). *The History of the GPL*. GNU Project. www.gnu.org/copyleft/

Stallman, R. (2018). *What Is Copyleft?* GNU Project. www.gnu.org/copyleft/

StatCounter. (2020a). *Mobile Vendor Market Share Worldwide*. StatCounter Global Stats. https://gs.statcounter.com/vendor-market-share/mobile

StatCounter. (2020b). *Search Engine Market Share Worldwide*. StatCounter Global Stats. https://gs.statcounter.com/search-engine-market-share

StatCounter. (2020c). *Social Media Stats Worldwide*. StatCounter Global Stats. https://gs.statcounter.com/social-media-stats

Statista. (2020). Facebook users worldwide 2020. Statista. www.statista.com/statistics/264810/number-of-monthly-active-facebook-users-worldwide/

Stigler, G.J. (1957). Perfect competition, historically contemplated. *Journal of Political Economy*, 65(1), 1–17.

Stop Hate for Profit. (2020). Stop hate for profit. www.stophateforprofit.org

Story, L., & Helft, M. (2007, 14 April). Google buys DoubleClick for $3.1 billion. *The New York Times*. www.nytimes.com/2007/04/14/technology/14DoubleClick.html

Su, J. (2014). *Google Profits Billions with Motorola Sale to Lenovo, Keeps Patents*. Forbes. www.forbes.com/sites/jeanbaptiste/2014/01/29/google-profits-billions-with-motorola-sale-to-lenovo-keeps-patents/

Surette, S. (2018). Perks of the job. Notes from Below. https://notesfrombelow.org/article/perks-of-the-job

Sweezy, P. (1994). The triumph of financial capital. *Monthly Review*, 46(2). https://monthlyreview.org/1994/06/01/the-triumph-of-financial-capital/

Syll, L.P. (2016). When the model becomes the message – a critique of Rodrik. *Real-World Economics Review*, 74, 139–55.

Tech Workers Coalition. (2018). Tech workers, platform workers, and workers' inquiry. Notes from Below. https://notesfrombelow.org/article/tech-workers-platform-workers-and-workers-inquiry

Teixeira, R.A., & Rotta, T.N. (2012). Valueless knowledge-commodities and financialization: Productive and financial dimensions of capital autonomization. *Review of Radical Political Economics*, *44*(4), 448–67. https://doi.org/10.1177/0486613411434387

Terranova, T. (2000). Free labor: Producing culture for the digital economy. *Social Text*, *18*(2), 33–58.

Testimony of David Chavern, President and CEO News Media Alliance (2019). Testimony of David Chavern. www.congress.gov/116/meeting/house/109616/witnesses/HHRG-116-JU05-Wstate-ChavernD-20190611.pdf

The Economist. (2017, 6 May). The world's most valuable resource is no longer oil, but data. *The Economist*. www.economist.com/leaders/2017/05/06/the-worlds-most-valuable-resource-is-no-longer-oil-but-data

Thompson, P. (2013). Financialization and the workplace: Extending and applying the disconnected capitalism thesis. *Work, Employment and Society*, *27*(3), 472–88. https://doi.org/10.1177/0950017013479827

TruePublica. (2019, 10 July). Personal data – The skyscraper of data you knew nothing about. *TruePublica*. https://truepublica.org.uk/united-kingdom/personal-data-the-skyscraper-of-data-you-knew-nothing-about/

Turow, J. (2011). *The Daily You: How the New Advertising Industry Is Defining Your Identity and Your Worth*. Yale University Press.

van Dijck, J. (2013). *The Culture of Connectivity: A Critical History of Social Media*. Oxford University Press.

van Dijck, J. (2014). Datafication, dataism and dataveillance: Big data between scientific paradigm and ideology. *Surveillance & Society*, *12*(2), 197–208. https://doi.org/10.24908/ss.v12i2.4776

van Dijck, J., de Waal, M., & Poell, T. (2018). *The Platform Society: Public Values in a Connective World*. Oxford University Press.

Vanoli, A. (2017). The future of the SNA in a broad information system perspective. *Review of Income and Wealth*, *63*(s2), S238–65. https://doi.org/10.1111/roiw.12332

Vercellone, C. (2007). From formal subsumption to general intellect: Elements for a Marxist reading of the thesis of cognitive capitalism. *Historical Materialism*, *15*(1), 13–36. https://doi.org/10.1163/156920607X171681

von Lohmann, F. (2017). The new wave: Copyright and software interfaces in the wake of Oracle v. Google Special issue: Software interface copyright. *Harvard Journal of Law & Technology (Harvard JOLT)*, *31*(Special Issue), 517–34.

vpnMentor. (2019). *The Real Influencers: Amazon, Apple, Facebook, Google and Microsoft have Spent $582 Million Lobbying Congress since 2005.* www.vpnmentor.com/blog/big-tech-lobbying-report/

Waddell, K. (2016, 19 January). *Why Google Quit China – And Why It's Heading Back.* The Atlantic. www.theatlantic.com/technology/archive/2016/01/why-google-quit-china-and-why-its-heading-back/424482/

Wei, X., & Heinrich, M. (2011). The interpretation of capital: An interview with Michael Heinrich. *World Review of Political Economy*, *2*(4), 708–28.

Whittaker, M., Crawford, K., Reisman, D., & Schultz, J. (2018). *Algorithmic Impact Assessments: A Practical Framework for Public Agency Accountability.* AI Now Institute.

Wiggershaus, R. (1995). *The Frankfurt School: Its History, Theories, and Political Significance.* MIT Press.

Williams, A. (2020, 10 July). US threatens $1.3bn worth of French goods with 25% tariff. *The Financial Times.* www.ft.com/content/f51be172-746f-48f2-9b9d-ac782b707c76

Williams, S. (2002). *Free as in Freedom: Richard Stallman's Crusade for Free Software.* O'Reilly Media.

WIPO. (2003). *Patentability of Computer Software and Business Methods.* Ministry of Science and Technology of the Republic of China and the World Intellectual Property Organization.

WIPO. (2020). *Patenting Software.* www.wipo.int/sme/en/documents/software_patents_fulltext.html

Woodcock, J., & Graham, M. (2020). *The Gig Economy: A Critical Introduction.* Polity.

World Bank. (2019). *World Development Indicators Database.* https://databank.worldbank.org/data/download/GDP.pdf

Wright, I. (2018). Silicon Valley startups: Being evil, again and again. Notes from Below. https://notesfrombelow.org/article/silicon-valley-startups-doing-evil-again-and-again

Written Testimony of David Heinemeier Hansson, CTO & Cofounder, Basecamp (2020). Testimony of David Heinemeier Hansen. https://judiciary.house.gov/calendar/eventsingle.aspx?EventID=2386

Wu, T. (2018). *The Curse of Bigness: Antitrust in the New Gilded Age.* Columbia Global Reports.

Zeichick, A. (2008). *How Facebook Works*. MIT Technology Review. www.technologyreview.com/s/410312/how-facebook-works/

Zuboff, S. (2015). Big other: Surveillance capitalism and the prospects of an information civilization. *Journal of Information Technology*, *30*(1), 75–89. https://doi.org/10.1057/jit.2015.5

Zuboff, S. (2019). *The Age of Surveillance Capitalism: The Fight for a Human Future at the New Frontier of Power* (1st edn). PublicAffairs.

Zukerfeld, M. (2017). The tale of the snake and the elephant: Intellectual property expansion under informational capitalism. *The Information Society*, *33*(5), 243–60. https://doi.org/10.1080/01972243.2017.1354107

Zwick, D., & Denegri Knott, J. (2009). Manufacturing customers: The database as new means of production. *Journal of Consumer Culture*, *9*(2), 221–47. https://doi.org/10.1177/1469540509104375

Index

Page numbers in *italic* type refer to figures; those in **bold** type refer to tables. References to endnotes show both the page number and the note number (231n3).